The Campus History Series

MEDICAL UNIVERSITY OF SOUTH CAROLINA

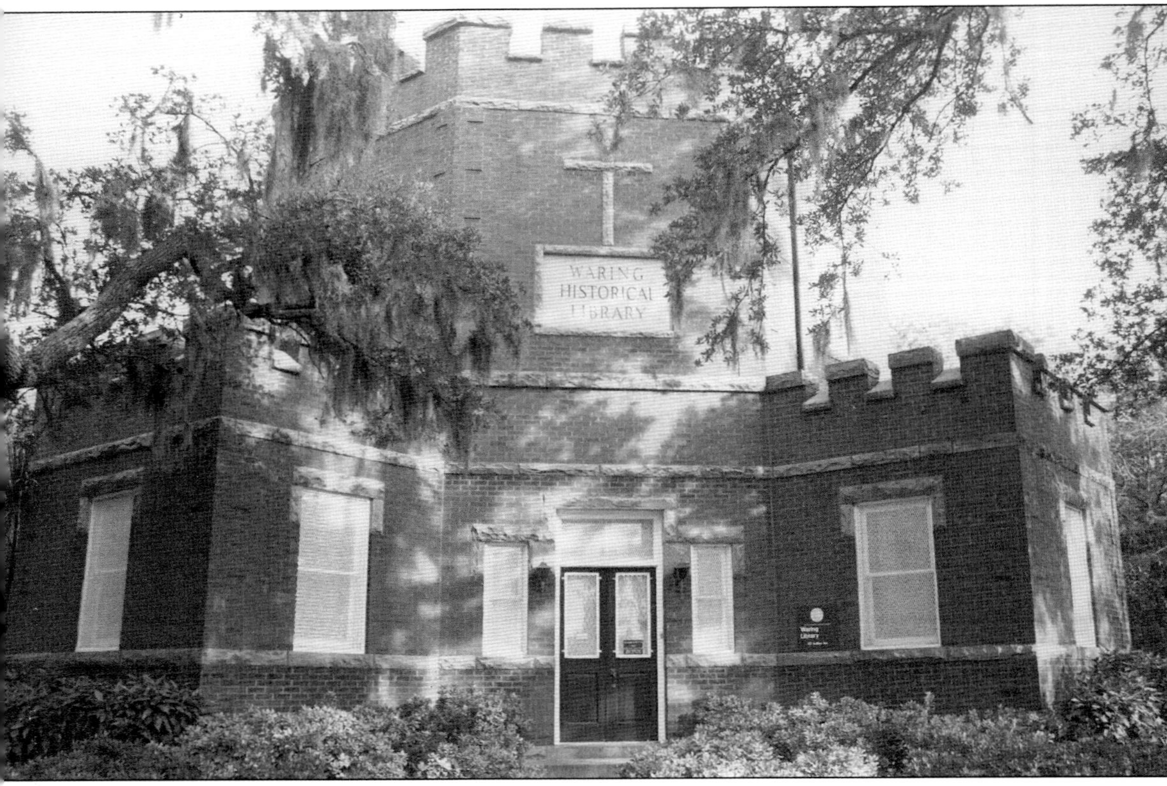

The Waring Historical Library is the special collections library for the Medical University of South Carolina (MUSC). The mission of the Waring Historical Library is to collect and preserve the history of the health sciences in South Carolina. The library's book collection, which now numbers over 14,000 volumes, dates predominantly from the 18th and 19th centuries and derives in large part from the library of the Medical Society of South Carolina. In addition to its book collection, the library holds manuscripts, images, and artifacts documenting the history of medicine in the state. The university acquired the building in 1963 during the purchase of the Porter Military Academy campus. The library was originally built in 1894 and named in honor of the benefactor, Rev. Charles Frederick Hoffman of New York, who provided the funds for its construction. In 1969, the library was renamed for Dr. Joseph Ioor Waring Jr., a pediatrician and medical historian who authored the three-volume set *History of Medicine in South Carolina*. The Waring Historical Library administers the MUSC University Archives and the Macaulay Museum of Dental History. (Courtesy of the Waring Historical Library, MUSC.)

On the Cover: Roper Hospital staff and school of nursing students pose in front of the hospital around 1924. (College of Nursing collection, MUSC University Archives.)

The Campus History Series

Medical University of South Carolina

Susan Dick Hoffius and E. Brooke Fox

ARCADIA
PUBLISHING

ISBN 978-0-7385-7996-2

Published by Arcadia Publishing
Charleston, South Carolina

Printed in the United States of America

Library of Congress Catalog Card Number: 2010936406

For all general information, please contact Arcadia Publishing:
Telephone 843-853-2070
Fax 843-853-0044
E-mail sales@arcadiapublishing.com
For customer service and orders:
Toll-Free 1-888-313-2665

Visit us on the Internet at www.arcadiapublishing.com

Dedicated with affection to W. Curtis Worthington Jr., MD

CONTENTS

ACKNOWLEDGMENTS

The authors wish to thank Dr. Raymond S. Greenberg, president of the Medical University of South Carolina, for his support of the Waring Historical Library and appreciation for the place of history at MUSC. We also thank Dr. Thomas G. Basler, director of the MUSC Library, for his support, both moral and financial, in the production of this book. We are indebted to Dr. W. Curtis Worthington Jr., director of the Waring Historical Library, for his years of dedication to the facility and his unwavering support of the library and its staff. Given his long history with the university and his elephantine memory, Dr. Worthington was our primary fact-checker, though of course the authors accept responsibility for all of the text. Jennifer M. Welch, Rebecca Powers, and Jana Meyer all provided crucial scanning work for which we are grateful. Thanks to Sophia Vasilos for her help with the artifacts and to Kay Carter for minding the store while we wrote. Thanks to Heather Woolwine in the MUSC Office of Public Relations and Beth Bilderback at the South Caroliniana Library at the University of South Carolina for providing a few important shots. Every writer needs an editor, and we appreciate Stephen Hoffius for his careful editing and thoughtful suggestions.

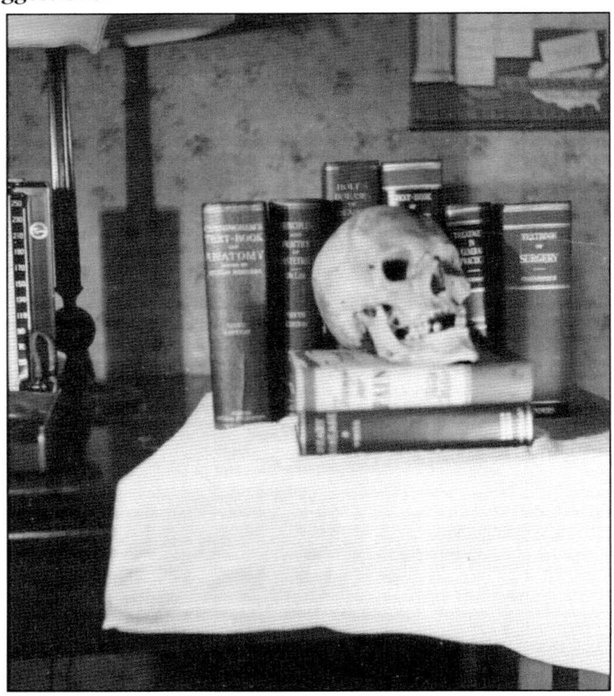

INTRODUCTION

The Medical University of South Carolina traces its origin to the Medical Society of South Carolina, whose members as early as 1791 advocated for the creation of a medical school in the state. The Medical College of South Carolina opened its doors to its first class on November 8, 1824; the five students were graduated the following year. Nearly 60 years later, the Medical College was joined by the Schools of Pharmacy (1881) and Nursing (1883). The school endured its share of disruptions from war, disease, and disasters. Yet despite these adversities, the college persevered, grew, and prospered. Since 1825, the Medical College (and now University) of South Carolina has educated thousands of physicians, nurses, pharmacists, dentists, scientists, and health-care professionals. The first medical college in the Deep South has grown to enjoy an international reputation in the field of health care.

This book surveys the history of the Medical University of South Carolina. For each photograph, pages could be written. Individual college histories are beyond the scope of this book. Our hope is that readers who are familiar with MUSC will enjoy the reminders of people, places, and events long gone and learn new stories along the way. For readers unfamiliar with MUSC, consider this book a visual primer. Above all, our goal is to present the history of MUSC—a diverse history, with many distinct chapters—as the history not just of six different colleges, but as the foundation for the story of health-care education and delivery in South Carolina.

The authors wish to alert readers to a number of stylistic peculiarities throughout the book. The name "Medical University of South Carolina" is a recent appellation. Originally the school was named the Medical College of South Carolina (1824), then the Medical College of the State of South Carolina (1832), then again the Medical College of South Carolina (1952), and finally the Medical University of South Carolina (1969). In the captions, we refer to the school by its name relative to the image or story within the narrative. Similarly, the Colleges of Pharmacy, Nursing, Graduate Studies, Dental Medicine, and Health Professions were originally the schools of same. We have preserved the names appropriate to the time period in question. Finally, unless otherwise noted, the illustrations are drawn from the collections of the Waring Historical Library and the MUSC University Archives.

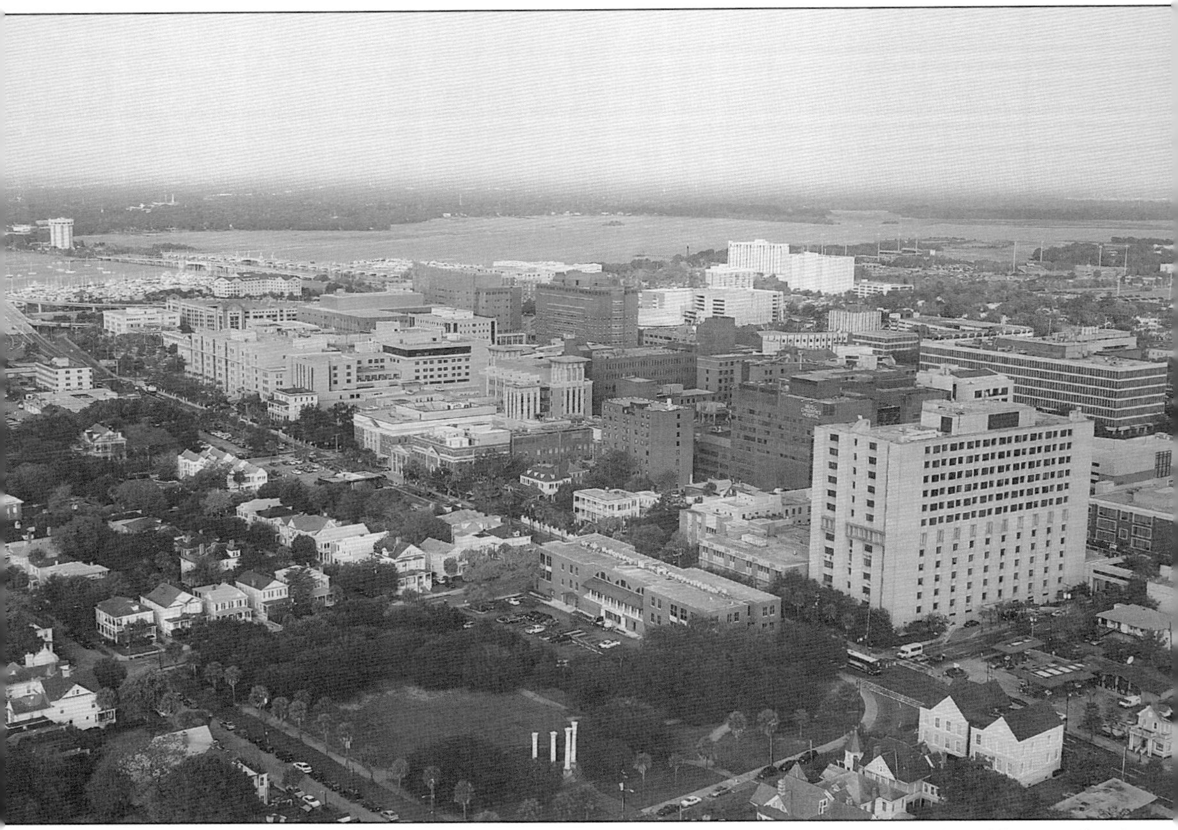

Founded in 1824 in Charleston, the Medical University of South Carolina is the oldest medical school in the Deep South. Today, MUSC continues a tradition of excellence in education, research, and patient care. MUSC educates and trains more than 3,000 students and residents and has nearly 11,000 employees, including 1,500 faculty members. The university and its affiliates are the largest nonfederal employer in Charleston. MUSC operates a 750-bed medical center, which includes a nationally recognized Children's Hospital, the Ashley River Tower (cardiovascular, digestive disease, and surgical oncology), and a leading Institute of Psychiatry. This 2010 aerial photograph of the MUSC campus is courtesy of the MUSC Office of Public Relations.

One

The Birth and Evolution of the Medical University of South Carolina

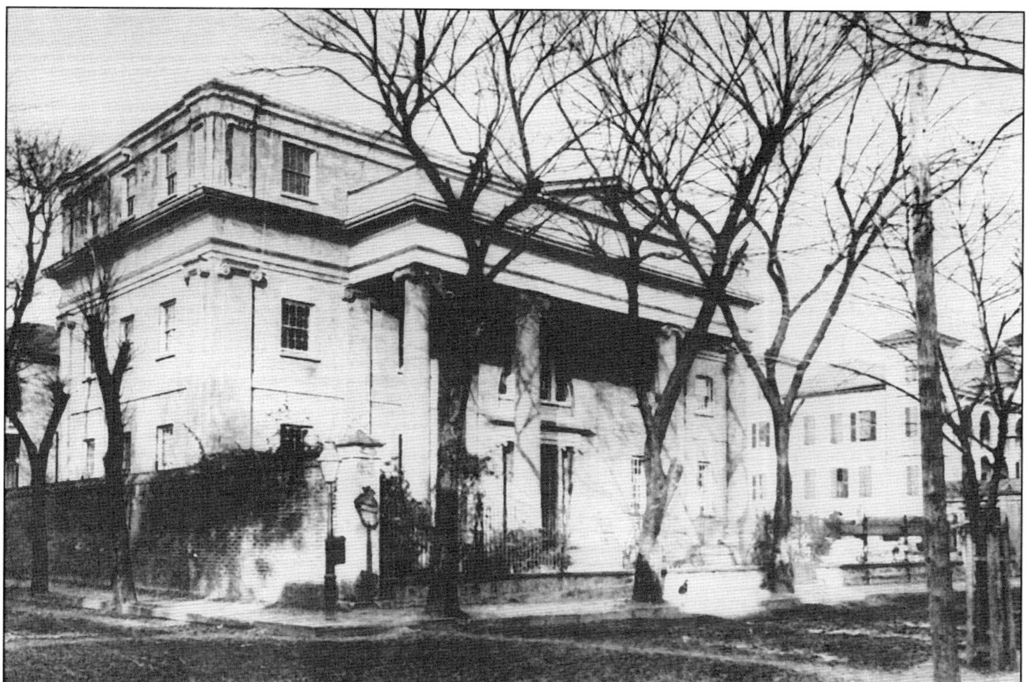

In 1823, the Medical Society of South Carolina petitioned the South Carolina General Assembly to establish the Medical College of South Carolina in Charleston. The Medical Society itself was founded in 1789 to "improve the science of medicine, provide liberality of the profession and harmony amongst the practitioners in this city." The first building of the Medical College of South Carolina, seen here, was erected in 1826 at the corner of Queen and Back (now Franklin) Streets. The building boasted a dissecting room, medical museum, library, lecture halls, and proximity to the city's hospitals.

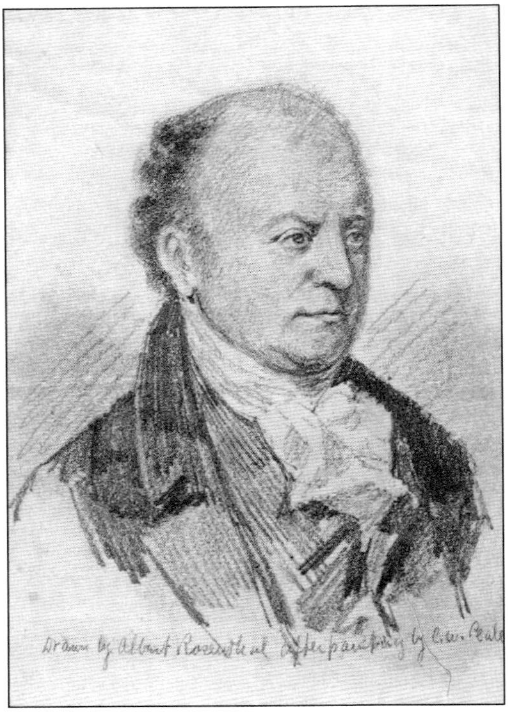

In the early 19th century, discussion emerged about the necessity of establishing a medical school in South Carolina. Thomas Cooper, president of the South Carolina College (now University of South Carolina in Columbia), urged the state's medical community to set up a school that would be divided between Columbia and Charleston. Charleston's medical community successfully advocated for the school to be located in Charleston on the grounds that Charleston had a larger population than Columbia, and it already had a hospital to provide clinical education.

Among the most ardent supporters of the effort to establish a medical college in South Carolina was David Ramsay, a student and friend of the noted American physician Benjamin Rush. Dr. Ramsay graduated from the University of Pennsylvania School of Medicine and eventually settled in Charleston, where he immersed himself in the city's culture, politics, and society. He was a Revolutionary War hero who served on the Charleston Council of Safety, in the Continental Congress, and later in the state legislature. In addition to his medical and political achievements, Ramsay is considered by some scholars to be the first historian of the United States for his books *History of the American Revolution*, *History of the United States*, and *History of South Carolina*. Unfortunately, Dr. Ramsay never lived to see the medical college as he was murdered in Charleston on May 8, 1815, by a patient whose insanity he had recently certified.

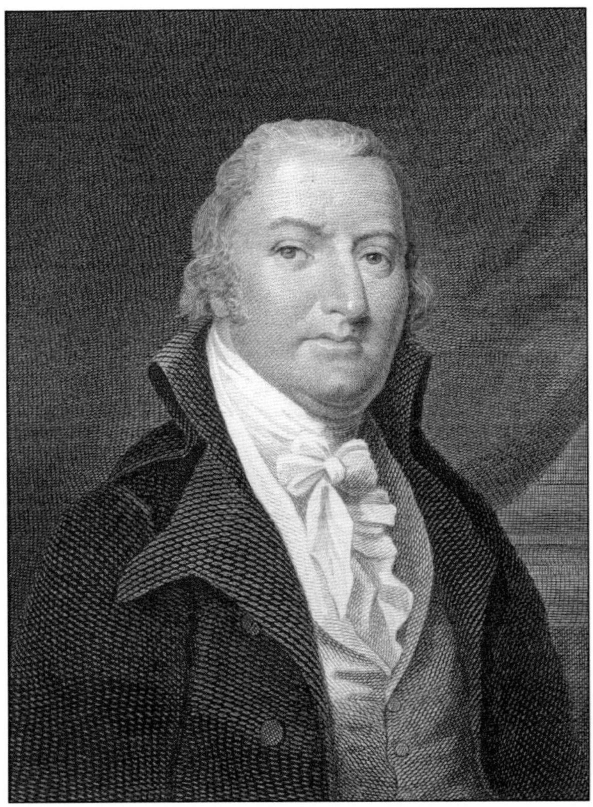

In November 1824, the school enrolled a class of five, all of whom graduated the following year. (Each candidate had completed at least one year of medical education elsewhere.) Medical instruction at the time consisted of four months of study in each of two consecutive years, with the second year being a repetition of the first year. Due to the very real danger posed by yellow fever, the academic year ran November to April to avoid the times of the year in which the fever was most prevalent in the city.

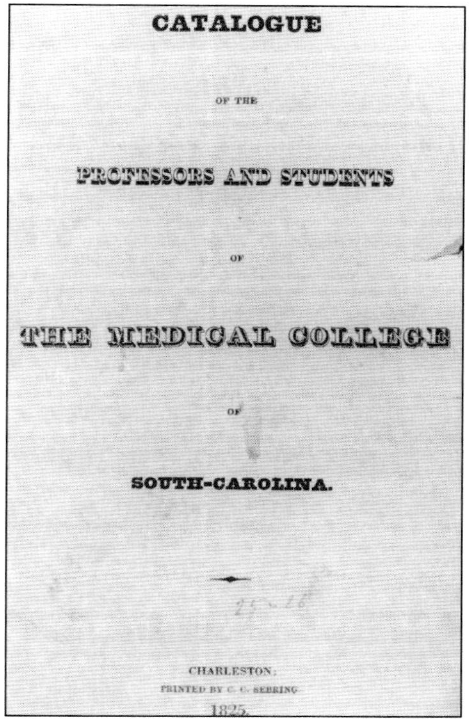

CATALOGUE

OF THE

PROFESSORS AND STUDENTS

OF

THE MEDICAL COLLEGE

OF

SOUTH-CAROLINA.

CHARLESTON:
PRINTED BY C. C. SEBRING
1825.

The South Carolina General Assembly granted the school a charter but provided no funding for the enterprise. Thus, the faculty of the school bore the entire expense for the operation of the college. Lecturers sold tickets to their classes, such as the one below from 1859–1860, which generated the only income for the faculty. When a student took a class, the faculty redeemed these tickets with the Medical Society for payment.

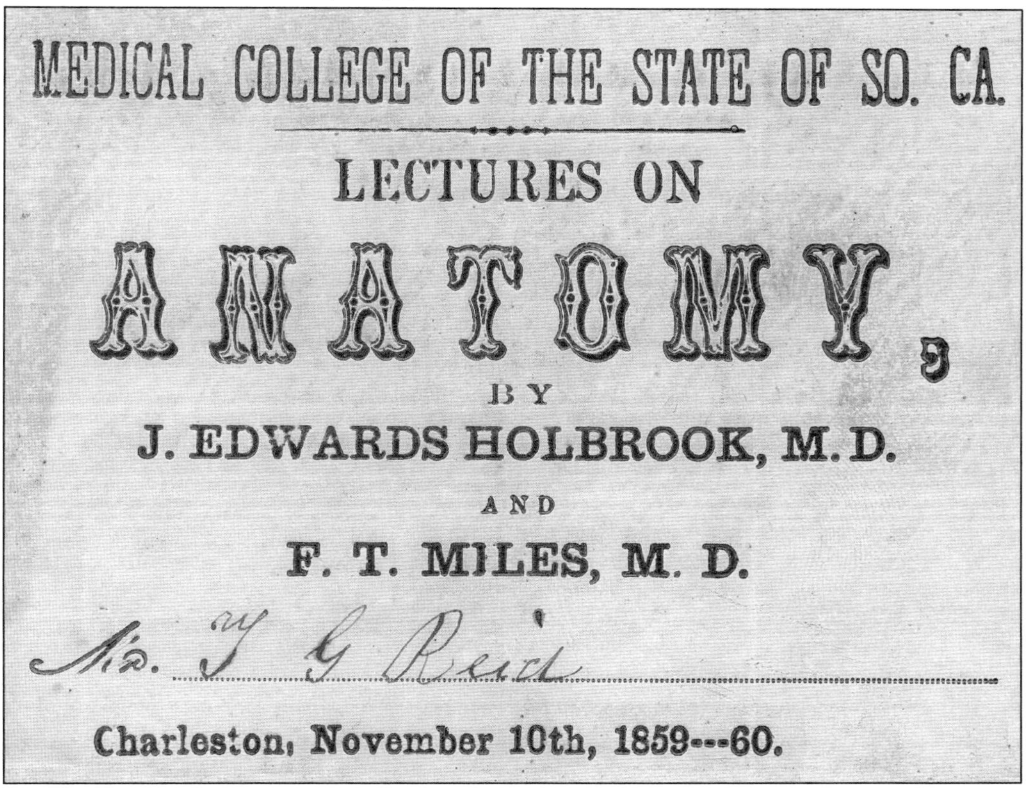

MEDICAL COLLEGE OF THE STATE OF SO. CA.

LECTURES ON

ANATOMY,

BY

J. EDWARDS HOLBROOK, M.D.

AND

F. T. MILES, M. D.

Charleston, November 10th, 1859---60.

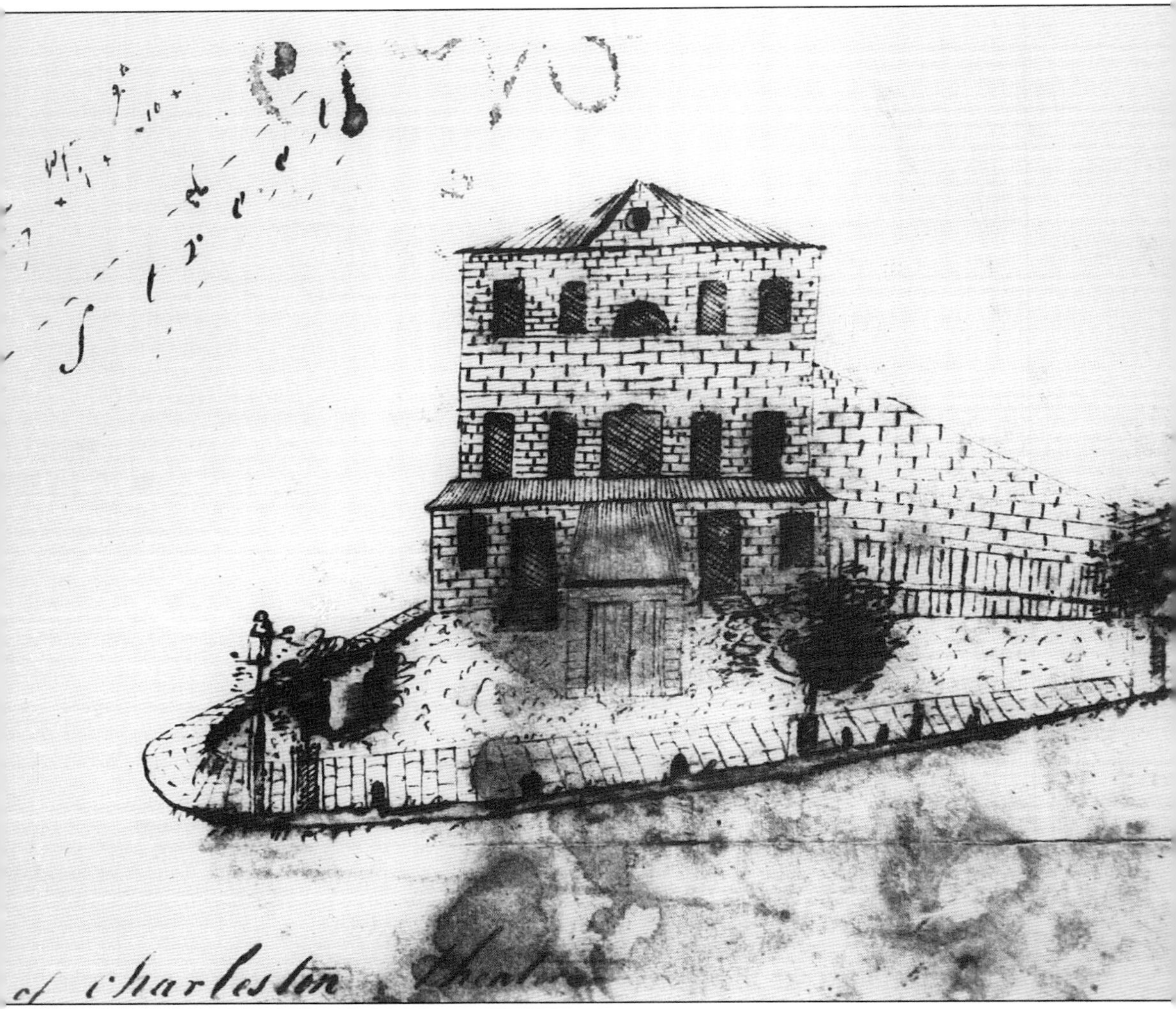

In 1832, a fissure between the faculty and the Medical Society erupted over the appointment of a new faculty member. Unhappy with the selection process for replacing a colleague, the entire faculty resigned and established its own institution, named the Medical College of the State of South Carolina. The Medical Society hired a replacement faculty, largely from the North, and continued to operate in the building on Queen Street. The new college purchased the old Charleston Theatre building (above) at the corner of New and Broad Streets, and the two schools operated in competition for nearly six years just blocks from each other. Ultimately, the new college (with the original faculty) was more successful, and after years of competition the two merged back together under the name Medical College of the State of South Carolina. It was not until 1952 that the "of the State" was dropped from the name. (Image is a detail from the McCrady Plat Collection, No. 7115, Charleston County Register of Mesne Conveyance.)

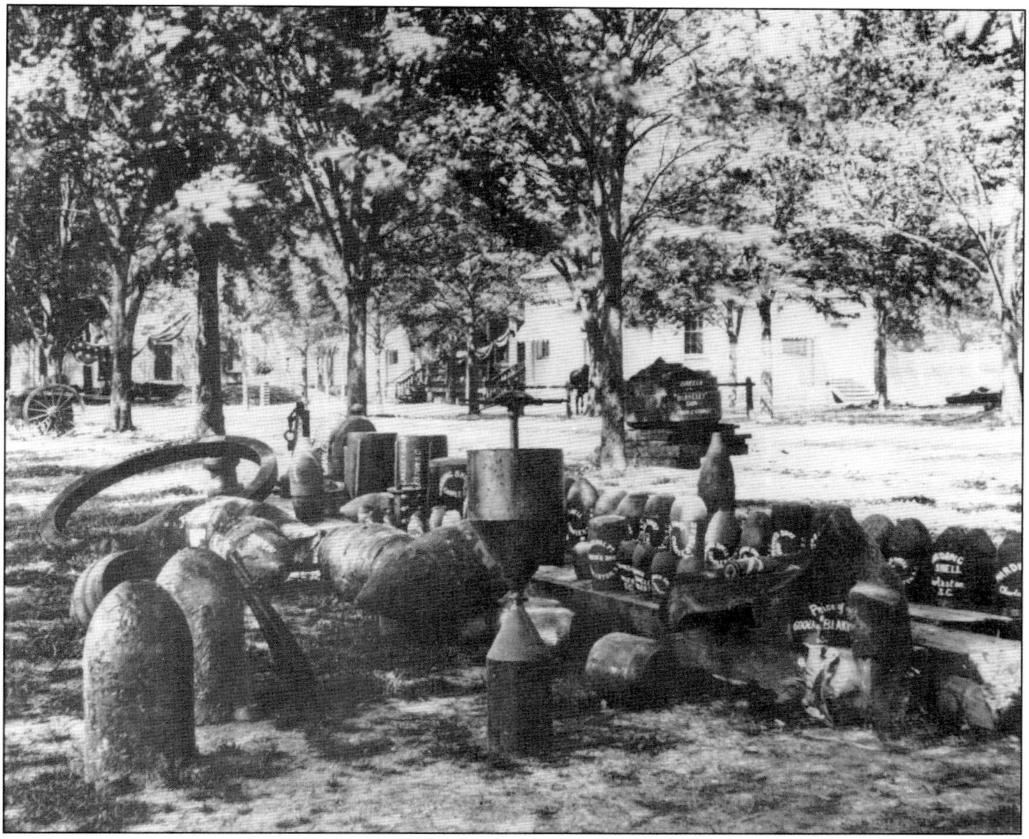

The Medical College suspended classes after the March 1861 graduation as faculty and students rushed off to serve in the Civil War. After an interval of nearly five years, classes resumed and the first postwar graduation was held in March 1866. "The Session was a most satisfactory one, when we take into consideration the condition of the country and the people, just emerging from an exhaustive war, which carried desolation into every household, broke up communications, isolated the various sections of the State from each other, and suspended the daily and weekly journals, the only means of extending information," reads the *Annual Circular*, 1865–1866. Above is a photograph of the Charleston Arsenal yard from about 1865. Below is a Confederate States of America belt buckle found in a medical bag in the collections of the Waring Historical Library. (Above, courtesy Library of Congress.)

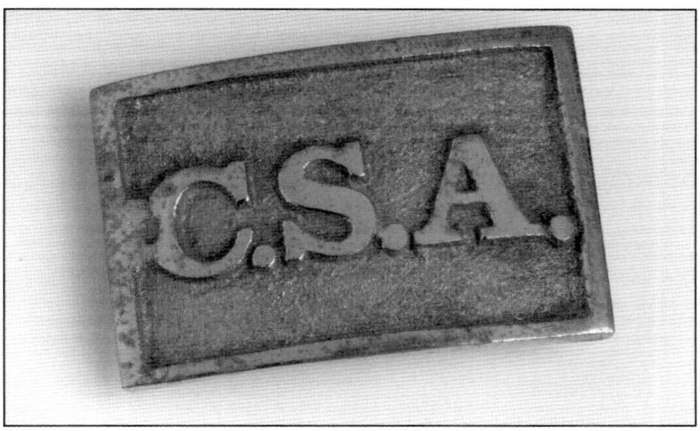

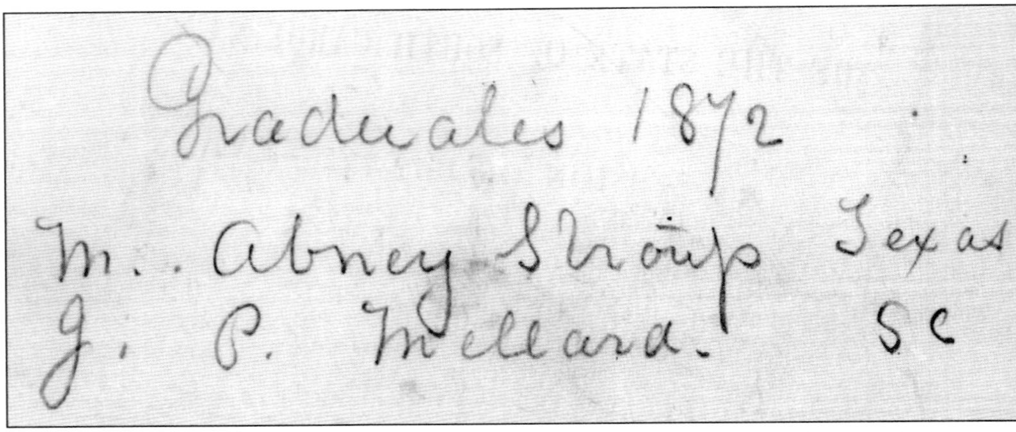

Graduates 1872

M. Abney Shoup Texas

J. P. Mclard. SC

When the college reopened after the Civil War, enrollment was low and continued to decline until 1872, when there were only two graduates, as shown above in the college's annual announcement. Times were so hard that the college offered free tuition from 1872 to 1876. The addition of the Schools of Pharmacy (1882) and Nursing (1883) enhanced the opportunities available to students, including women who were allowed to enroll in the college of medicine for the first time in 1894.

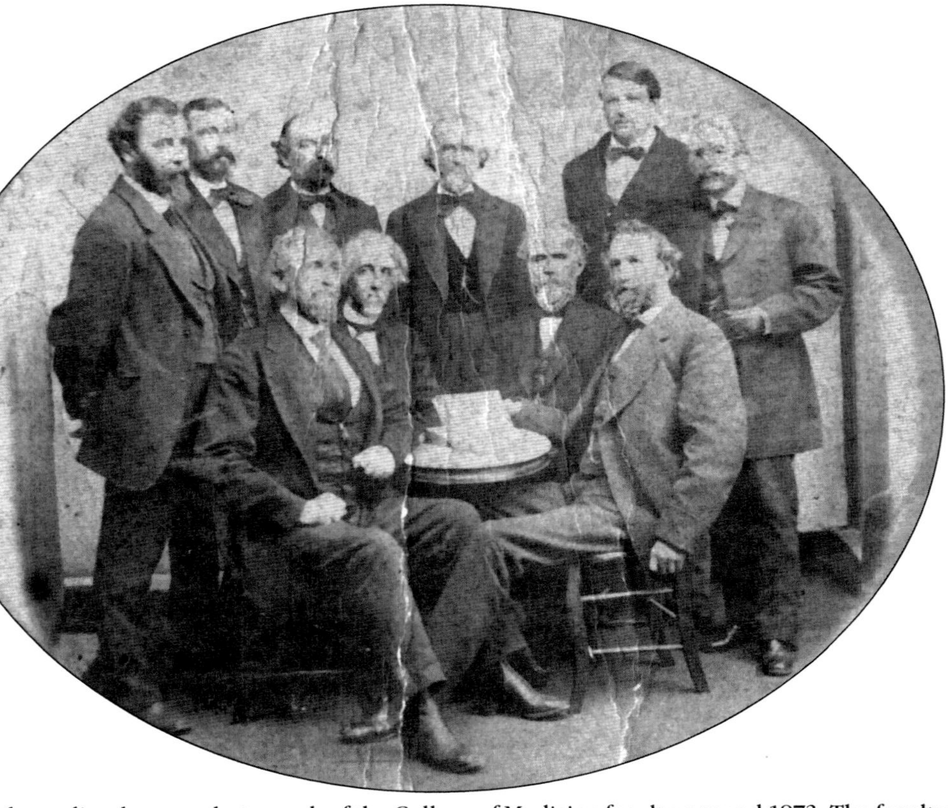

This is the earliest known photograph of the College of Medicine faculty, around 1873. The faculty included Eli Geddings, Robert A. Kinloch, John P. Chazel, Middleton Michel, George E. Trescot, Charles U. Shepard, J.F.M. Geddings, Francis LeJau Parker, Francis Marion Robertson, J. Ford Prioleau, F. Peyre Porcher, and Manning Simmons.

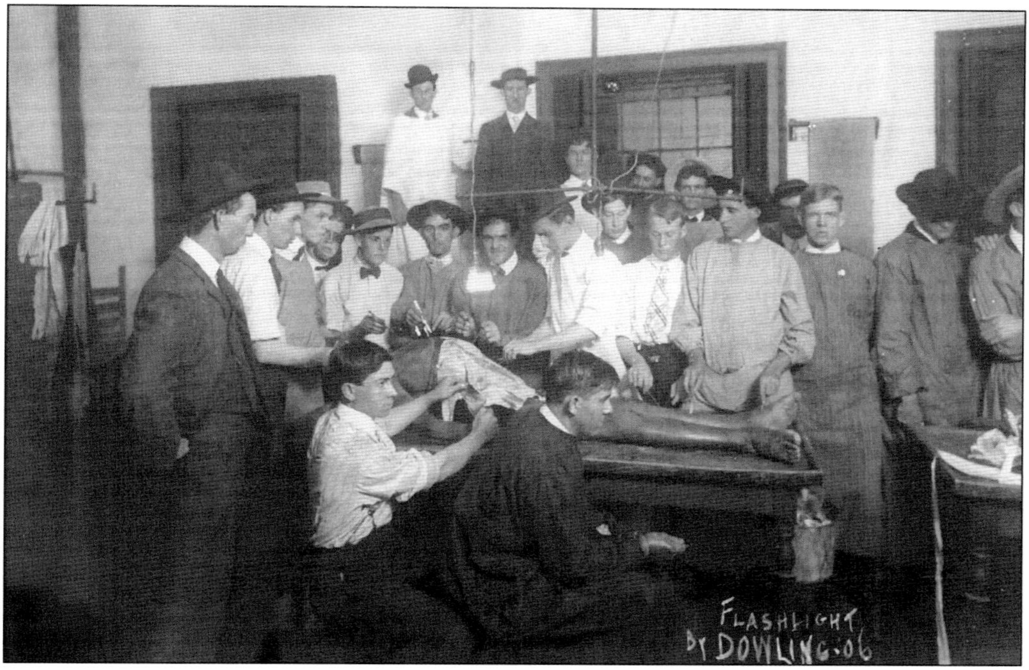

For many students, medical education begins with gross anatomy. Anatomy images such as these document the rite of passage for young medical students. These staged images provide a public view to a private, and well-guarded, world of dissection. The photograph above was taken in 1906; the one below in 1913.

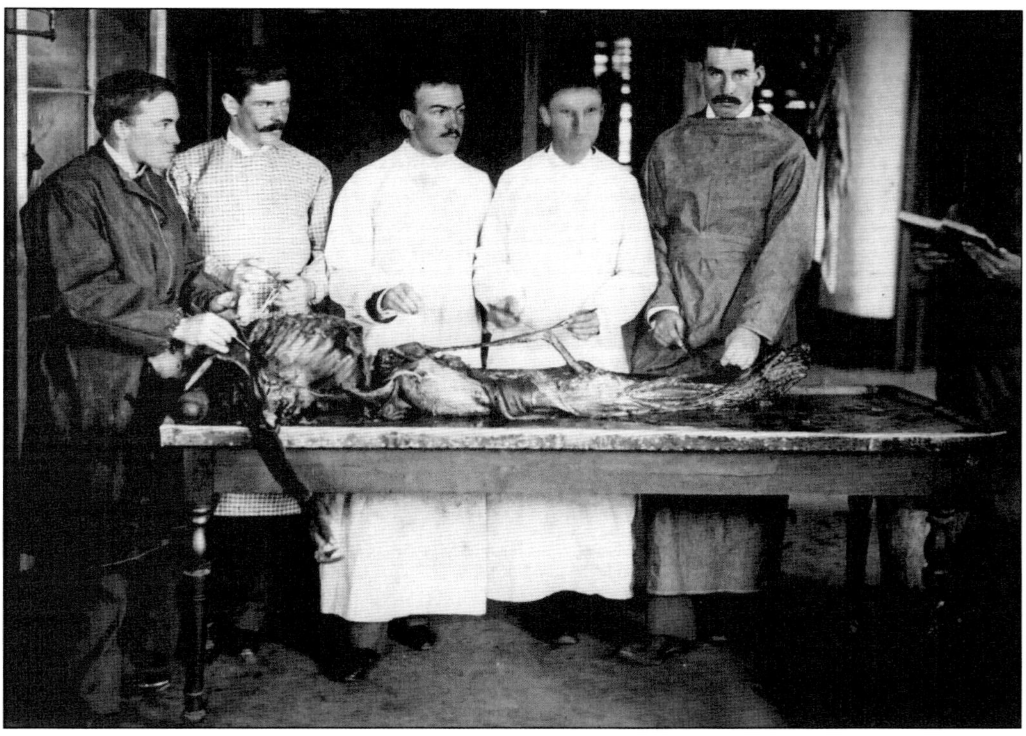

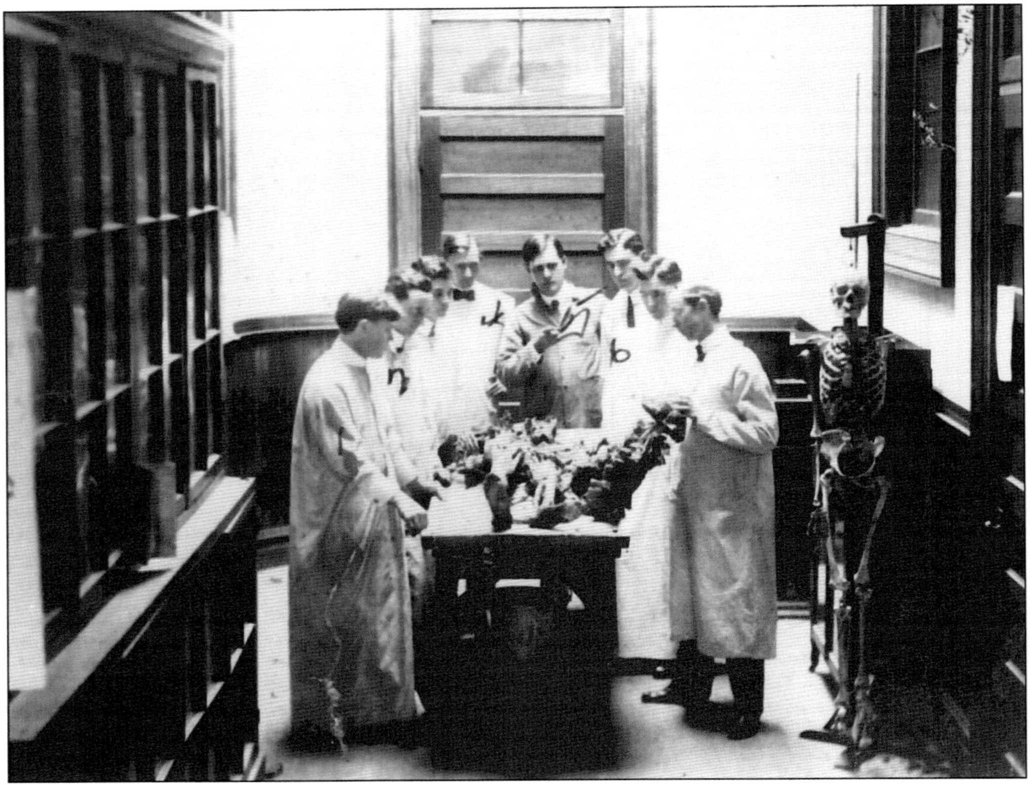

The 1837 *Annual Announcement* reports, "Anatomy, so indispensable as a ground work of Medical and Chirurgical science, can be no where more advantageously cultivated than in Charleston. While in many of the medical schools of the United States, subjects for dissection cannot be obtained, and in most of them the supply is very inadequate, students who resort to Charleston, experience no difficulty in obtaining them in sufficient abundance to subserve all the purposes of dissection and operations." The image above is from 1900, and the image below from 1894.

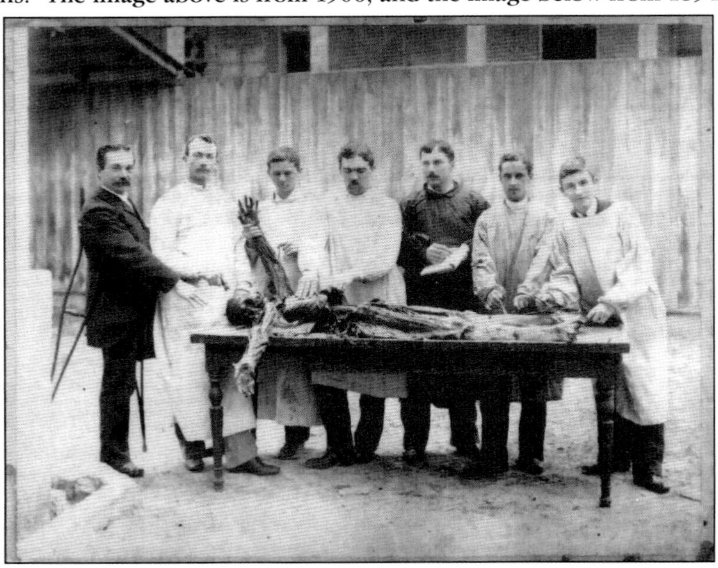

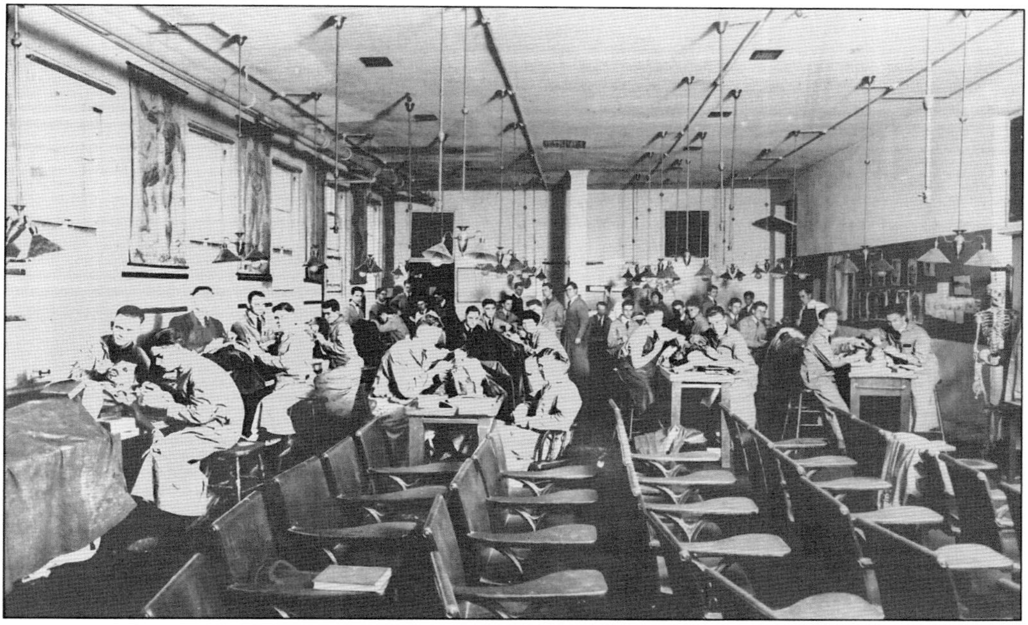

Above is an anatomy classroom in the new Medical College Building at Calhoun and Lucas Streets in 1926. Below, Dr. W. Cyril O'Driscoll works with his students in the anatomy room around 1950. For 53 years, Dr. O'Driscoll was a professor of anatomy at the Medical College, where he was known as a gifted, charismatic, and commanding teacher. A former student, H. Biemann Othersen, remembered, "During the first lecture the students sat in stark terror while Dr. O'Driscoll lectured about the bones. One student nervously produced a cigarette and began to smoke. Dr. O'Driscoll stopped lecturing, looked at the student, and thundered, 'Dammit, man, you've got so much gall, if your gallbladder burst, you'd drown.' "

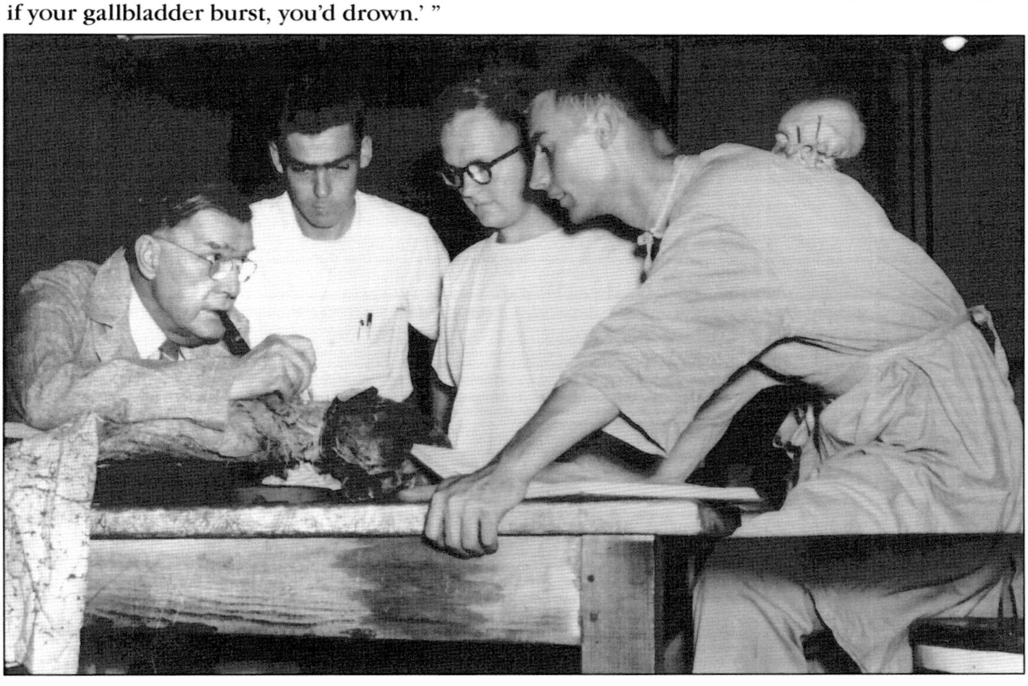

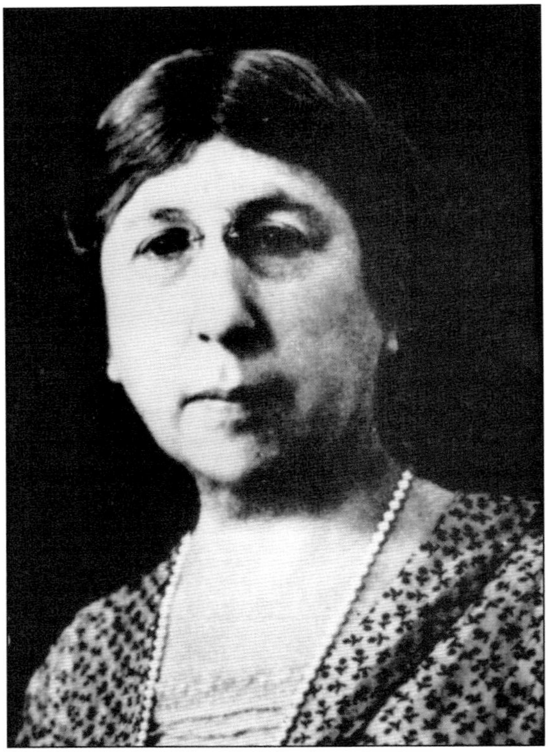

Women were first permitted admission to the Medical College in 1894, but it was not until 1901 that the first women graduated from the College of Medicine. Two women were members of that class—Love Rosa Hirschmann Gantt (left) and Emilie Melanie Viett Rundlett (below). Both achieved many "firsts" during their careers. Dr. Gantt was the first female to practice medicine in Spartanburg, where she was very involved in public health issues, including tuberculosis, rural health, maternal health, and school health. In 1939, Dr. Rundlett moved to New York, where she practiced medicine, specializing in women's and children's health. That same year, Rundlett became the first female president of the medical staff of the New Jersey Medical Center, one of the country's largest hospitals.

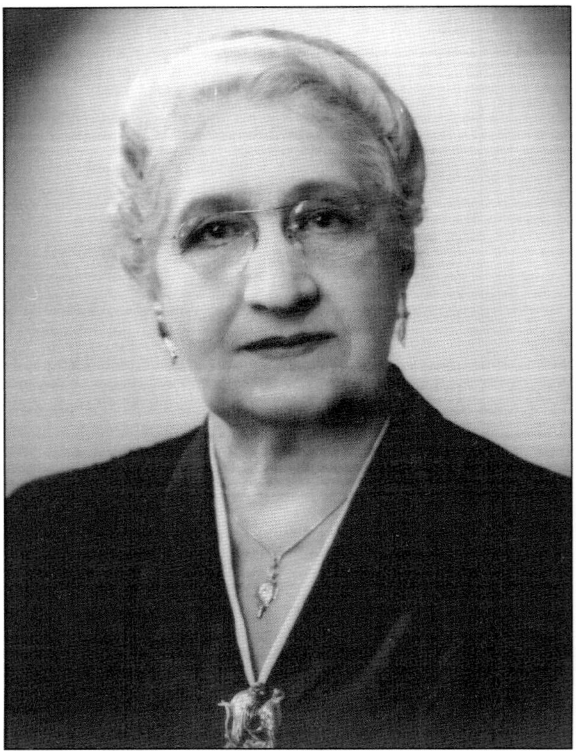

MEDICAL EDUCATION
IN THE
UNITED STATES AND CANADA

A REPORT TO
THE CARNEGIE FOUNDATION
FOR THE ADVANCEMENT OF TEACHING

BY
ABRAHAM FLEXNER

The early 1900s saw growing concern nationally about the number of medical schools churning out doctors with little or inadequate instruction. In February 1909, Abraham Flexner, working for the Carnegie Foundation and the American Medical Association, visited Charleston and evaluated the Medical College as part of his national tour. In his 1910 report (title page shown above), the assessment of the Medical College criticized poor equipment, poor physical facilities, lack of full-time professors, and lack of money. Flexner recommended that all medical education in the Southeast be focused at six locations, including Atlanta; Charleston would not make the cut.

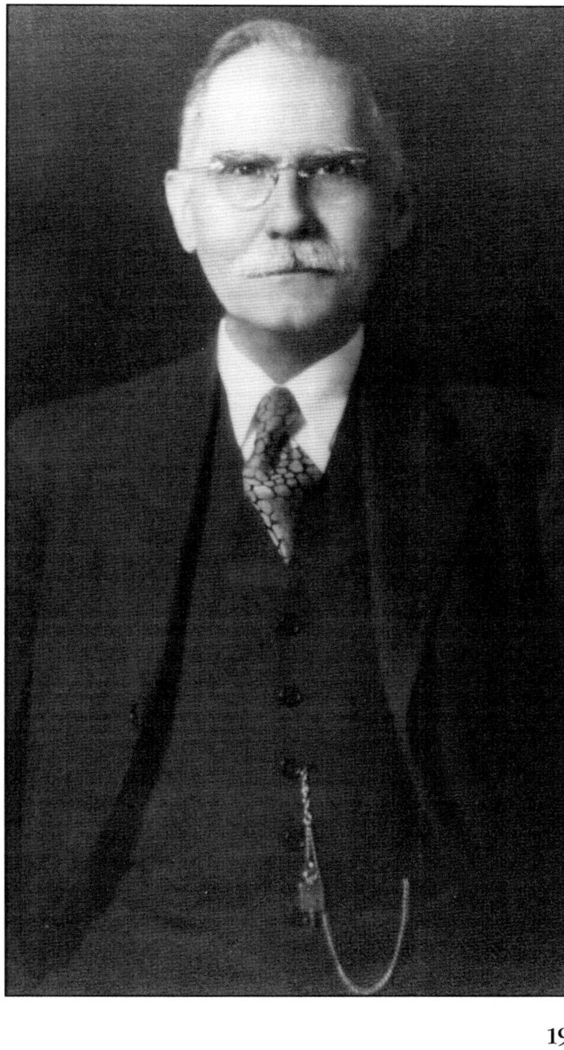

Dr. Robert Wilson, known as "The Dean," is credited with saving the school from closure in the wake of Flexner's report. He brokered a deal with Gov. Coleman L. Blease to turn the college over to the state, which would entitle it to state appropriations. In 1913, the Medical College of the State of South Carolina became an official state institution. Dr. Wilson had graduated from the Medical College in 1892 and joined the faculty as professor of medicine. He became dean of the Medical College in 1908 and served as such until his retirement in 1943.

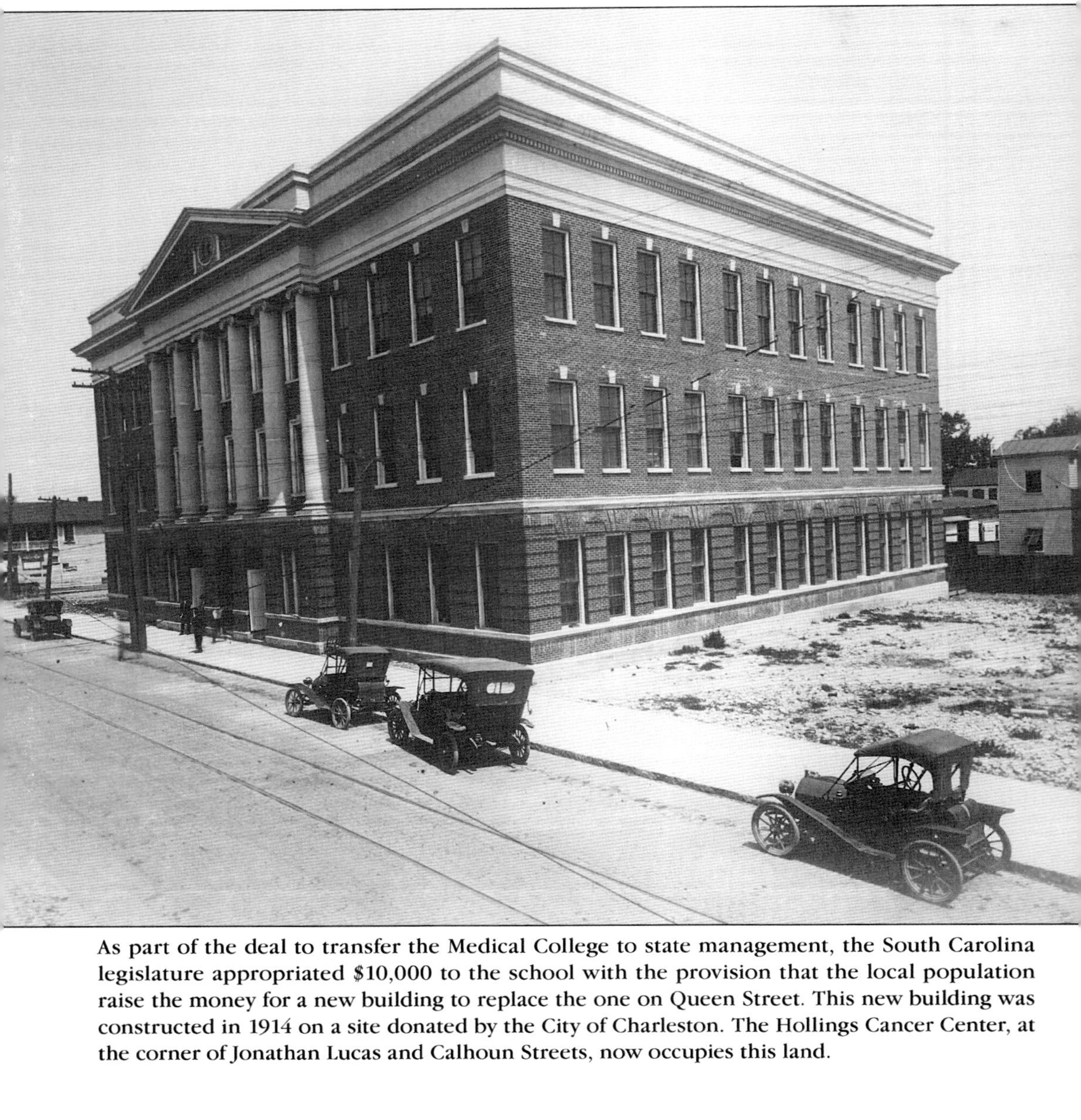

As part of the deal to transfer the Medical College to state management, the South Carolina legislature appropriated $10,000 to the school with the provision that the local population raise the money for a new building to replace the one on Queen Street. This new building was constructed in 1914 on a site donated by the City of Charleston. The Hollings Cancer Center, at the corner of Jonathan Lucas and Calhoun Streets, now occupies this land.

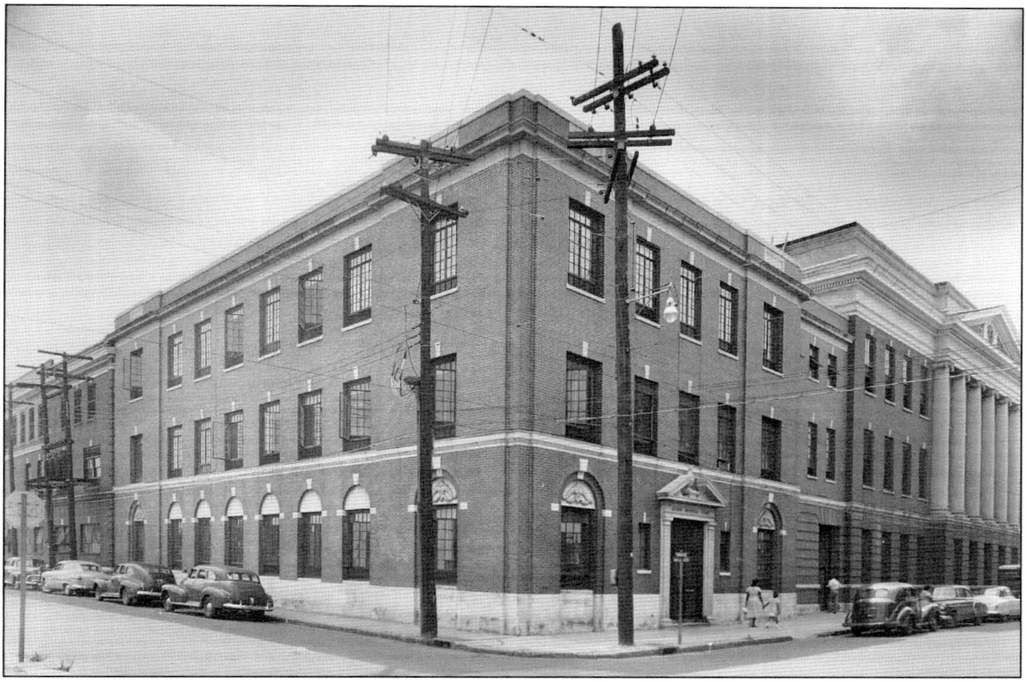

With construction of the 1914 building, the campus shifted from Queen Street to an area formerly known as the Lucas property. In the first half of the 20th century, additional buildings were erected to form what became known as the Quadrangle, which included the Medical College Building (above far right), research building, laboratory-clinic building, library-pathology building, physiology-pharmacology building (above foreground), and Baruch Auditorium.

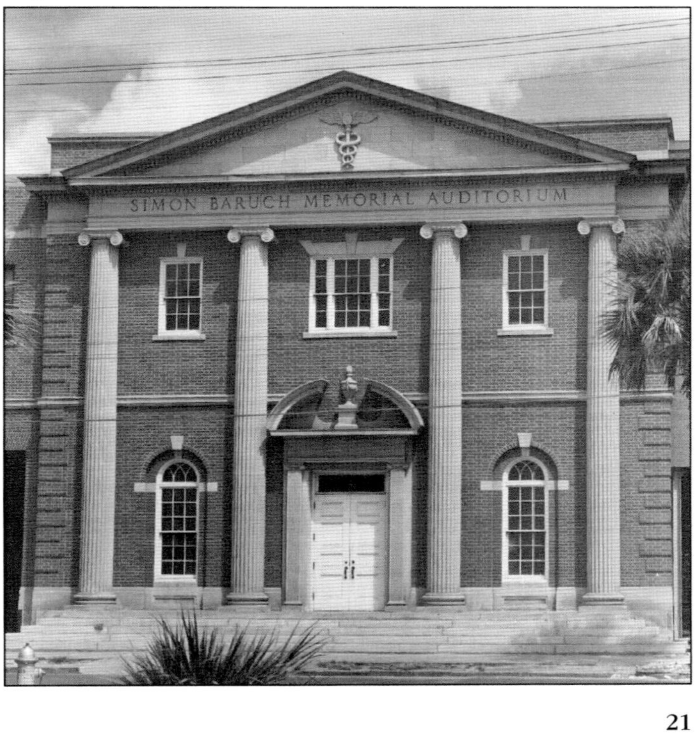

The Simon Baruch Memorial Auditorium was added to the campus in 1940. It was paid for by financier Bernard M. Baruch and named for his father, Dr. Simon Baruch, who served as president of the South Carolina Medical Association and chairman of the South Carolina Board of Health.

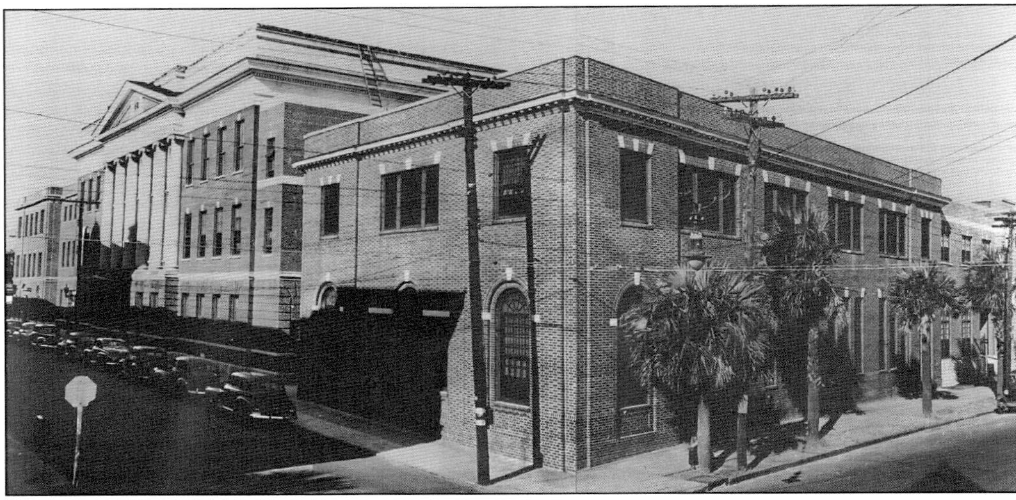

The library-pathology building was constructed on the corner of Lucas and Calhoun Streets in 1930. The first floor housed the college library; the second floor was home to the pathology department. When a new library was constructed in 1971, the building continued to house offices until 1982, when it was demolished to make way for the Hollings Cancer Center. Below is the physiology-pharmacology building constructed in 1920 on the north edge of the Quadrangle.

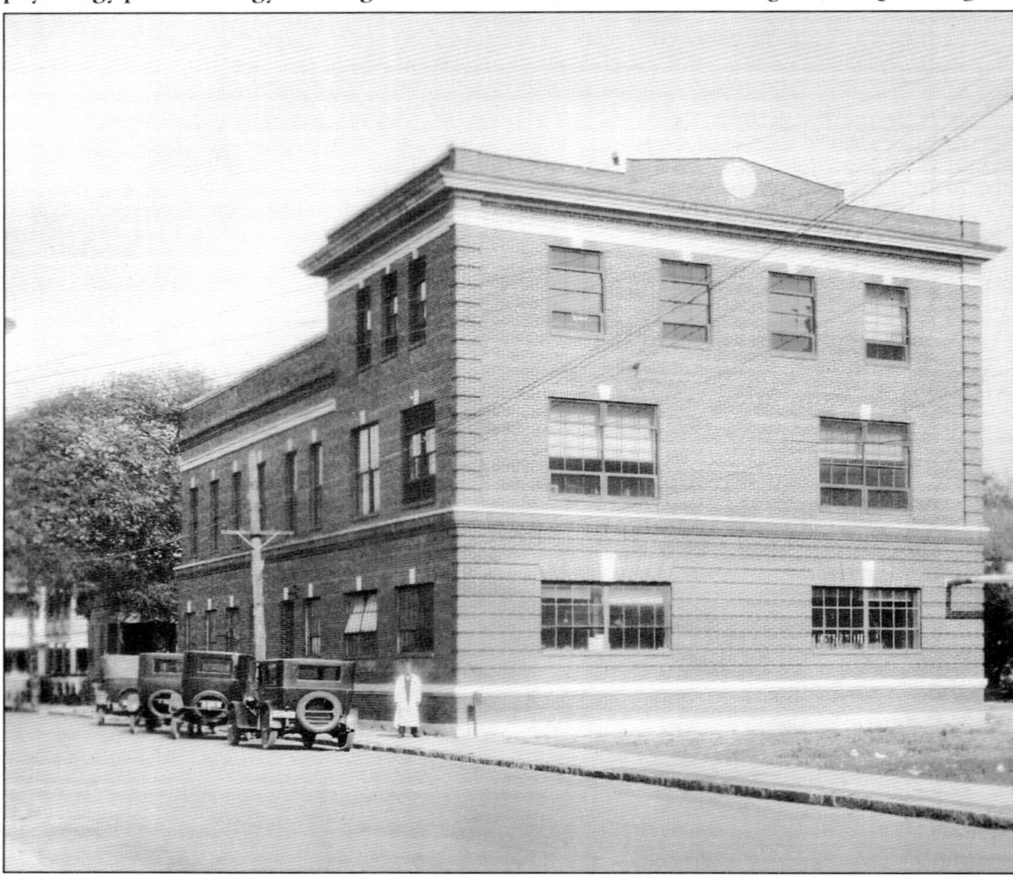

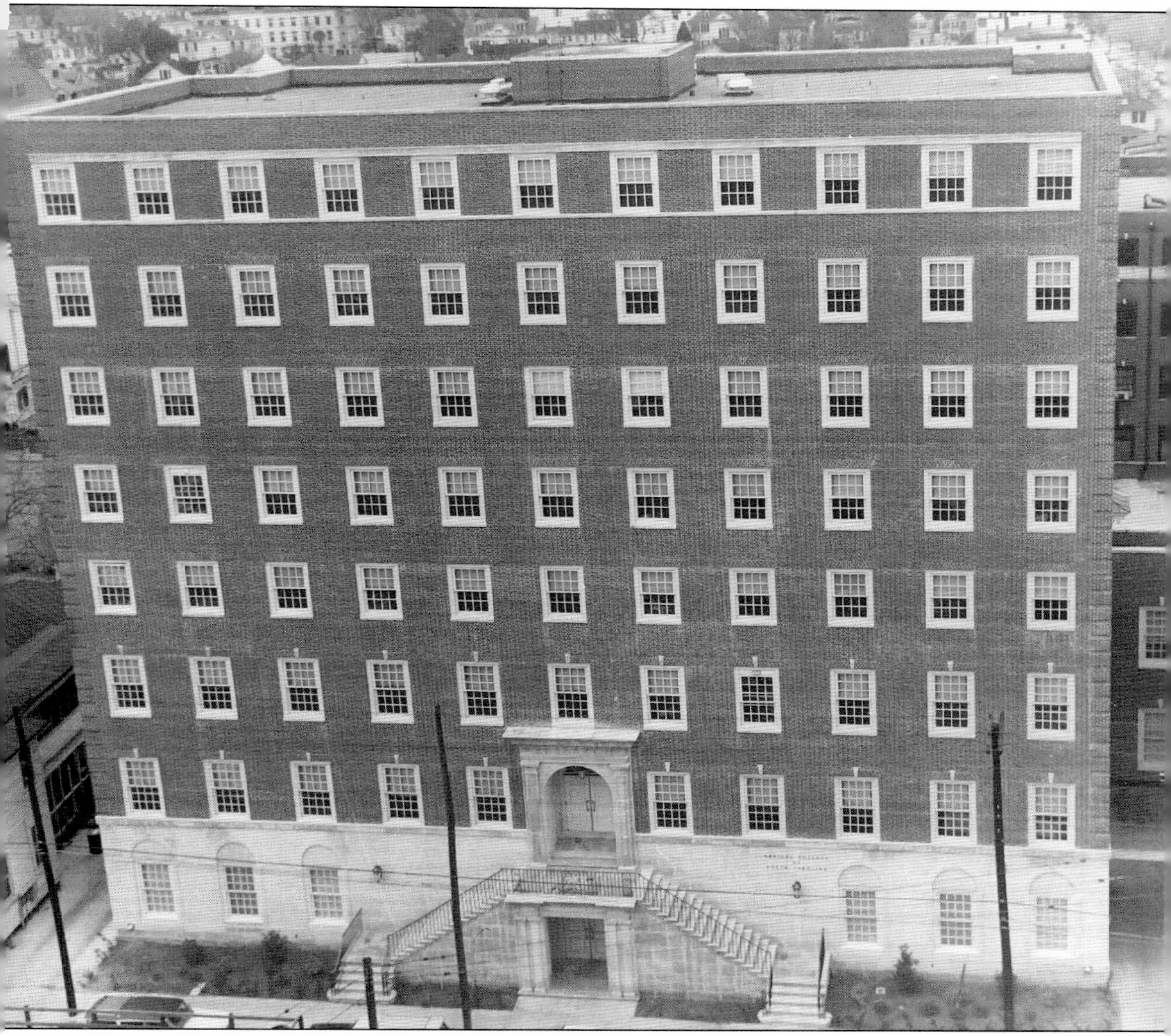

The research building was constructed on the Quadrangle in 1962 and renamed in honor of Robert Petrie Walton in 1982. When the facility was first publicized in the 1963–1964 announcement, the building boasted "a wide variety of experimental facilities and is a central focus of investigative activity for the program of graduate studies." Among the research-supporting services housed in the structure were "radio-autography, animal x-ray, animal autopsy, manuscript typing, drafting and illustrating, color micro-photography, glass blowing, volatile solvent storage, sterilizers and ovens, cold rooms, electronic repair and development shop, mechanical shop, etc."

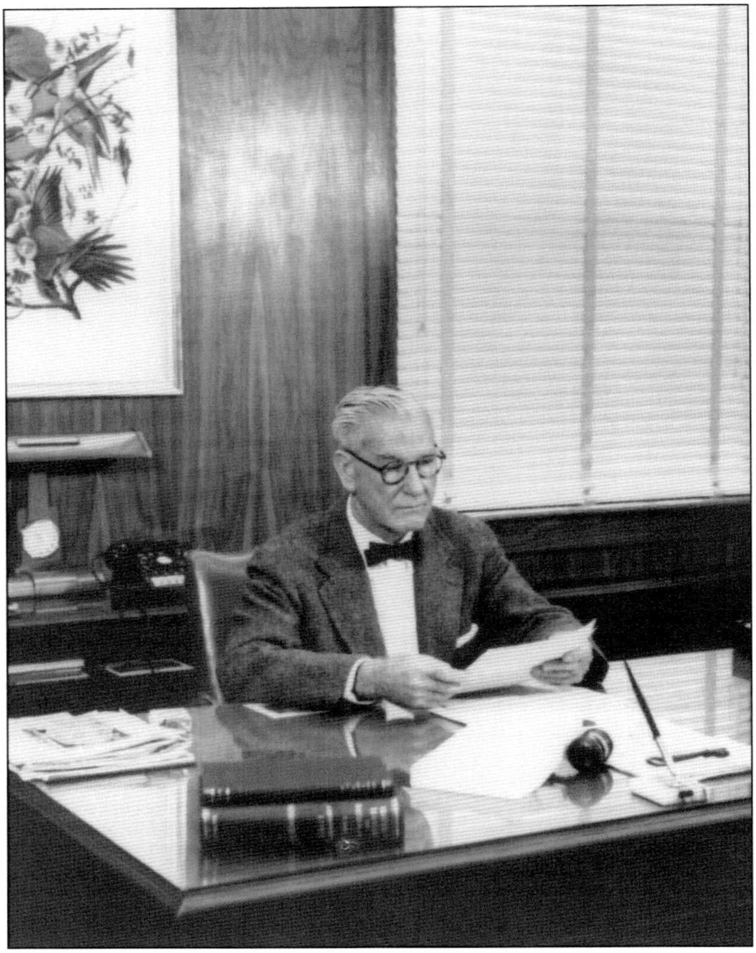

The arrival of Kenneth Lynch in 1913 coincided with the school's initial efforts to transition from college to university. Lynch was educated in Texas and joined the Medical College in 1913 as the first full-time faculty member in the pathology department. His major focus of research was on the link between asbestos and lung cancer. He succeeded Robert Wilson as dean of the college in 1943 and served until 1949, when he was named president of the college, a position he held until 1960. Below Dr. Lynch is at the head of the table with members of the building committee.

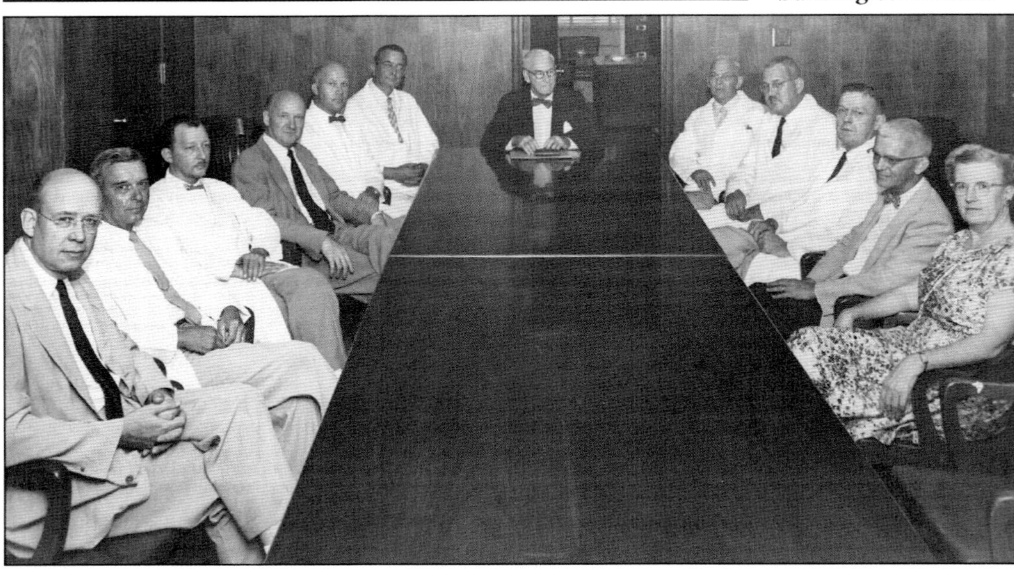

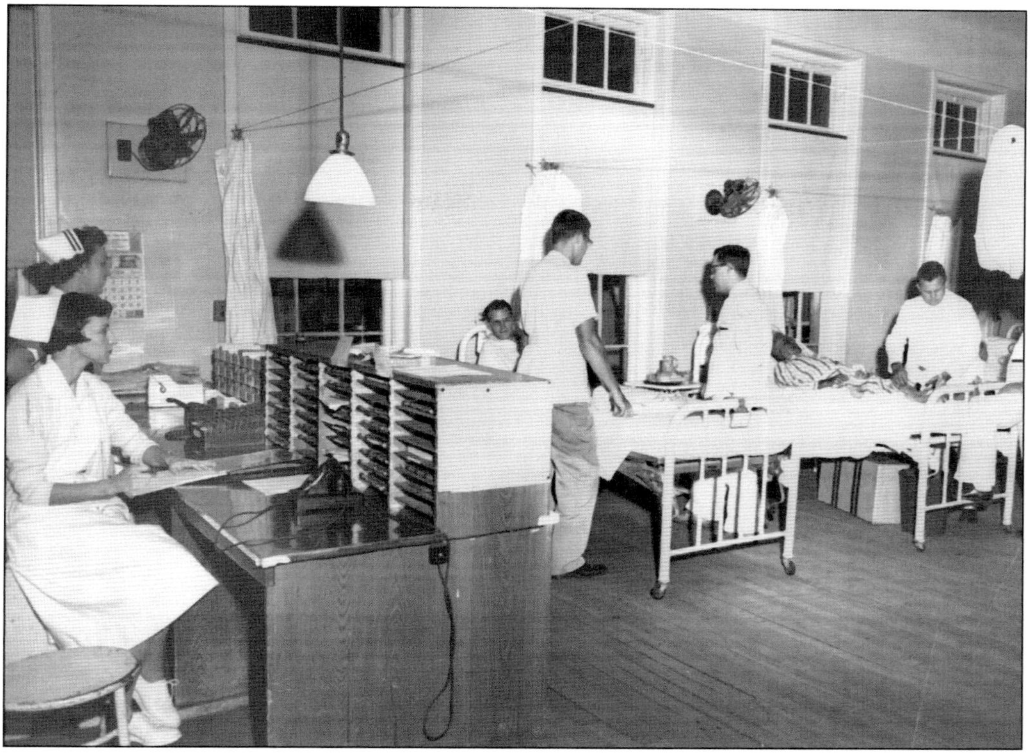

For the first two decades after the transfer to the state, funding and space continued to be problems. Perhaps Kenneth Lynch's most important contribution to the college was the construction of the 1955 Medical College Hospital on Doughty Street. Since 1856, Roper Hospital had served as the primary teaching hospital for the college. Lynch realized that in order to advance, the school had to have a teaching hospital under its own authority and as early as 1944 began planning for the new hospital. Above, nurses-in-training and doctors-in-training work the Roper wards sometime between 1937 and 1942. Below is a construction view of the Medical College Hospital.

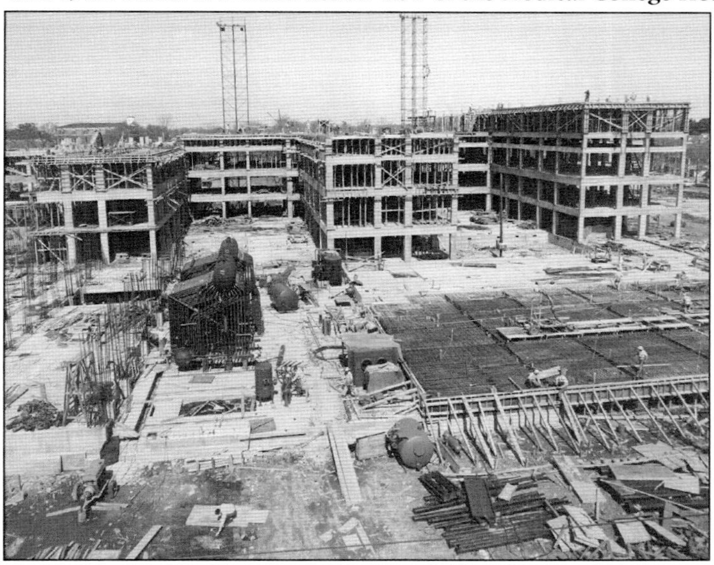

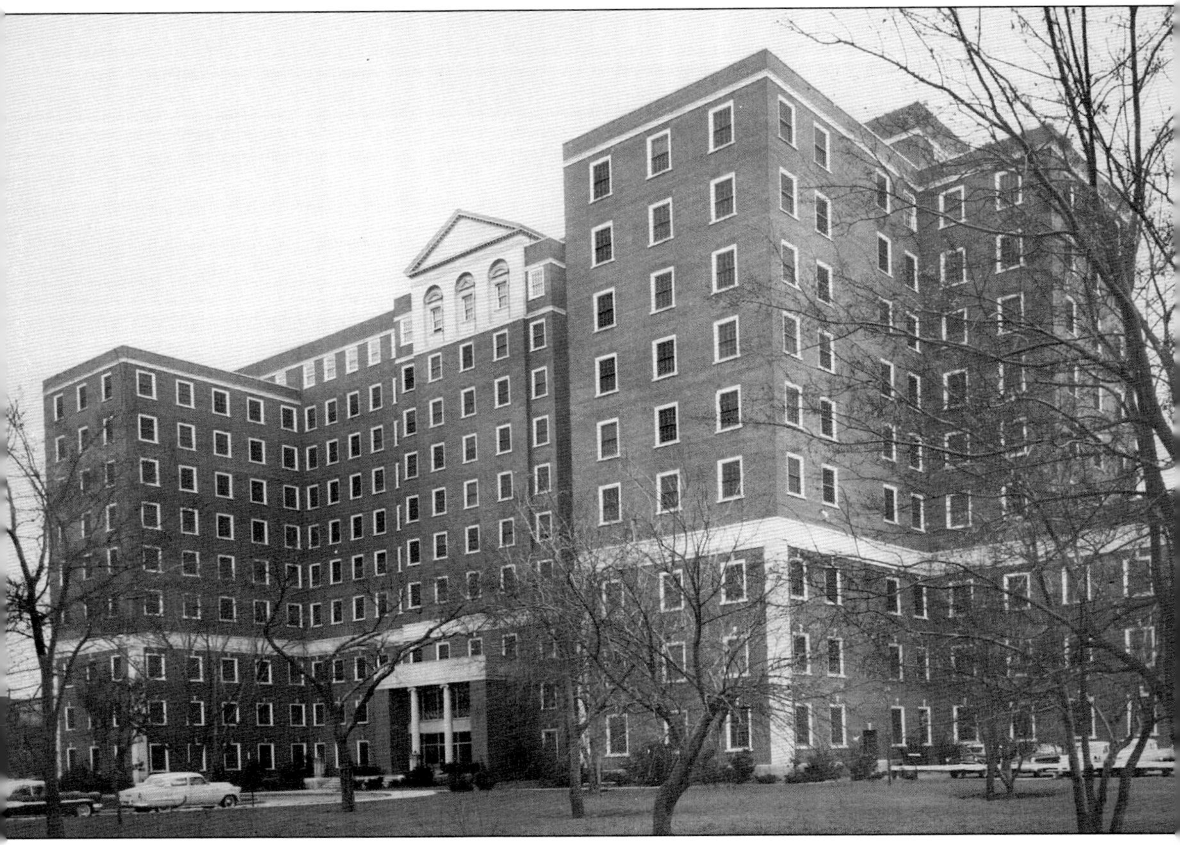

In 1955, the Medical College Hospital was opened, having been built with funds allocated from the federal government. This hospital has subsequently been renovated: in 1975, the Clinical Sciences Building was attached to the west side and the Storm Eye Institute to the east side; in 1987, the Children's Hospital moved into the east side; and in 1993, the North Tower was attached to the front. So, while the building looks very different today, its original structure can still be seen despite its many changes. The 1955 Medical College Hospital represented the first in a long line of facilities expansions that would greatly enlarge the campus footprint and building capacity.

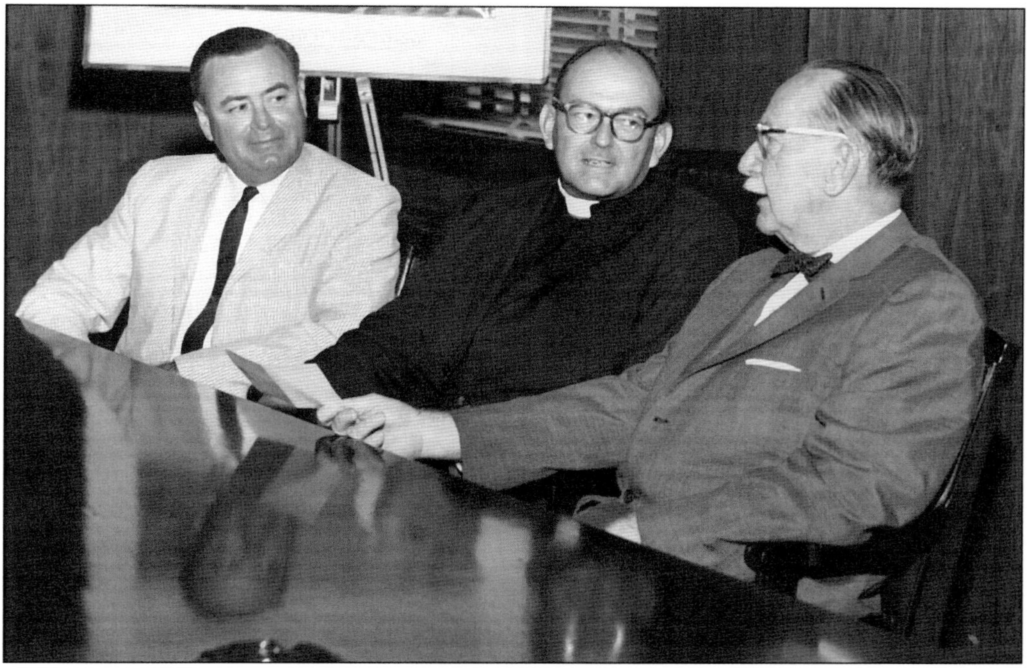

In the early 1960s, Porter Military Academy merged with the Gaud School and the Watt School and relocated to a new site on Albemarle Road west of the Ashley River. In 1963, the Medical College of South Carolina purchased the 11-acre former site of the military academy at a cost of $1,136,000. Pictured here at the time of the sale are, from left to right, Dr. H. Rawling Pratt-Thomas, president of the Medical College; the Right Reverend Gray Temple, bishop of the Episcopal Diocese of South Carolina; and Dr. Thomas A. Pitts, chairman of the Medical College's board of trustees.

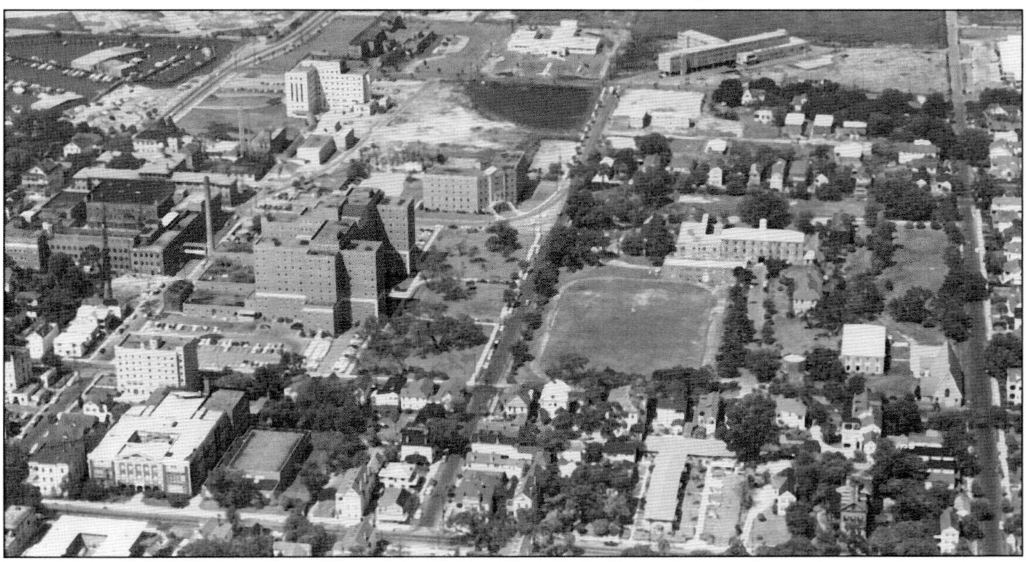

This is an aerial view of the Porter property before the purchase. In the lower right-hand corner of the photograph are the only surviving buildings from the Porter campus—St. Luke's Chapel, Colcock Hall, and Waring Historical Library. To the far left is the Medical College Hospital and nearby the College of Nursing (CON) building. In the upper left is Roper Hospital.

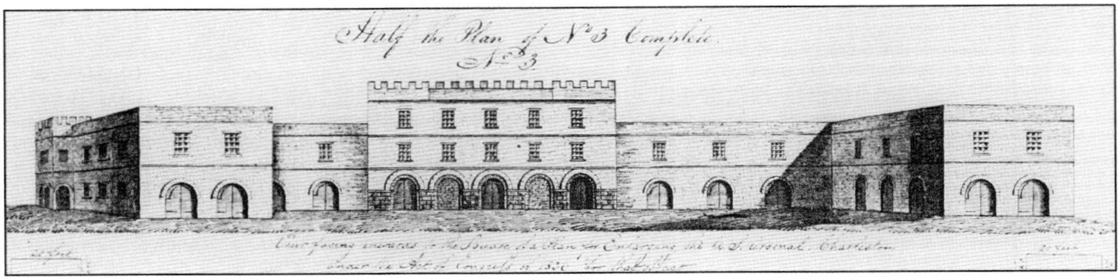

The Porter campus was built on the site of the Charleston Arsenal (above), on land now bound by Bee, Doughty, and President Streets and Ashley Avenue. In 1825, the US government acquired the property, and Charleston architect Edward Brickell White designed the complex of buildings, constructed between 1825 and 1832. On November 7, 1860, the South Carolina militia seized the arsenal, making it one of the first federal properties to fall into Confederate hands. At the war's end, Federal troops reclaimed it and occupied the site from 1865 until 1879, when it was decommissioned as a military installation. Porter Military Academy was established in 1867 by Rev. Anthony Toomer Porter as a school for boys orphaned by the Civil War. In 1880, the school changed its name to the Holy Communion Church Institute and that same year took over the site of the federal arsenal. In 1886, the name of the school was changed to the Porter Military Academy to honor its founder. Below is the entrance to the campus viewed from Ashley Avenue.

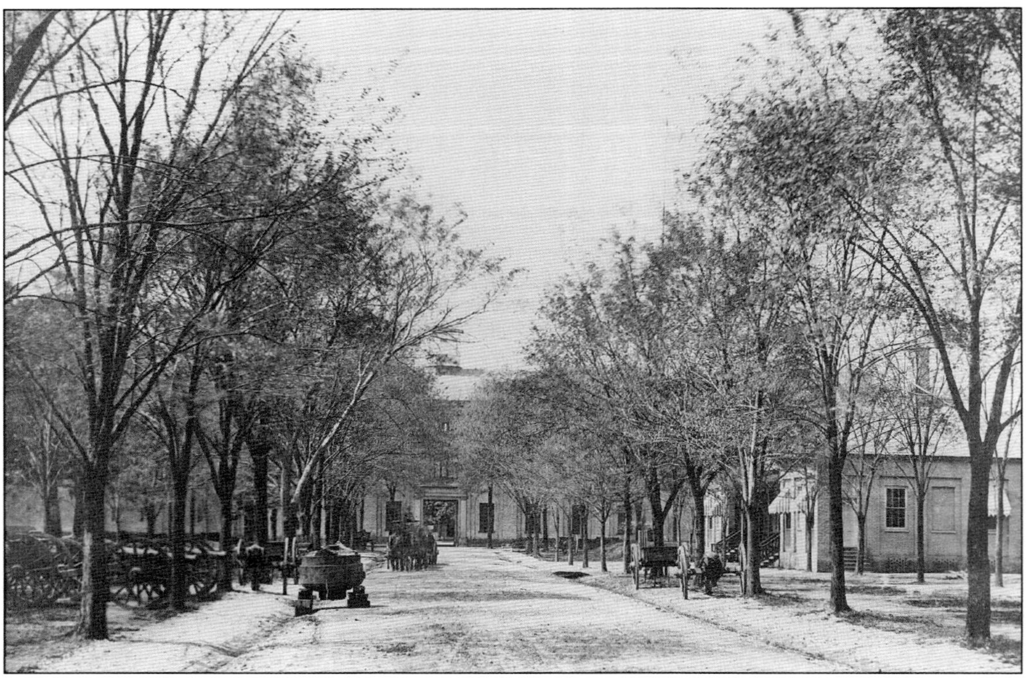

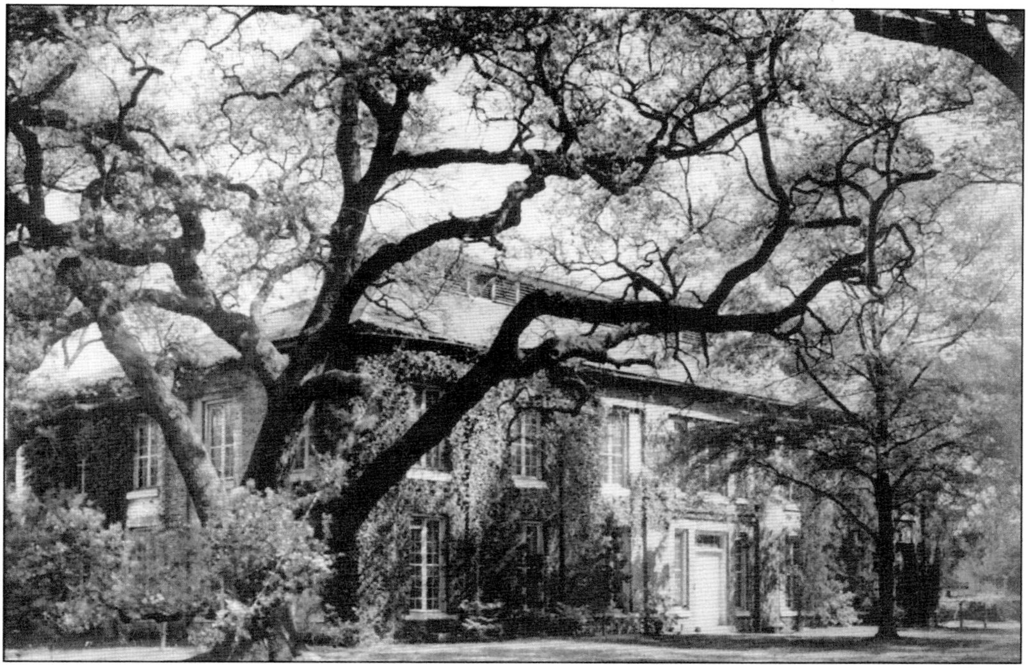

The building now known as Colcock Hall (above) was constructed by the Confederacy in 1861–1862 as a facility for the manufacture and repair of small arms. It later served as classroom space for Porter Military Academy. After being purchased by the Medical College, Colcock Hall, Waring Historical Library (below), and St. Luke's Chapel were added to the National Register of Historic Places in 1996. The rest of the Porter buildings were demolished to make room for the Medical College campus expansion.

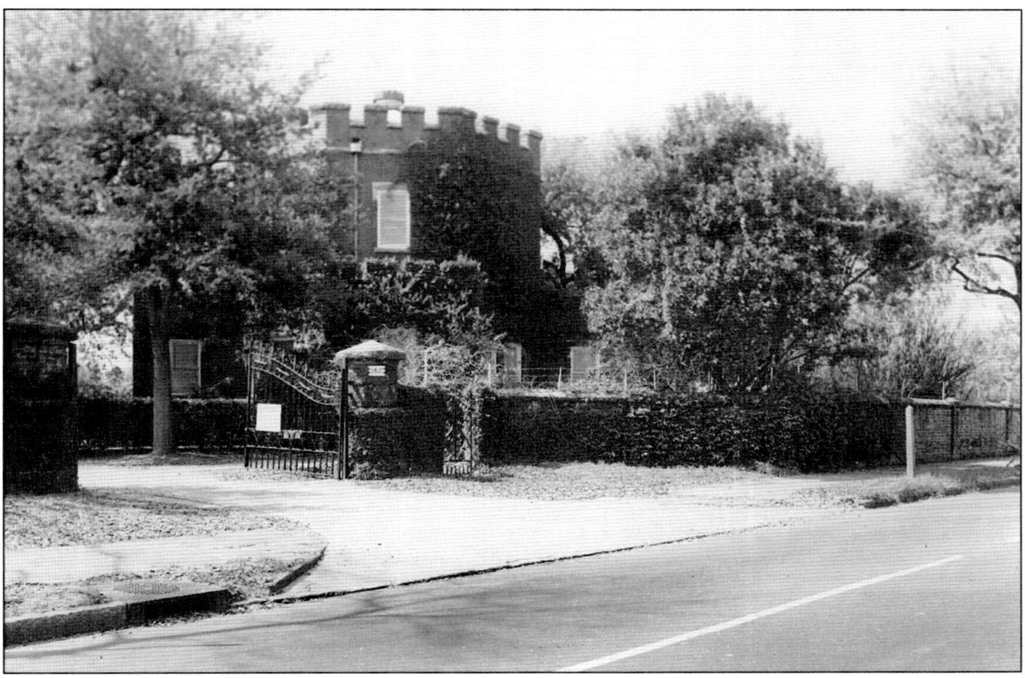

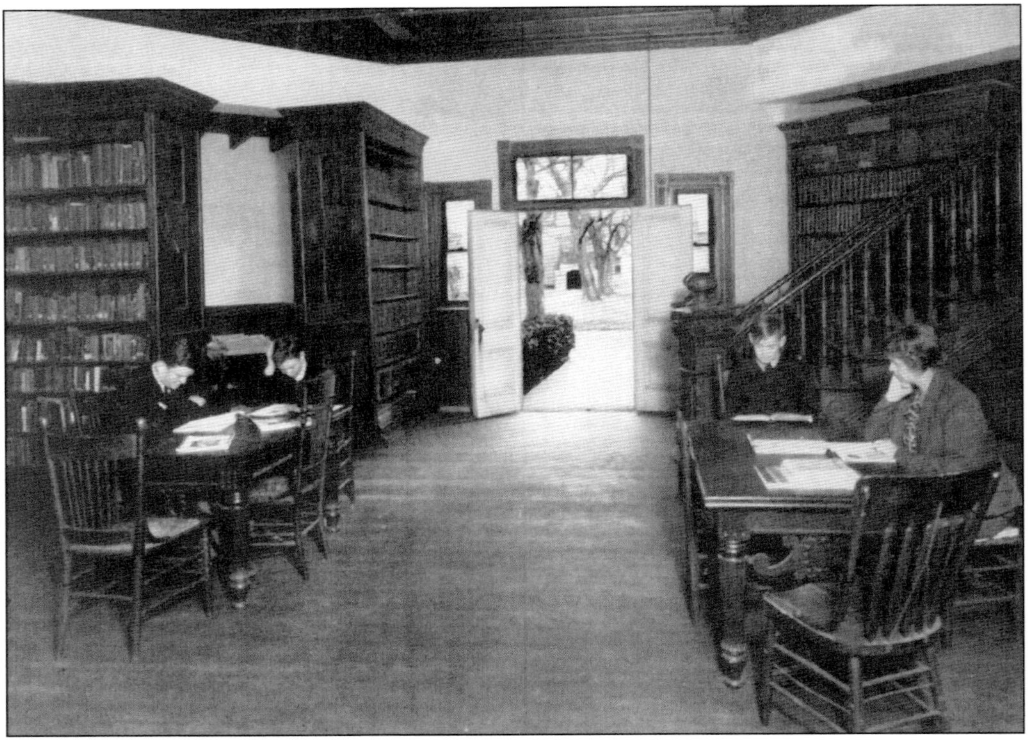

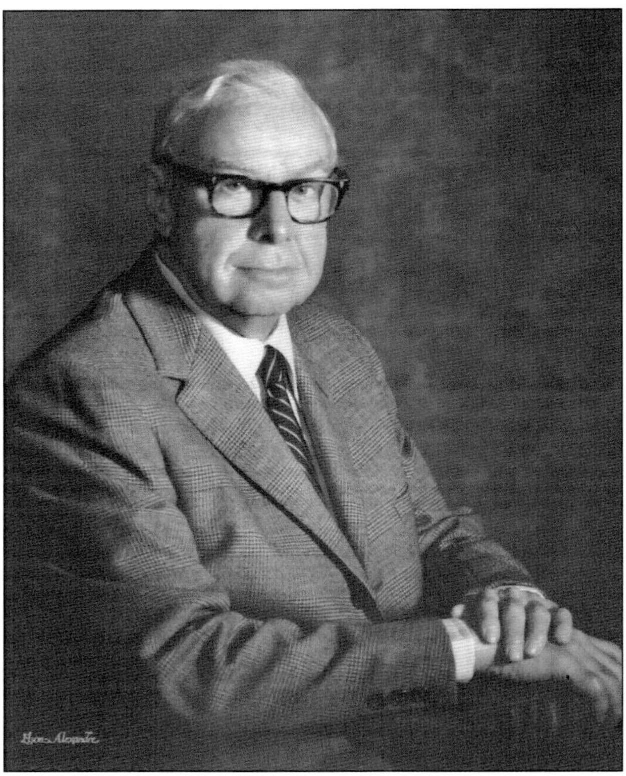

The building now known as the Waring Historical Library was constructed for and served as the library for Porter Military Academy. It was built in 1894 at a cost of $7,500. In 1949, Dr. Joseph I. Waring Jr., for whom the library was later renamed, was elected librarian for the Medical Society of South Carolina and soon thereafter advocated for the collection thusly, "It would be a fine contribution to itself and future generations of the Society . . . to gather them [the books] all in one place where they will be available, visible, and inspiring." Above is an interior view of the Waring Historical Library from around 1920, when it was used by Porter Military Academy. At left is Dr. Joseph I. Waring Jr.

The nucleus of the Waring Historical Library is the library of the Medical Society of South Carolina, which began in 1791 when Drs. Robert and Samuel Wilson donated the first 14 titles to the Medical Society.

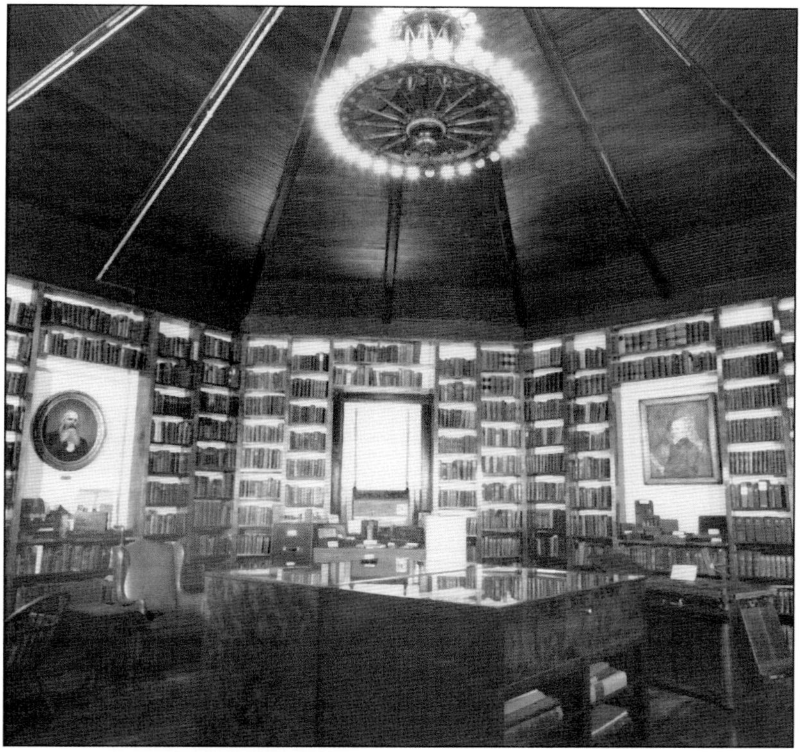

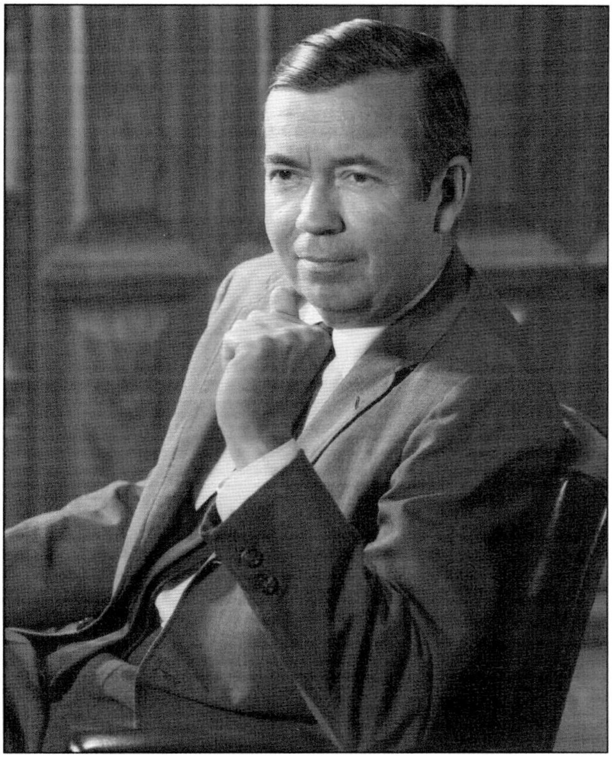

Since 1982, Dr. W. Curtis Worthington Jr. (left) has served as director of the Waring. A 1952 graduate of the Medical College, Dr. Worthington taught anatomy, chaired the anatomy department, and served as academic vice president from 1975 to 1982.

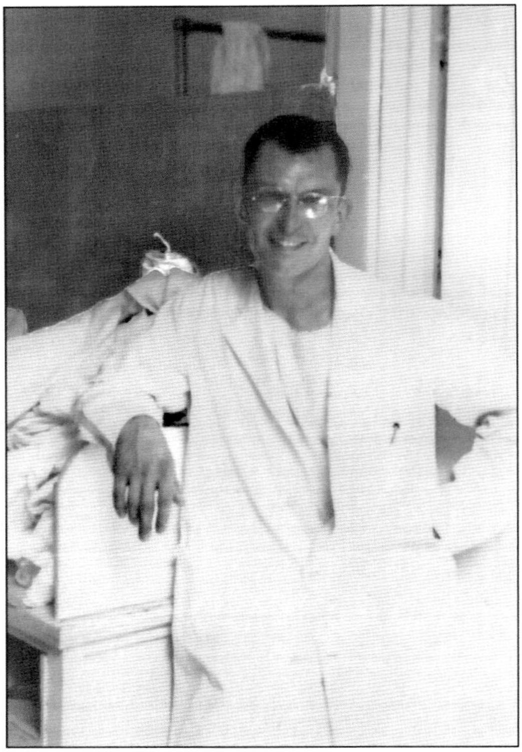

In addition to the improvements to the physical campus, there was increased effort to improve and encourage the college's research capabilities. One such example was that of Dr. Horace Gilbert Smithy's work on the valvulotome. Smithy (shown at left) was the chief surgical resident at Roper Hospital from 1940 to 1942 and a faculty member at the Medical College. Dr. Smithy invented the valvulotome to remove scar tissue from the heart. After conducting animal trials with the device, Dr. Smithy performed the first human operation in 1948. The surgery was a success, and Smithy received nationwide acclaim. Dr. Smithy's interest in the valvulotome was personal: he himself had scar tissue on the aortic valves of his heart as a result of rheumatic fever he suffered as a child. Unfortunately, Dr. Smithy died at age 34 in 1948 before the life-saving surgery he pioneered could be performed on him.

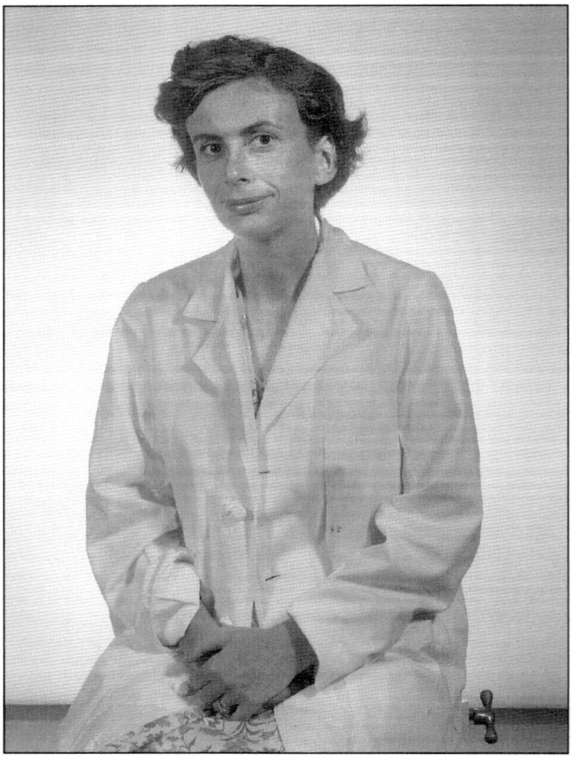

Dr. Maria G. Buse joined the faculty of the Medical College in 1957 in the department of medicine. She helped establish the Nuclear Medicine Laboratory and served as its director until 1983. With her husband, Dr. John Buse, she cofounded the division of endocrinology at the Medical College. Because she was foreign educated, born in Budapest and educated there and in Switzerland, it was not until 1960 that she was able to obtain her license to practice medicine in South Carolina. Dr. Buse holds the record for a continuously funded grant by the NIH—spanning more than 50 years.

On December 3, 1968, MCSC performed the first major organ transplant in its history and the first in the state of South Carolina when 24-year-old William Ashley of Iva, South Carolina, received a kidney from his sister, Velma Ashley Madden. What made this relatively straightforward operation unique and the first of its kind was the use of lymphocyte depletion as the principal preoperative measure against organ rejection. Thomas Hargest, director of engineering and development for the department of surgery, developed the SCIRT pump to remove impurities from the lymph of uremic patients and return the purified lymph to the body. The operation was successful, and the donor was discharged eight days after the surgery. Ashley was discharged December 24. In this photograph, team members Dr. C. Thomas Fitts (right) and Lloyd Martin prepare for the operating room.

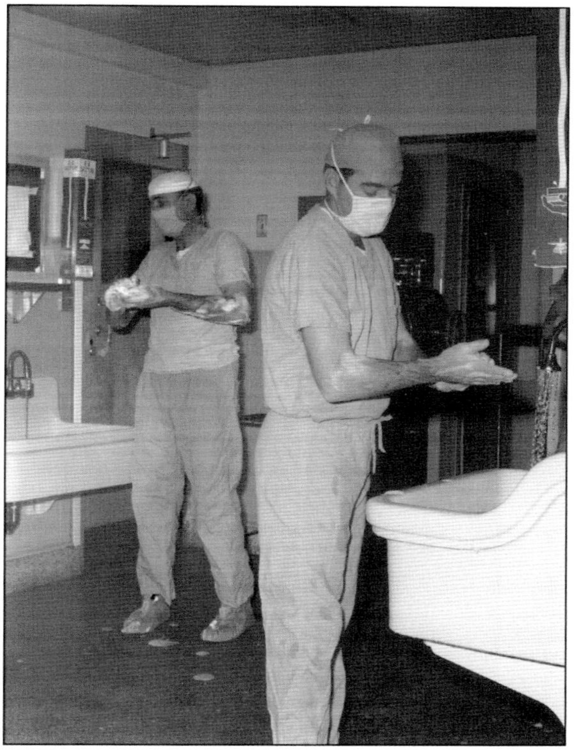

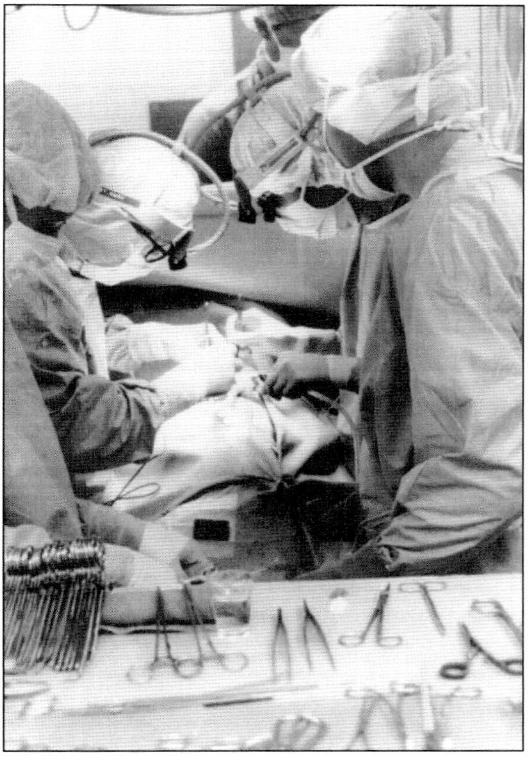

On June 30, 1987, twelve-year old Terrance Richardson of Edisto Island, South Carolina, became the first heart-transplant patient at MUSC. The four-hour surgery was performed by Drs. Fred A. Crawford, chief of cardiothoracic surgery; A. Jackson Crumbley, chief of cardiac transplantation; Henry B. Wiles, pediatric cardiologist; and Calvert C. Alpert, anesthesiologist.

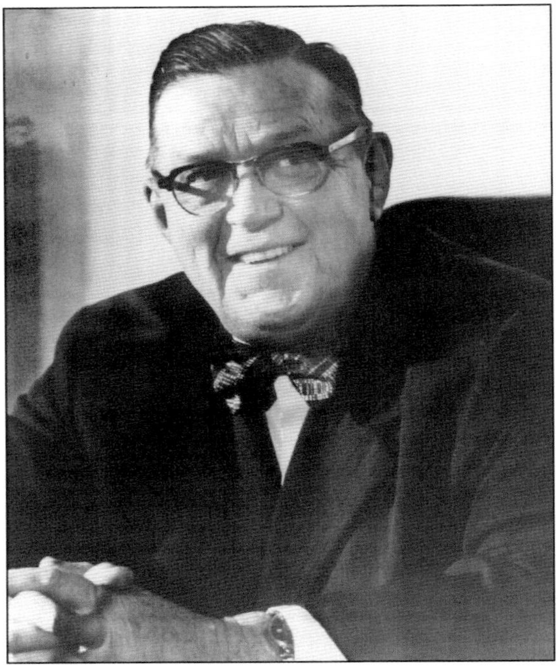

Even as the Medical College made enormous strides in education, research, and patient care, it was still very much a Southern institution with a legacy of racial discrimination. Four years after assuming the presidency from Dr. H. Rawling Pratt-Thomas, Dr. William M. McCord presided over the 1969 hospital workers strike, which started on March 20 when 12 black nonprofessional hospital workers were fired. This action triggered a strike of nonprofessional workers at the Medical College Hospital and Charleston County Hospital.

The strike drew Rev. Ralph Abernathy of the Southern Leadership Conference, Coretta Scott King, Andrew Young, and others in the national civil rights movement to Charleston in a show of solidarity. A nighttime curfew was declared, and the National Guard patrolled the streets.

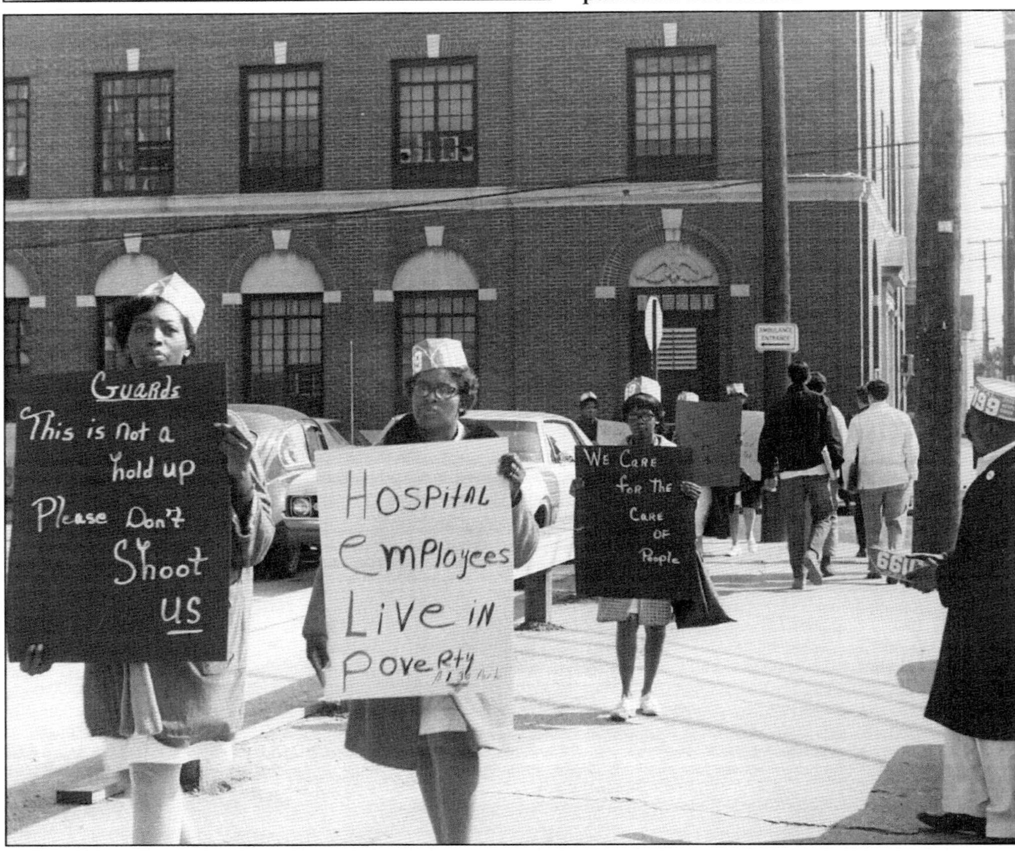

The strike was settled on June 27, ninety days after it started, when the university rehired the workers who were fired as a result of the strike and put in place grievance policies to help prevent future discrimination.

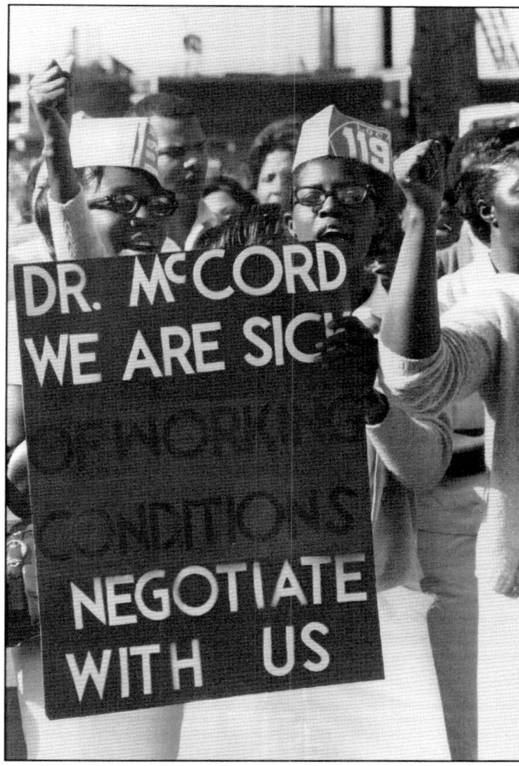

Photographs of the strikers taken by the college's public relations office were annotated to identify the strike participants. The image shown below is an example of this: individuals are identified by name, when known, or their ward or floor assignments.

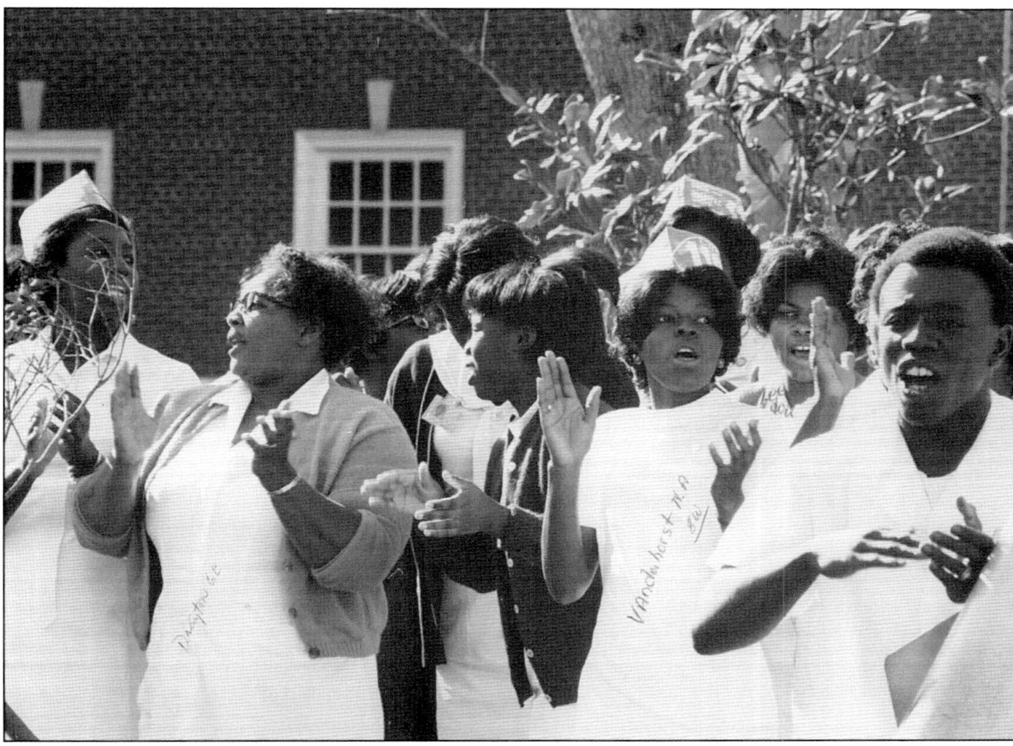

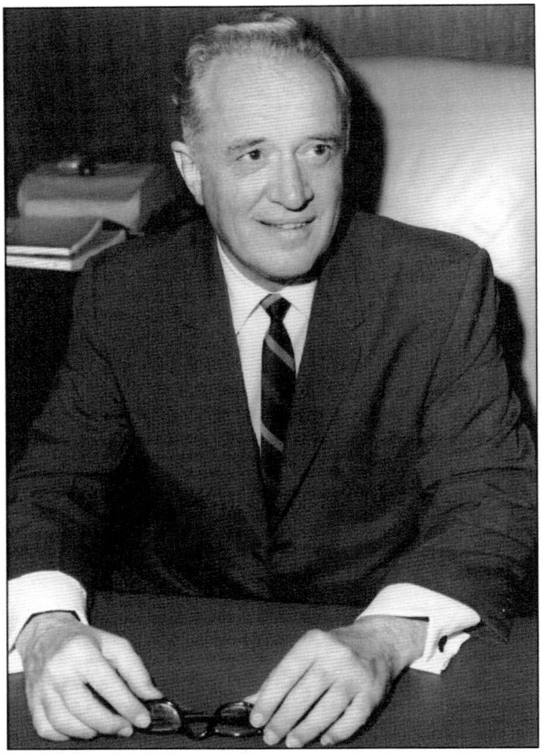

James W. Colbert Jr., MD, arrived at the Medical College as its first vice president for academic affairs on February 1, 1969, shortly before the start of the hospital workers strike, which he helped settle. During his five years of service, Dr. Colbert oversaw the Medical University during a period of unparalleled growth. A visionary, facilitator, and advocate, Dr. Colbert worked with faculty and staff to strengthen the university's core missions—education, research, and patient care. His work laid the foundation for MUSC's rise as a nationally renowned academic medical center. Dr. Colbert played a major role in the development of South Carolina's statewide system of health education, the Area Health Education Consortium (AHEC), and was instrumental in developing the Medical University's Family Practice program. Dr. Colbert's career was cut short by his death on September 11, 1974, in a plane crash in Charlotte. In 2009, the library and administration building was renamed in his honor.

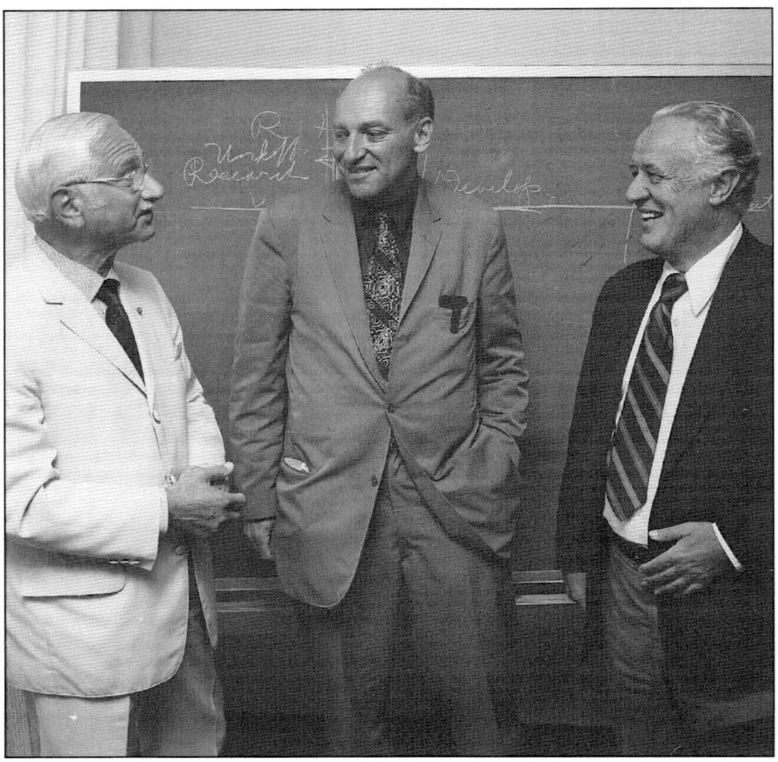

Dr. Colbert brought Dr. Albert B. Sabin, developer of the oral polio vaccine, to MUSC in 1974 as the distinguished research professor of biomedicine. Sabin called Colbert "my very good friend . . . whom I had known for over a quarter of a century." This 1974 photograph shows Drs. Albert B. Sabin (left), H. Hugh Fudenberg (center), and James W. Colbert Jr.

William H. Knisely received a doctorate from the Medical College of South Carolina in 1954. He returned to the Medical University in 1974 to take the position of vice president of academic affairs. After the untimely death of Dr. Colbert, Knisely was made president-elect. He was officially appointed president of MUSC in December 1975. He served in this office until 1982, when he left South Carolina for the University of Oklahoma College of Medicine.

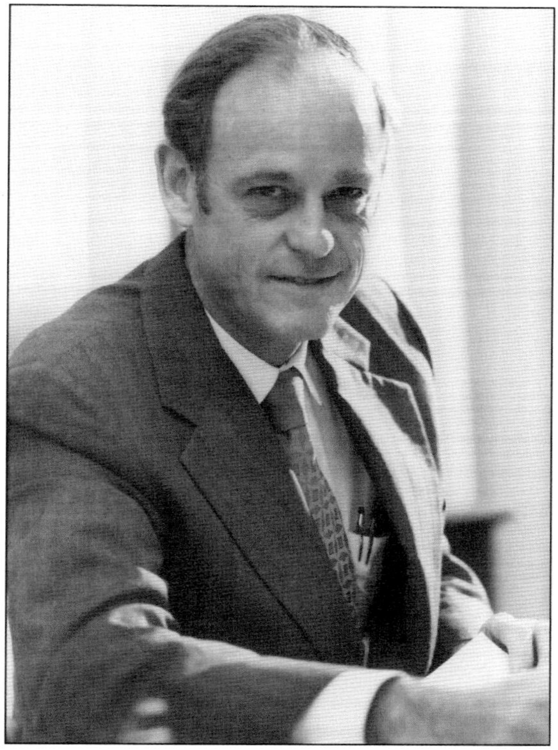

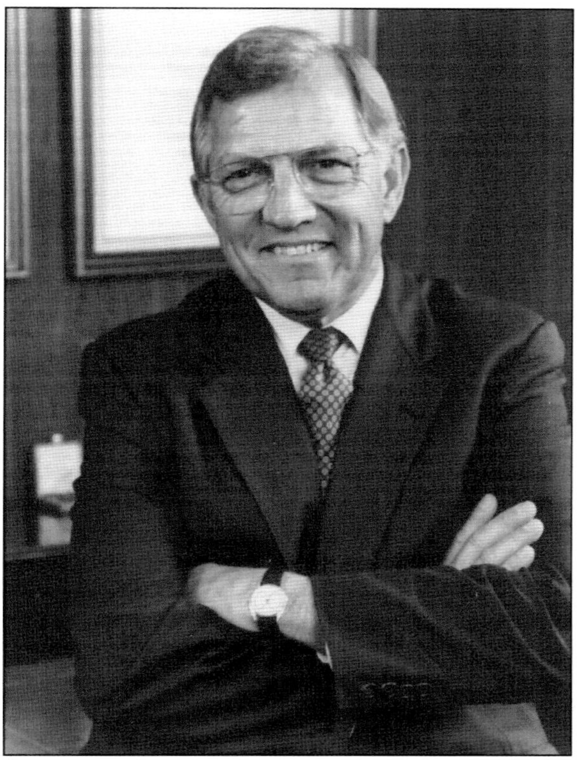

James Burrows Edwards, DMD, served as president of the Medical University from 1982 to 1999. During his 17 years, Edwards was instrumental in the creation of the Hollings Cancer Center, the Heart Center, the Digestive Disease Center, the Institute of Psychiatry, the Transplant Center, the Children's Hospital, and the Storm Eye Institute. Research funding grew tenfold, surpassing $100 million in 1999. The growth under Edwards's leadership made MUSC one of South Carolina's largest employers. In 2009, in recognition of his work on behalf of the university, the College of Dental Medicine was renamed the James B. Edwards College of Dental Medicine.

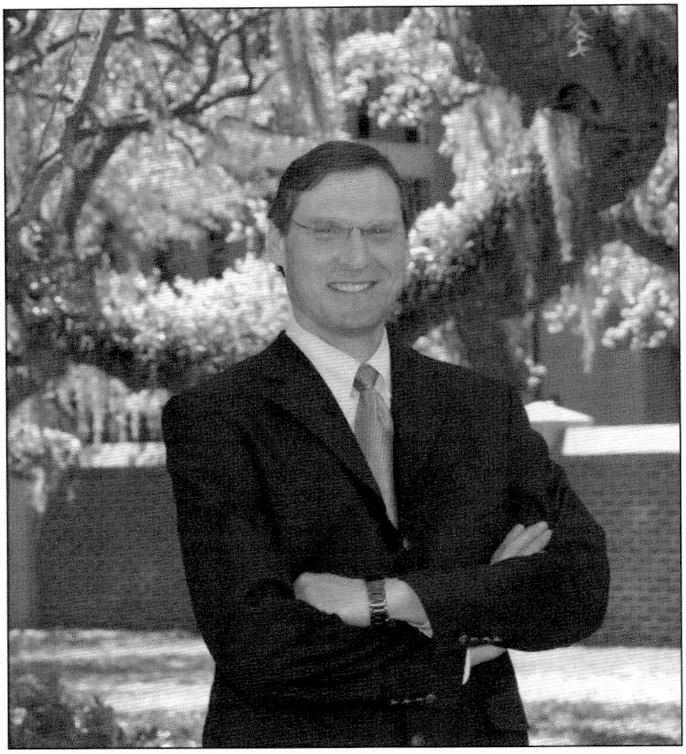

Raymond S. Greenberg, MD, PhD, became president of MUSC in January 2000. Greenberg has placed an emphasis on statewide outreach and collaboration. He has championed the progressive replacement of aging hospital facilities and the development of five new research buildings for children's health, cancer, drug discovery and development, bioengineering, and clinical research. Prior to coming to Charleston, Greenberg served on the medical school faculty at Emory University and was the founding dean of the Rollins School of Public Health there. He arrived at the Medical University in 1995 as the vice president for academic affairs and provost.

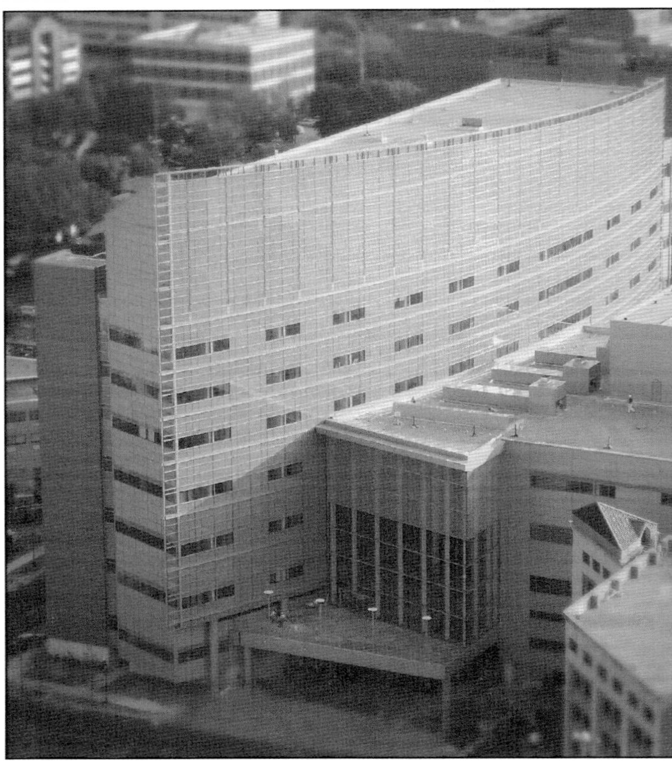

In 2007, Ashley River Tower was dedicated in the first phase of the hospital replacement effort. Seen here is the Ashley River Tower in 2010. (Courtesy of the MUSC Office of Public Relations.)

Two

College of Pharmacy

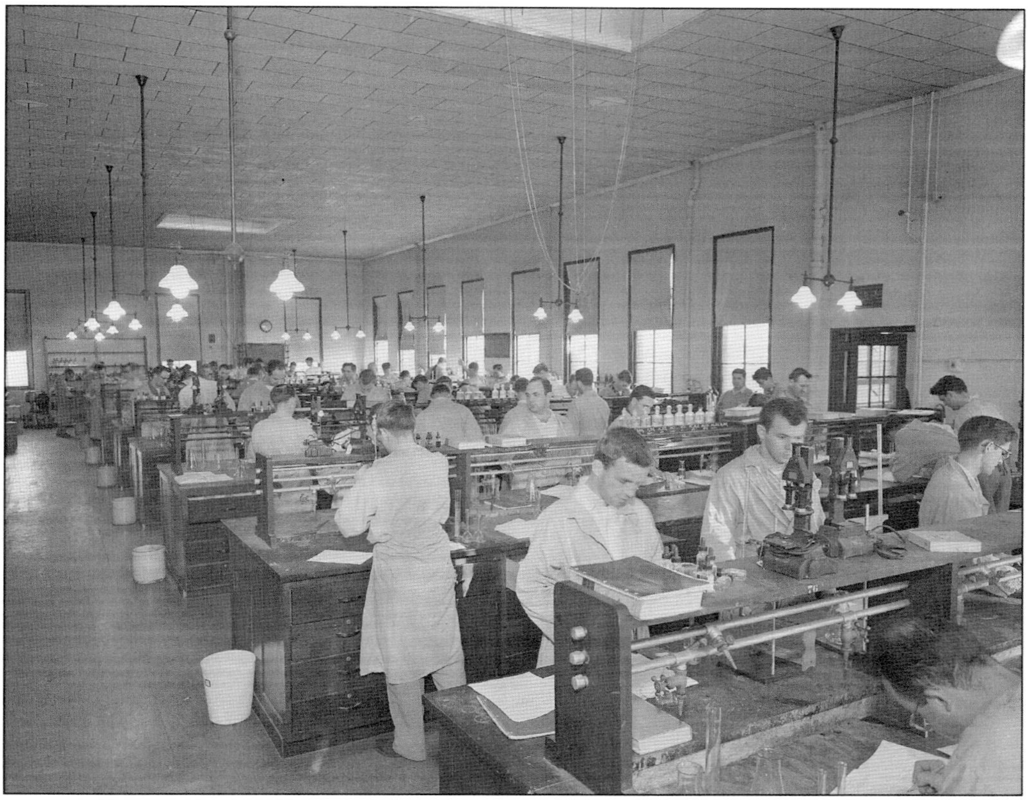

As early as 1824, the Medical College offered lectures on the topics of materia medica, botany and natural history, and chemistry and practical pharmacy—pharmacy courses that were also foundation courses for the study of medicine. During the next four decades, a handful of diplomas in pharmacy were awarded by the Medical College. It was not, however, until 1874 that the Medical College conferred its first official degree of pharmacy.

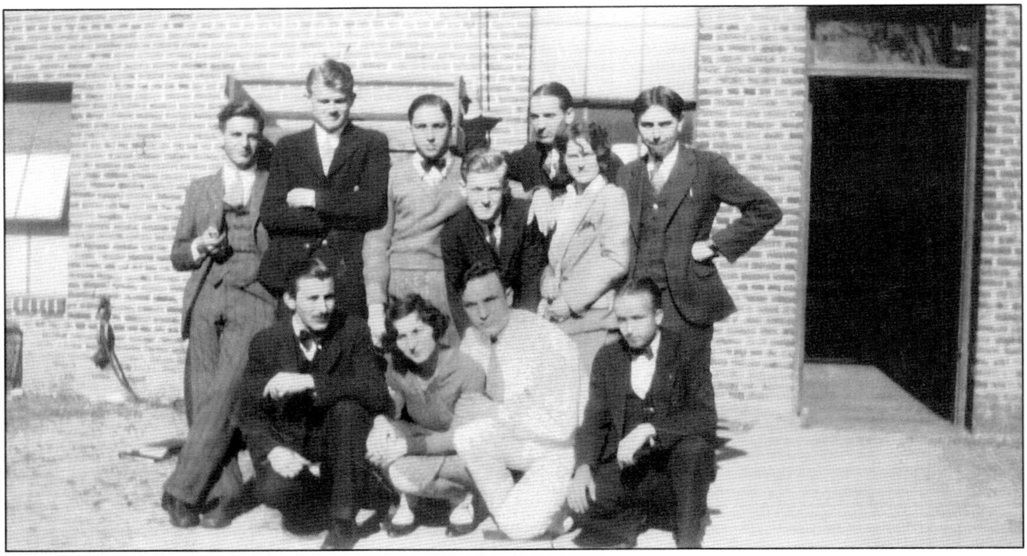

The 1876 Pharmacy Act reflected the efforts of South Carolina pharmacists to standardize and improve education and licensure in the state. By faculty resolution in 1881, the Medical College created a department of pharmacy that was the first of its kind in the Deep South. The first degree-seeking students were admitted in 1882, but the program was discontinued after two years. After some reorganization, the pharmacy school resumed on a permanent basis in 1894, offering the degree of Graduate in Pharmacy. In the 1925 photograph above, students gather outside the Medical College Building on Lucas Street. Below is the senior pharmacy class from 1963.

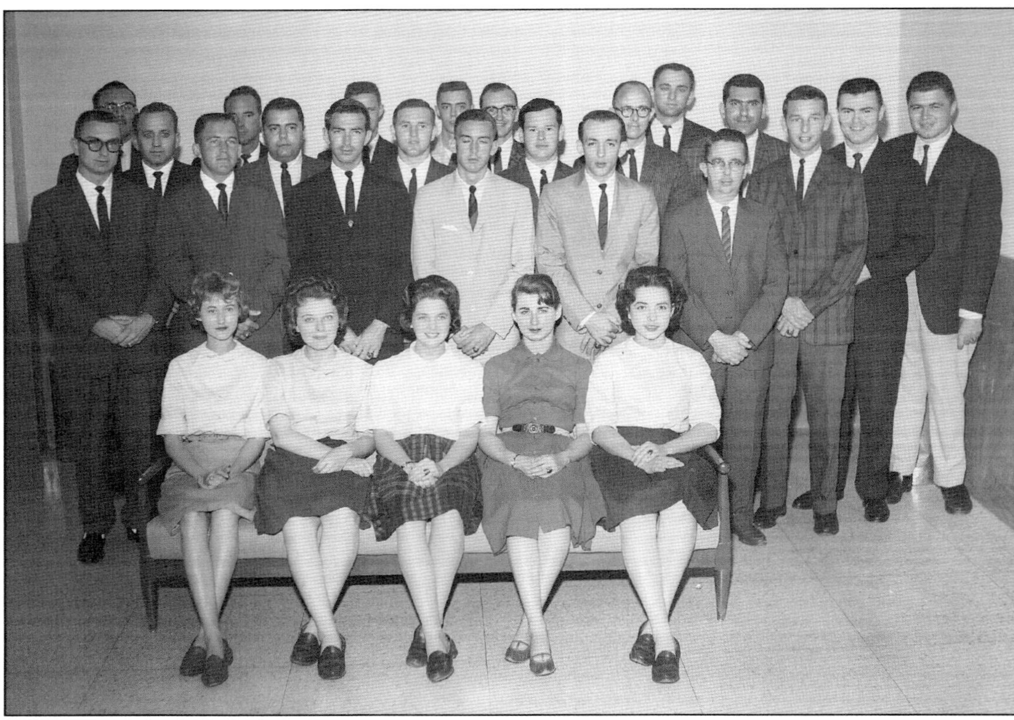

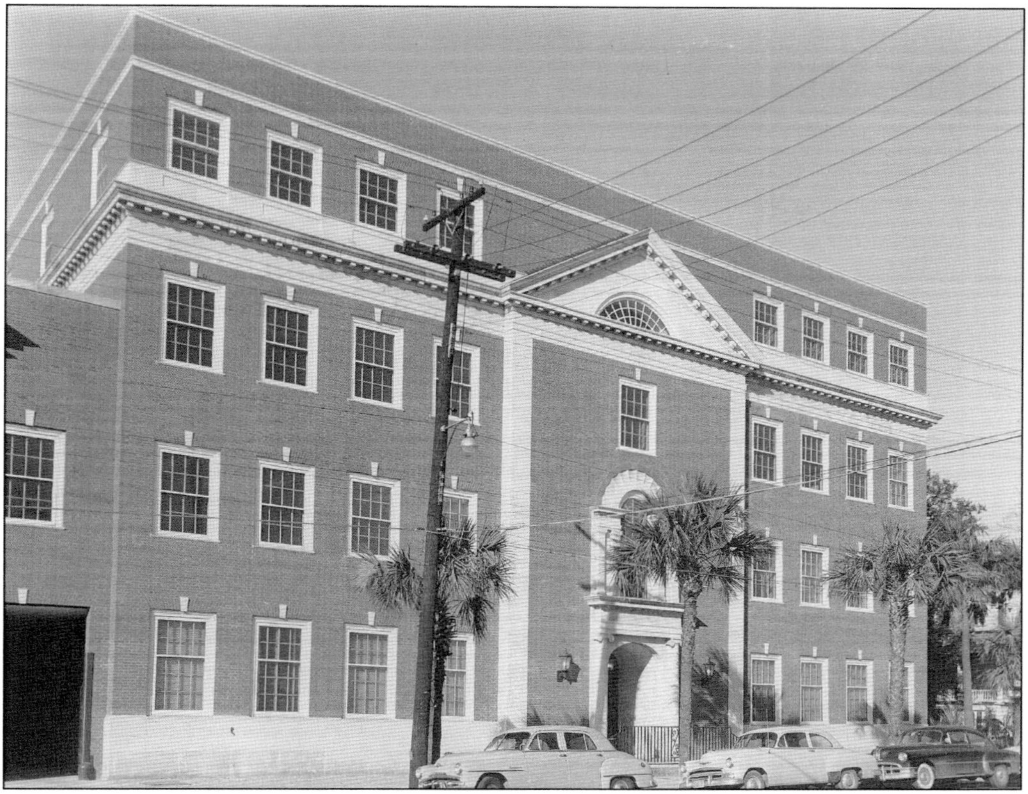

In the early years, the pharmacy program was located on the second floor of the main college building on Lucas Street. In 1952, the Laboratory-Clinic building, or Cancer Clinic, was constructed to the east of Baruch Auditorium, with the College of Pharmacy occupying the fourth floor, as identified in this wall marker (right). By the 1970s, the College of Pharmacy occupied the entire building.

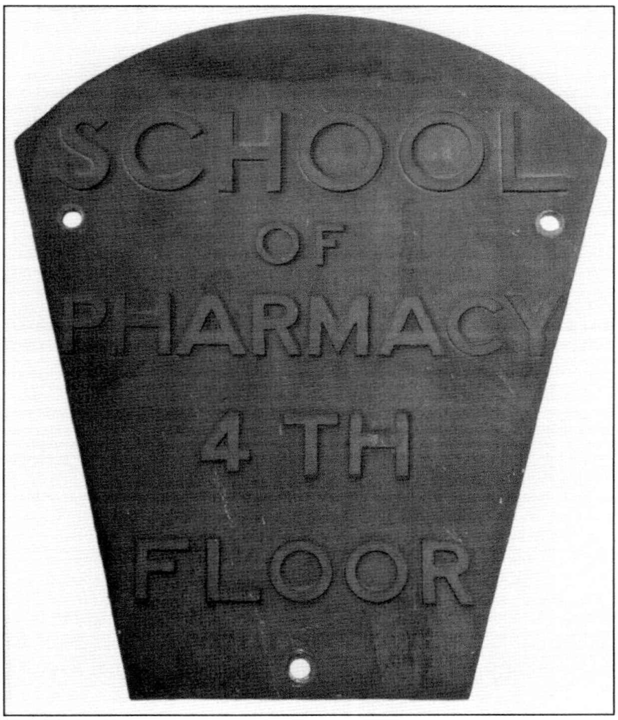

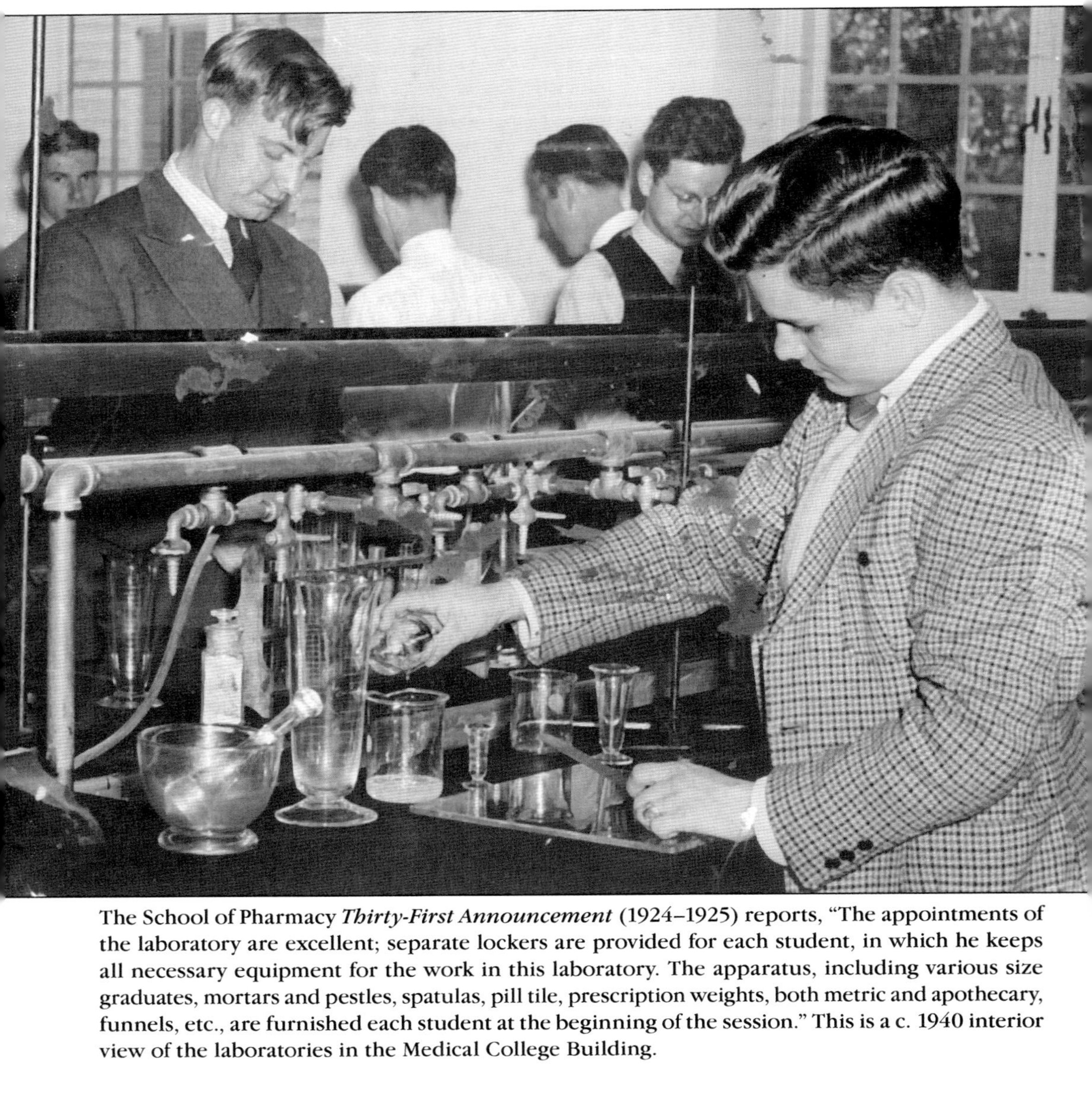

The School of Pharmacy *Thirty-First Announcement* (1924–1925) reports, "The appointments of the laboratory are excellent; separate lockers are provided for each student, in which he keeps all necessary equipment for the work in this laboratory. The apparatus, including various size graduates, mortars and pestles, spatulas, pill tile, prescription weights, both metric and apothecary, funnels, etc., are furnished each student at the beginning of the session." This is a c. 1940 interior view of the laboratories in the Medical College Building.

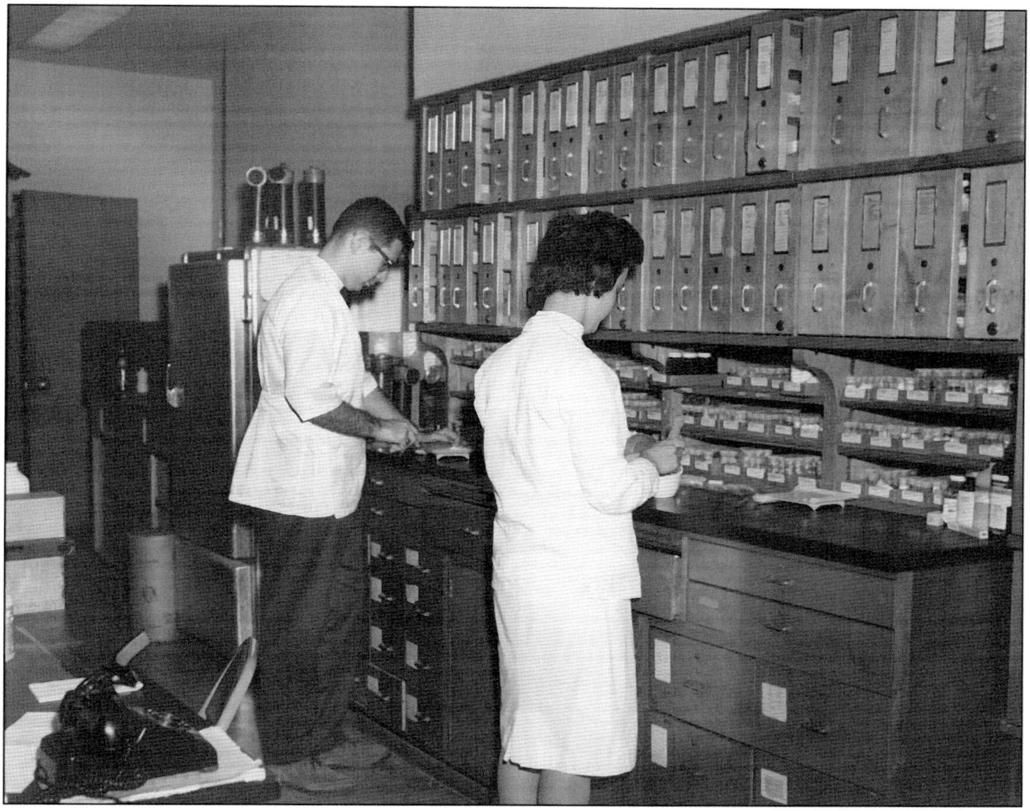

The announcement continues that "the laboratory fixtures are so arranged as to give as much similarity as possible to the drug store, and have on them the glass labeled stock bottles, herb cannisters [*sic*], ointment pots, etc., with abbreviated Latin titles. Equipment for manufacturing is also furnished, such as drug mills, powder mixers, suppository and tablet triturate machines, percolators, pill machines, tincture presses, bottle capping machines, etc." This c. 1965 photograph shows a pharmacy lab.

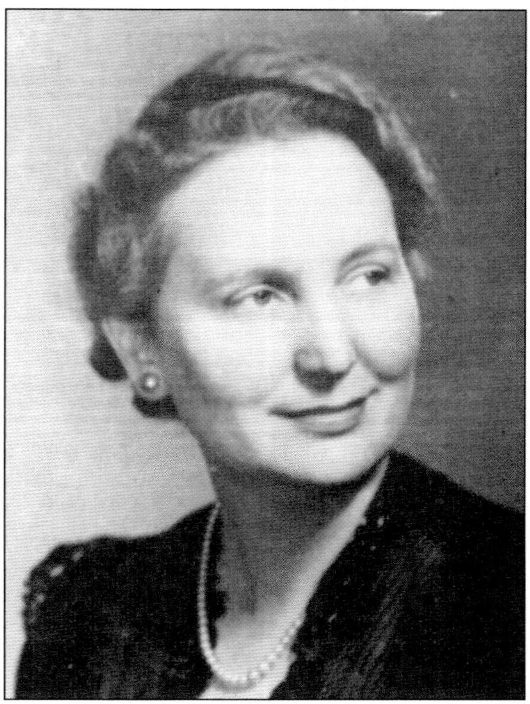

Dr. Maxine Larisey was born in Terre Haute, Indiana, in 1909. She earned degrees in botany from Washington University in St. Louis, Missouri. When Larisey joined the faculty of the College of Pharmacy as professor of biology and pharmacognosy in 1947, she became its first female professor. She taught botany at MUSC until her retirement in 1975.

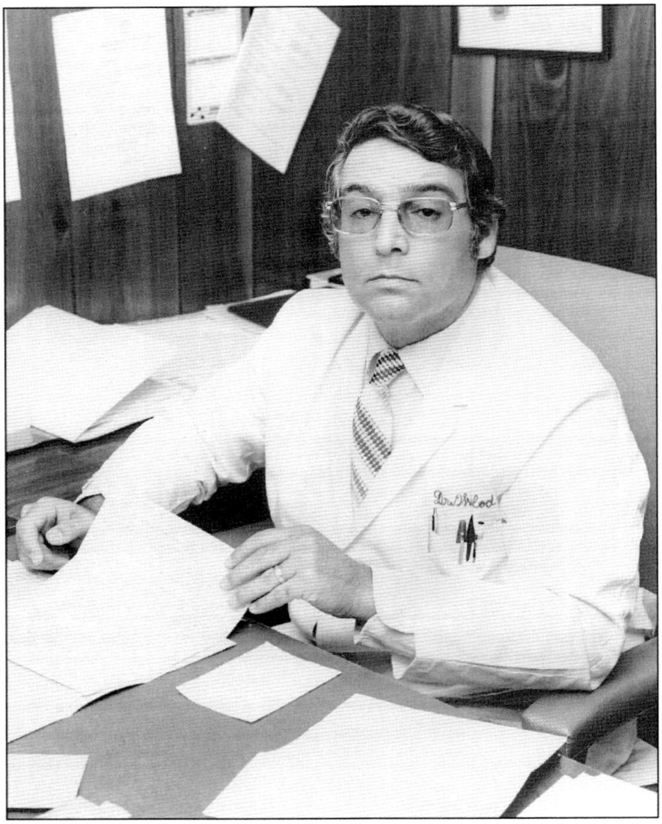

In its first 100 years, the college had only four deans—Edward S. Burnham, Washington Hayne Zeigler, William Allen Prout, and William H. Golod. Dr. Golod (left) served as dean of the College of Pharmacy from 1965 to 1994.

In 2004, the MUSC College of Pharmacy joined forces with the University of South Carolina (USC) to create the South Carolina College of Pharmacy. Both USC and MUSC have long histories of pharmacy education in the state. The University of South Carolina first offered degrees in pharmacy in 1888. The current school, however, dates to 1925 when it was officially established within the university. The mortar and pestle belonging to Dr. S. Napier was manufactured around 1870.

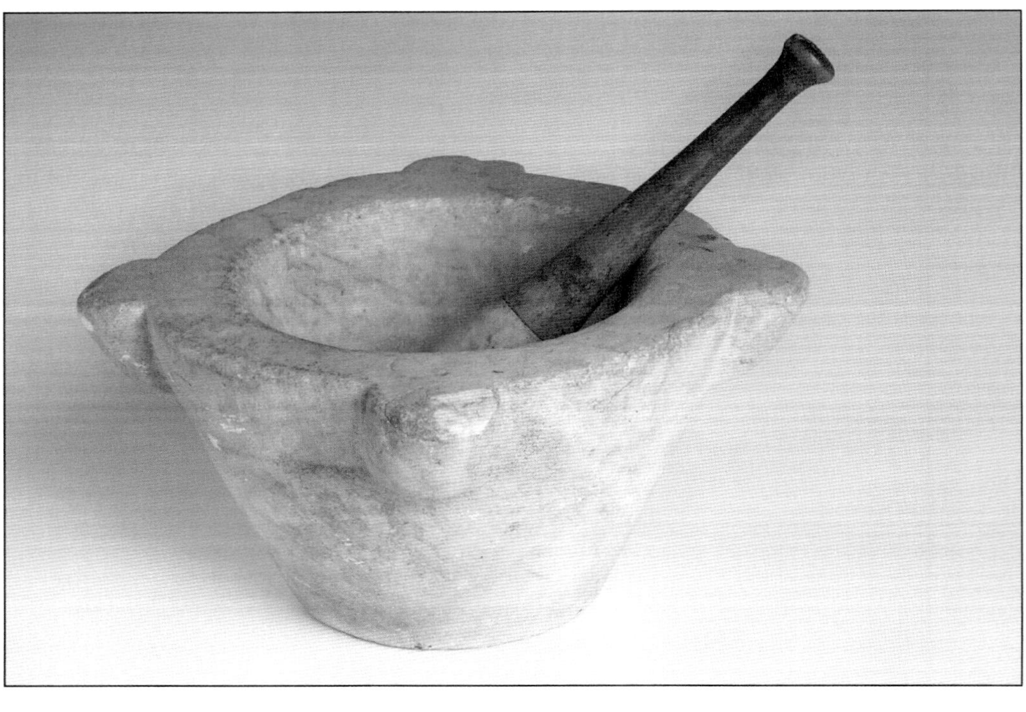

Three

COLLEGE OF NURSING

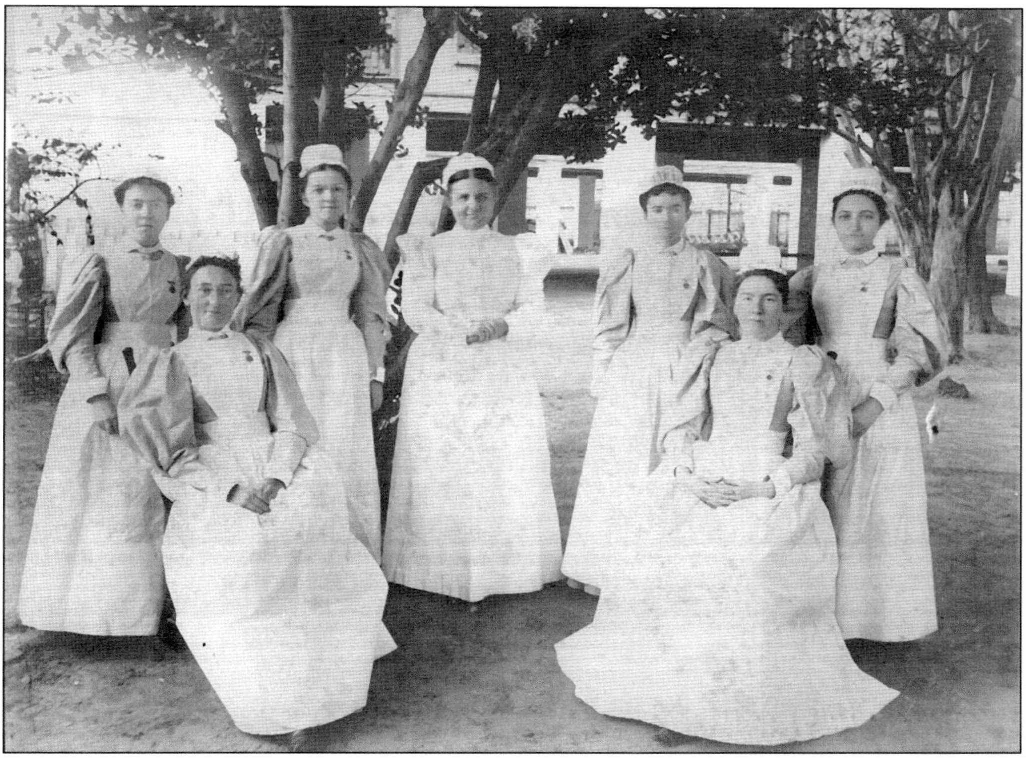

The College of Nursing had its origin in 1882 when the city council of Charleston approved a request by the City Hospital for $2,000 to establish a "Training School for Nurses." The school was opened in 1883 (first students accepted in 1884) and continued operating at the City Hospital until it was destroyed by an earthquake in 1886. The institution was reestablished as the Charleston Training School in 1895. Pictured are the nursing graduates of the Charleston Training School, class of 1897.

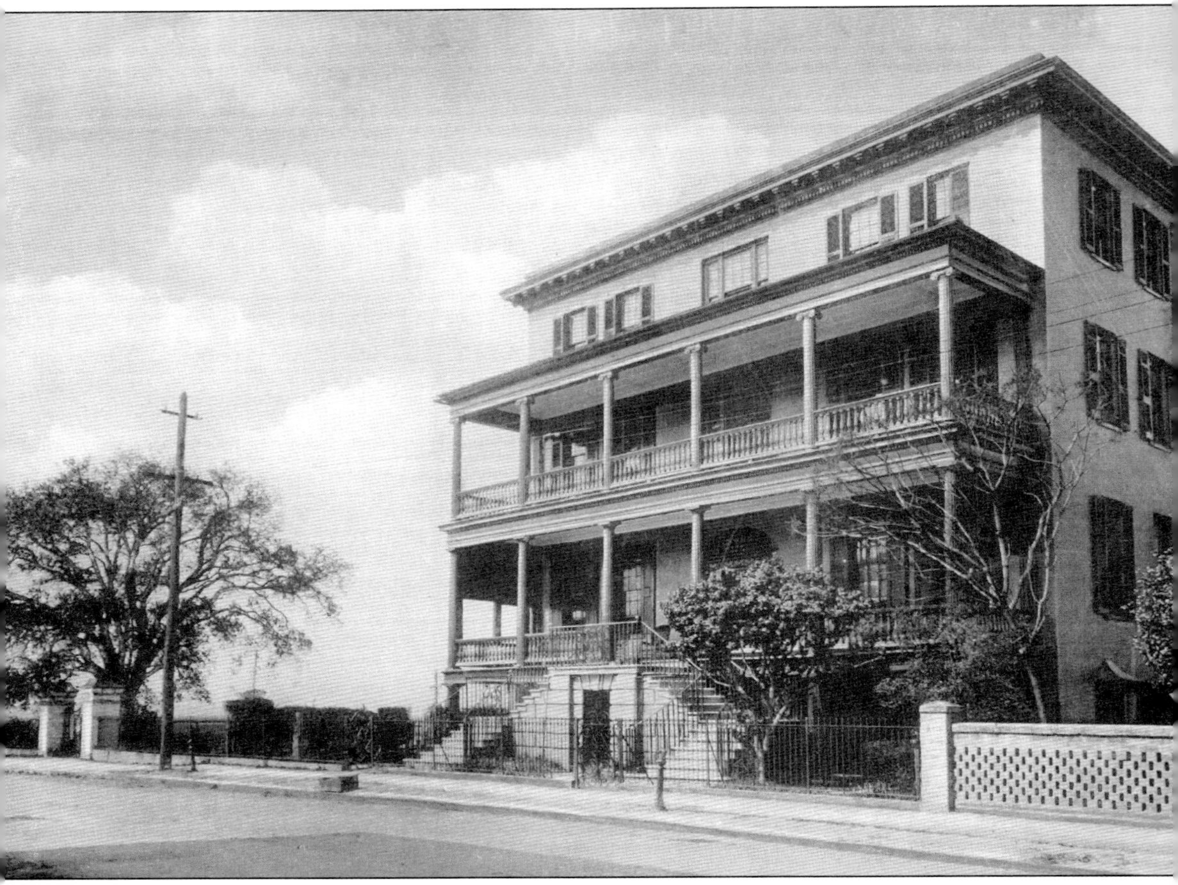

As early as 1895, student nurses were living on the top floor of what would later be called the Kinloch Home for Nurses at the west end of Calhoun Street. When the second Roper Hospital was built on Lucas and Calhoun Streets, this house, originally the residence for the Lucas family, which had owned the surrounding area, was used for private patients of Roper Hospital and known as the Riverside Infirmary. In 1922, when the Thompson Memorial Hospital was built for private patients, the Lucas House became the Robert A. Kinloch Home for Nurses. It accommodated 60 students and, according to the *School of Nursing Second Announcement* (1922–1923), was "provided with all the usual comforts. Reception rooms are provided for visitors, and entertainments under the direction and supervision of the Superintendent of Nurses. Every care is taken to make the life of the nurse pleasant to surround her with a home atmosphere and comfort."

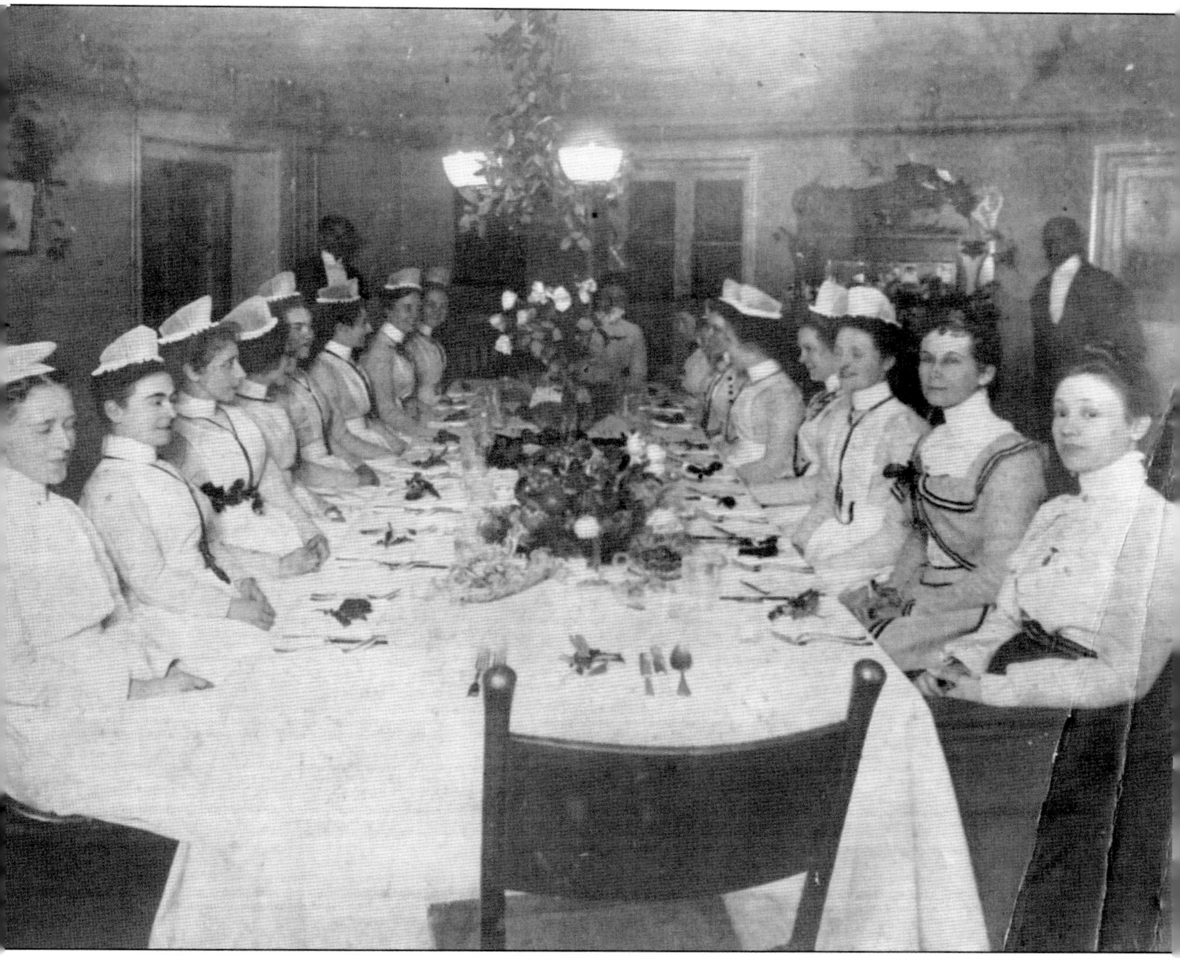

Nursing students were required to reside together while in school and also partake of meals together. This c. 1902 picture illustrates the home atmosphere and comfort provided to the student nurses during their courses of study.

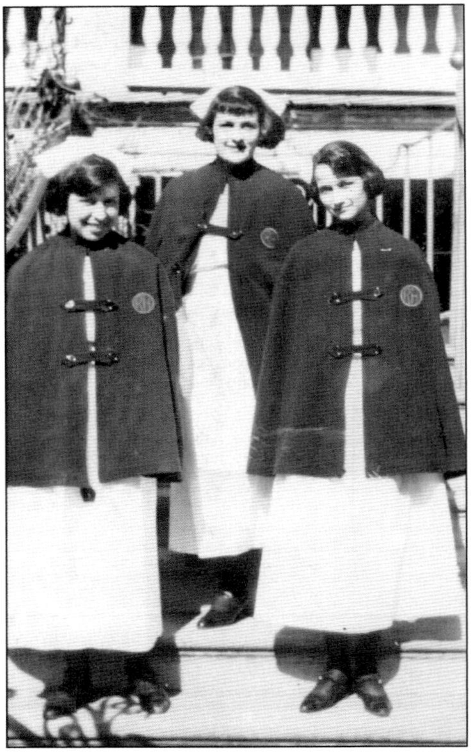

A two-year program of instruction was offered with some lectures given by the Medical College faculty. Between 1904 and 1916, Roper Hospital administered the nursing program until the hospital board of commissioners proposed incorporating the training school into the Medical College. In 1919, the Roper Training School for Nurses became the School of Nursing of the Medical College of the State of South Carolina and expanded to a three-year diploma program.

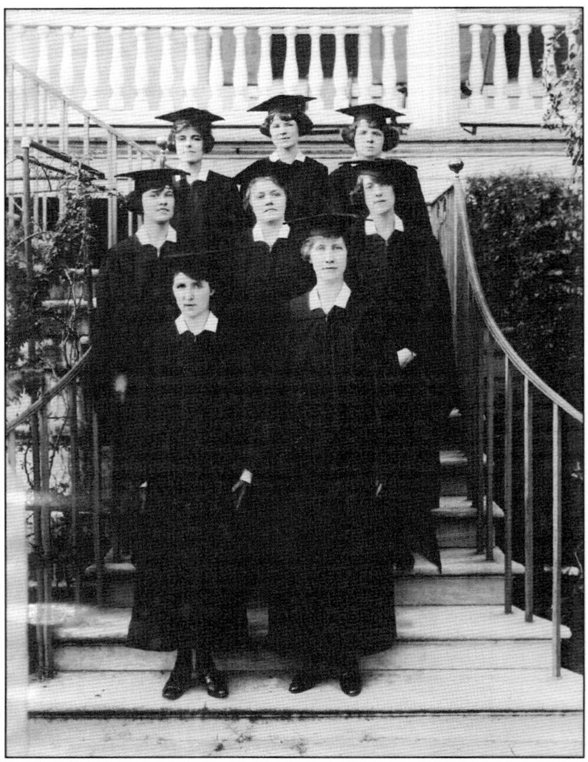

The 1922–1923 *School of Nursing Second Announcement* includes the following: "Requirements for Graduation—Candidates must be twenty-one years of age and of good moral character. They must have completed satisfactorily a three-year course of nursing, the last year being spent in this College."

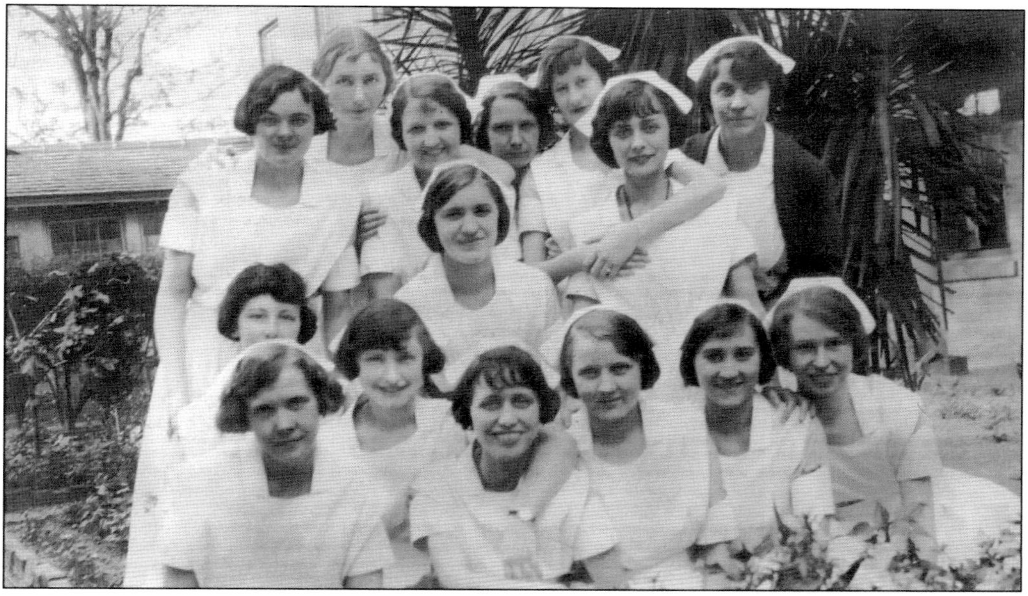

A class history recorded in a graduate's scrapbook in 1926 relates how students saw their educational experience: "We have watched the girls in the upper classes finish and as each one left we felt that we had gotten just a little nearer toward our goal. And now June the third, our commencement day is almost here, the goal is just in sight and we are very happy. We realize though that we are once more at the beginning and that we shall set a higher goal for which we must strive, however, we know that the training we have received at Roper will certainly help us on our way. As we think of the three years spent at Roper we can truly say that we are glad to have been here."

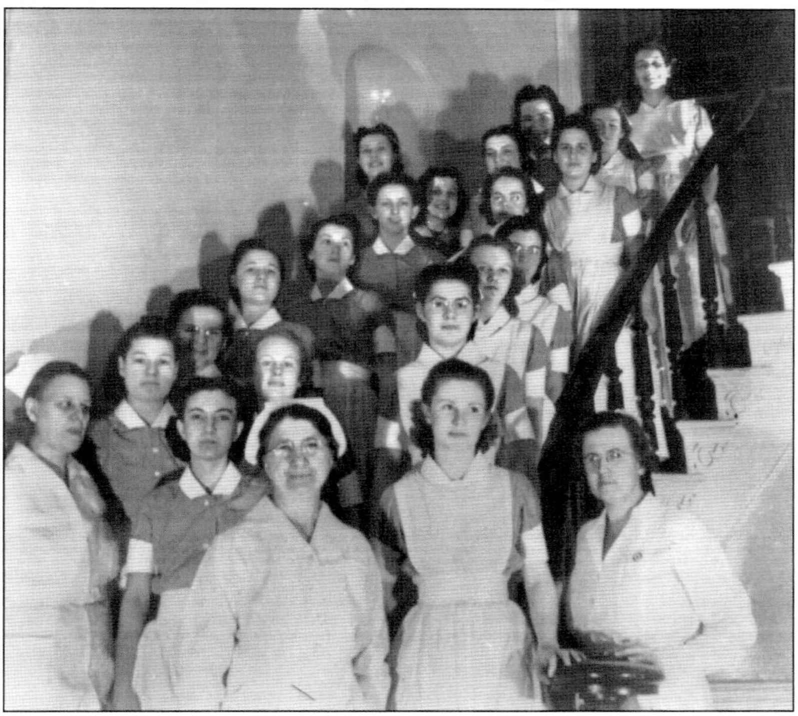

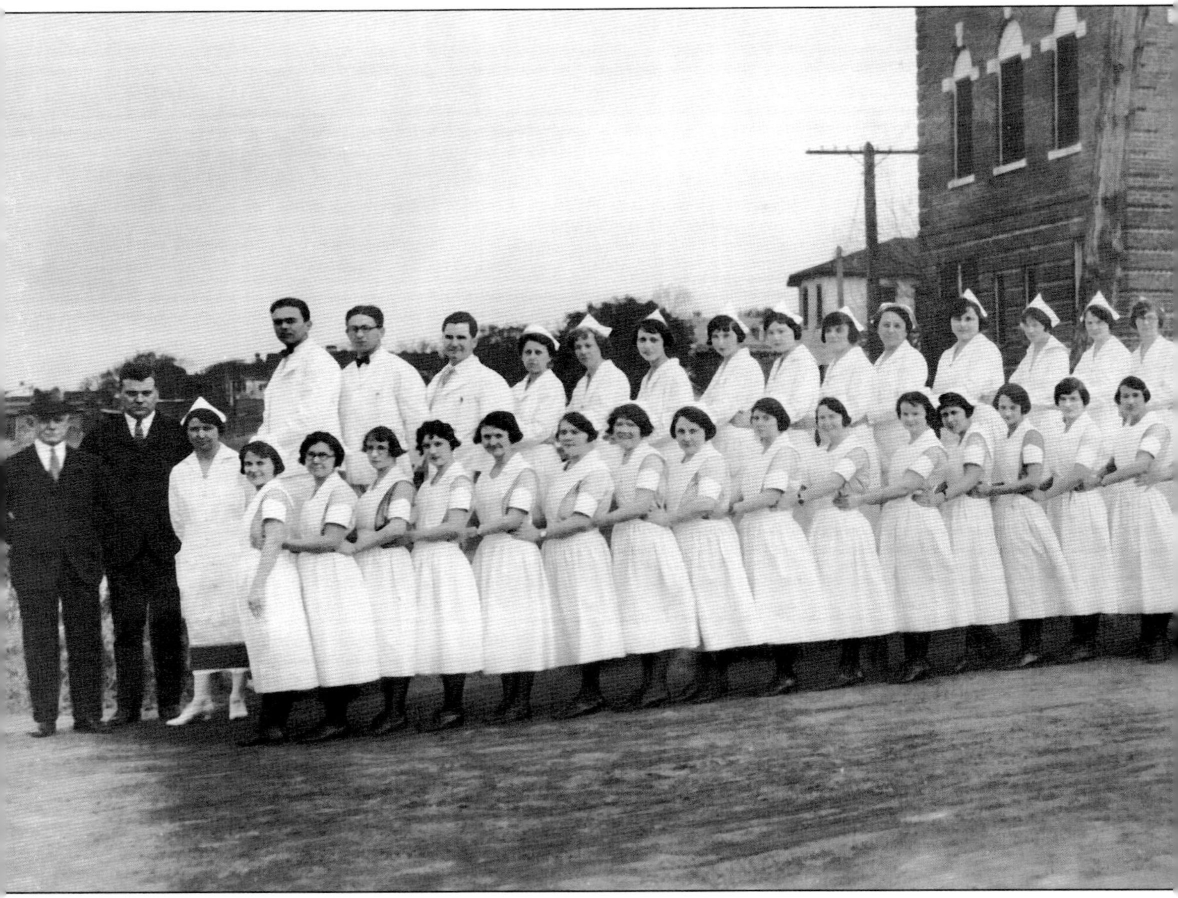

The College of Nursing class of 1927 stands with hospital staff in front of Roper Hospital. Marguerite Andell, superintendent of nursing, is the first woman on the left, standing beside Dr. George McF. Mood (far left), chairman of the Roper Hospital board of commissioners, and F. Oliver Bates, hospital superintendent. According to the 1920–1921 *School of Nursing Second Announcement*, "There is no tuition fee. The expenses of the student nurses are paid by the Roper Hospital, in

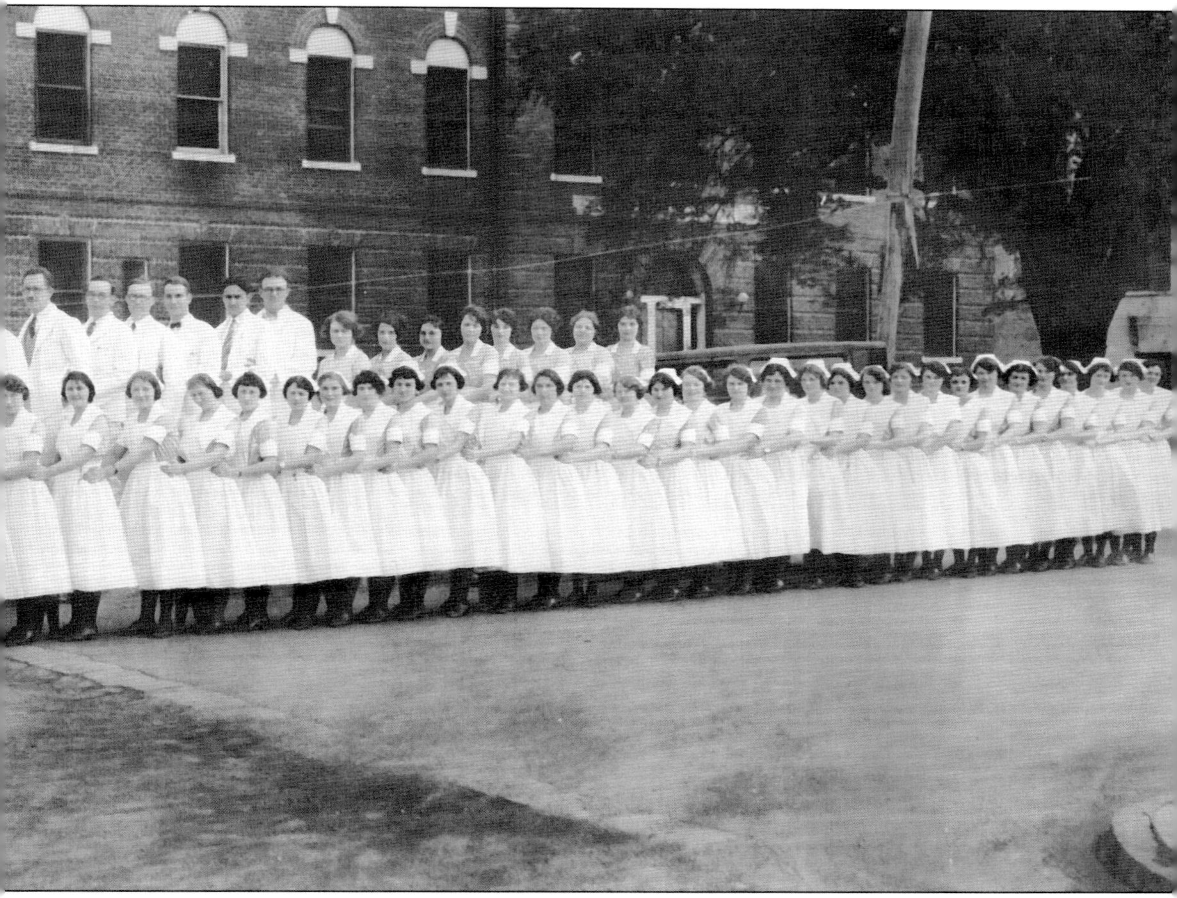

which she receives her practical training. In addition to expenses the hospital provides probation outfit which includes dresses, aprons, collars, cuffs, caps, and books on practical nursing, and after the third month allows the student $12 a month for incidental expenses. Therefore the student has all expenses in connection with her training and course of instruction paid."

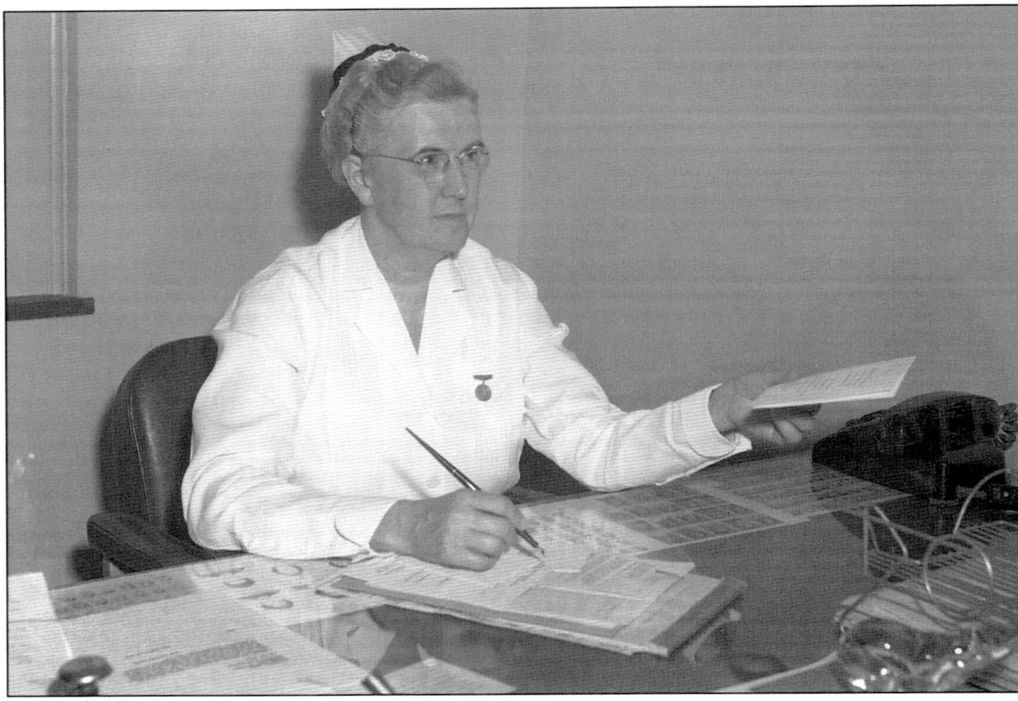

A native New Yorker, Ruth Chamberlin came to the Medical College in 1937 to serve as the educational director for the School of Nursing. Chamberlin was a 1932 graduate of the Teachers College at Columbia University in New York, where she also received a masters of arts in nursing administration in 1951. In 1946, after three years of military service during World War II, she returned to Charleston and served as director of the School of Nursing. In 1948, Chamberlin was also promoted to director of nursing at Roper Hospital and in 1949 was named dean of the School of Nursing, the first person to hold that title within the School of Nursing. She received the additional title of professor of nursing in 1956.

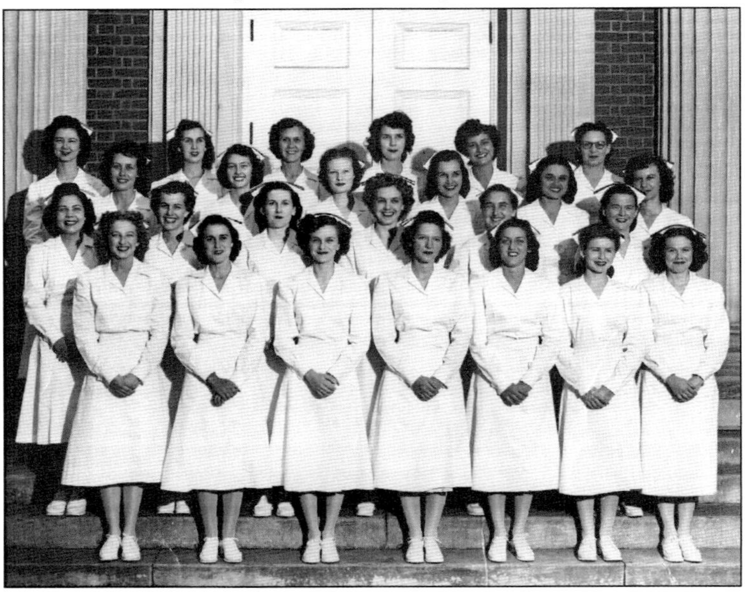

The 1946 publication *Tres Anni* reads, "Our success will depend upon our achievements of the past three years; the knowledge we have assimilated; the personalities we have become. If we catch the spirit that the Medical College offers, we can go forth to meet the future with courage and faith." Pictured is the class of 1949.

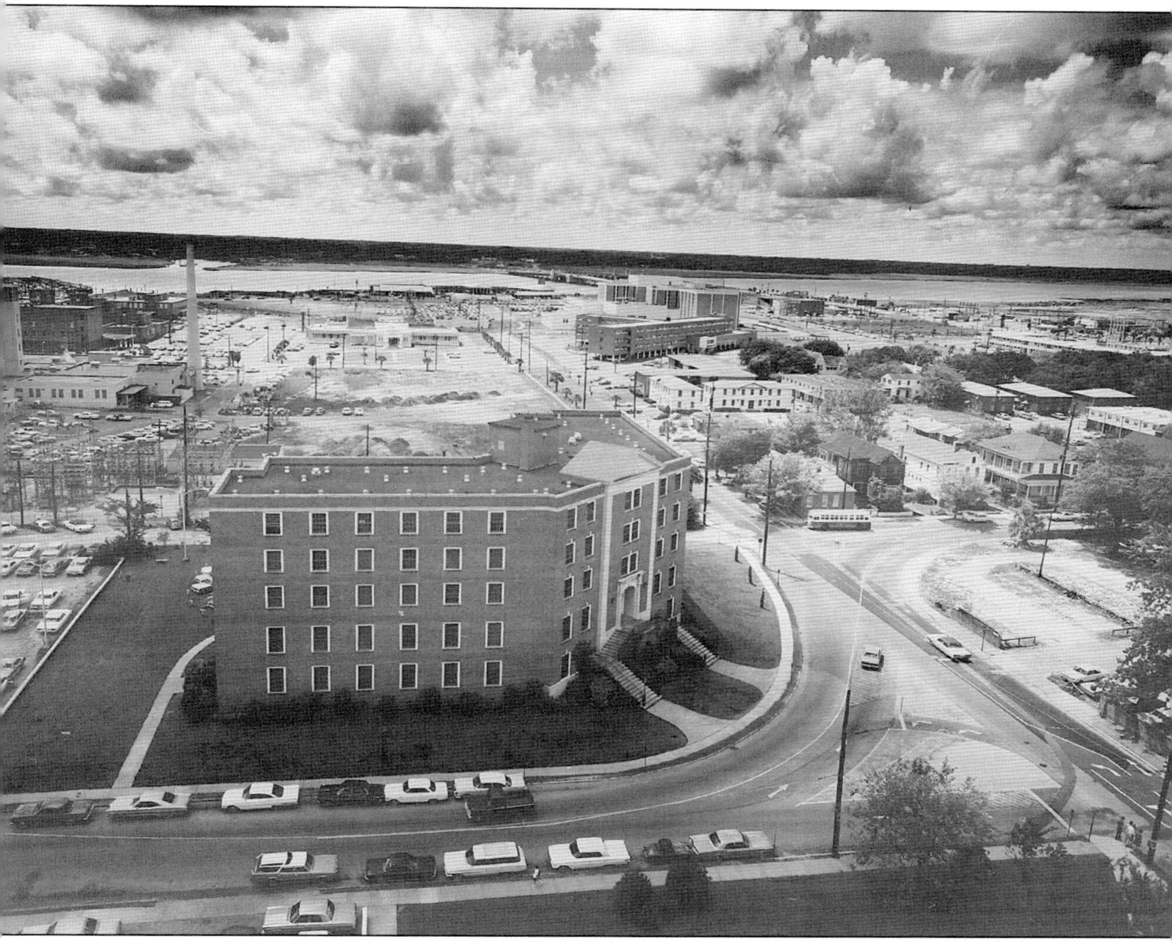

In 1956, the School of Nursing opened this new building, which provided both classroom and dormitory space. By design, the building is shaped like a nurse's cap. In the far right background is the Alumni Memorial House, and at the extreme left is Roper Hospital.

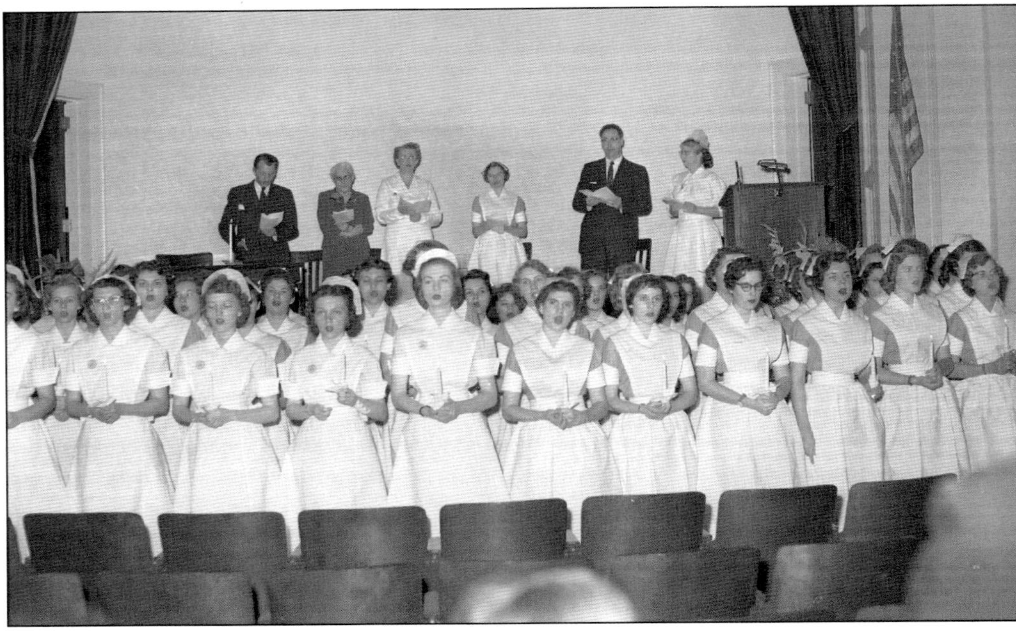

For many years, the nurse's cap was used in a ceremony for new nurses. The capping ceremony celebrated the end of a nurse's coursework and the start of her hospital training. In recent times, as a reflection of the fact that nurses no longer wear caps, new nurses receive stethoscopes instead of caps. In the image above, Dean Chamberlin presides over a 1956 capping ceremony. Below is a 1910s nurse's cap from the College of Nursing collection.

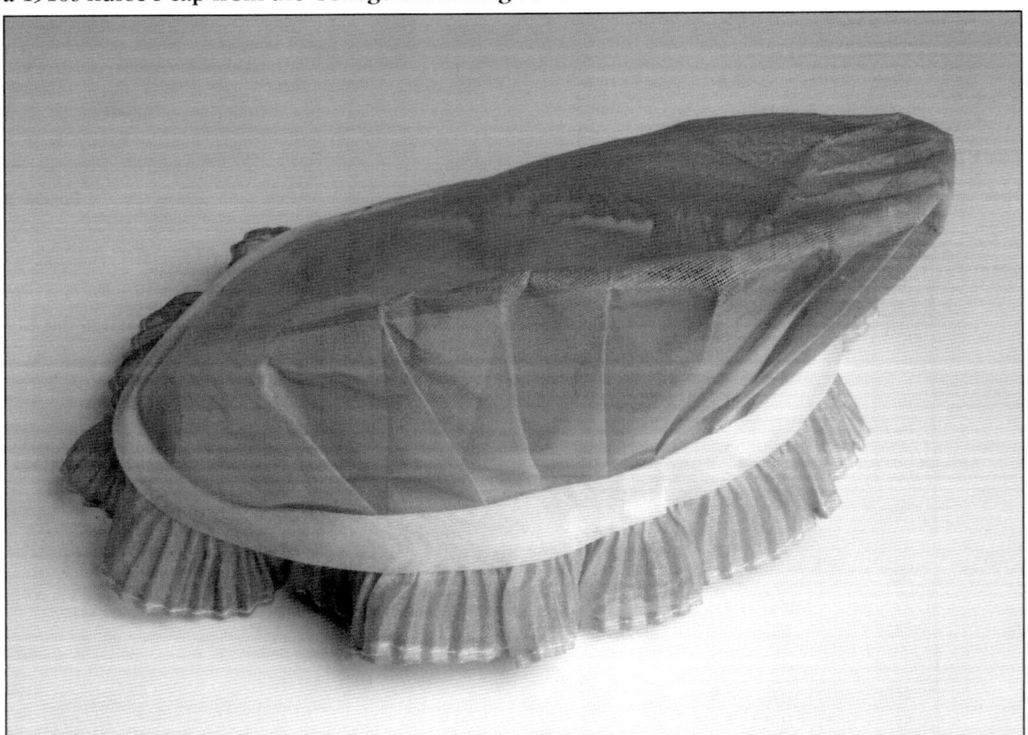

Rosslee Douglas (right) was born in Florence County, South Carolina, in 1928. She was educated in Charleston at the Buist School and graduated from the Avery Institute in 1947. In 1952, Douglas was awarded an RN from the Lincoln School for Nurses, the Bronx, New York. In 1972, Douglas was awarded her BSN with honors from the College of Nursing, becoming the first African American graduate to do so. In 1981, Douglas became Pres. Ronald Reagan's first African American female appointee as the director of the Office of Minority Economic Impact in the US Department of Energy.

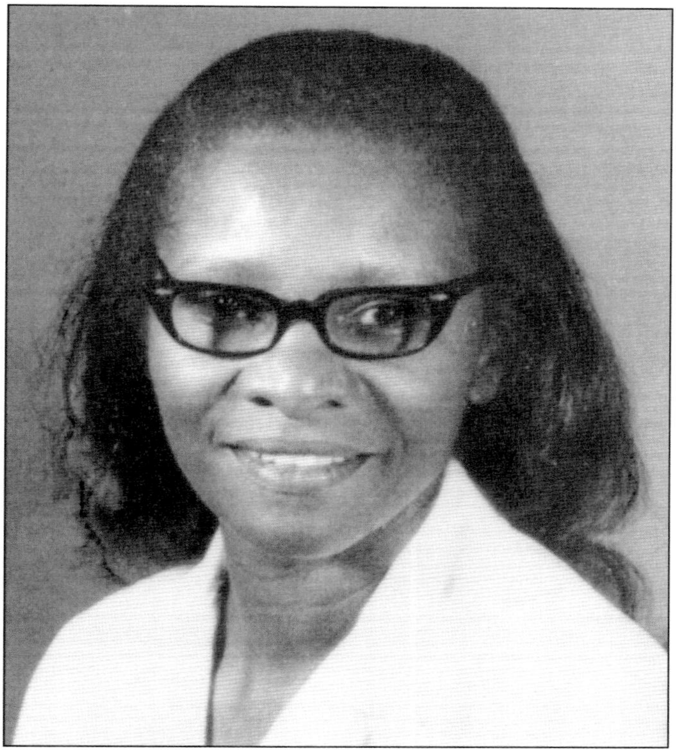

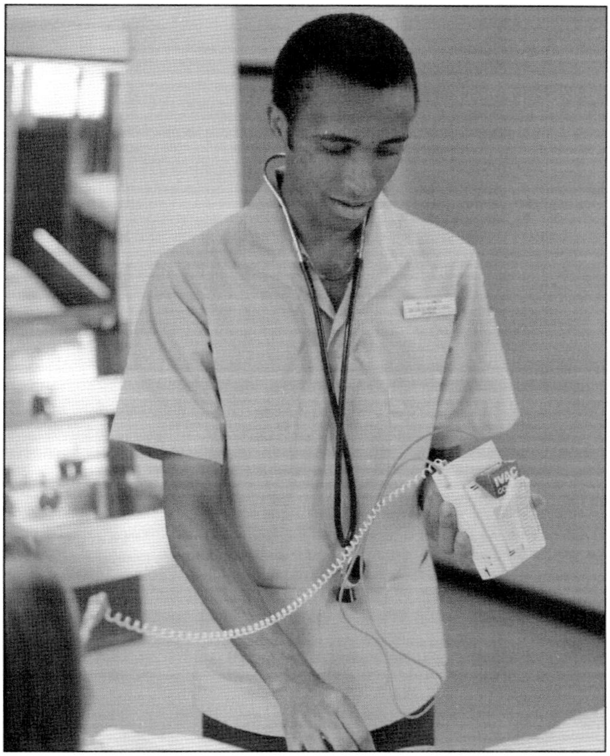

In 1975, the College of Nursing (CON) graduated its first African American male nurse, Joe Nelson Mitchell. This 1980 photograph is representative of the increased enrollment of male nurses in the CON program from the mid-1970s onward.

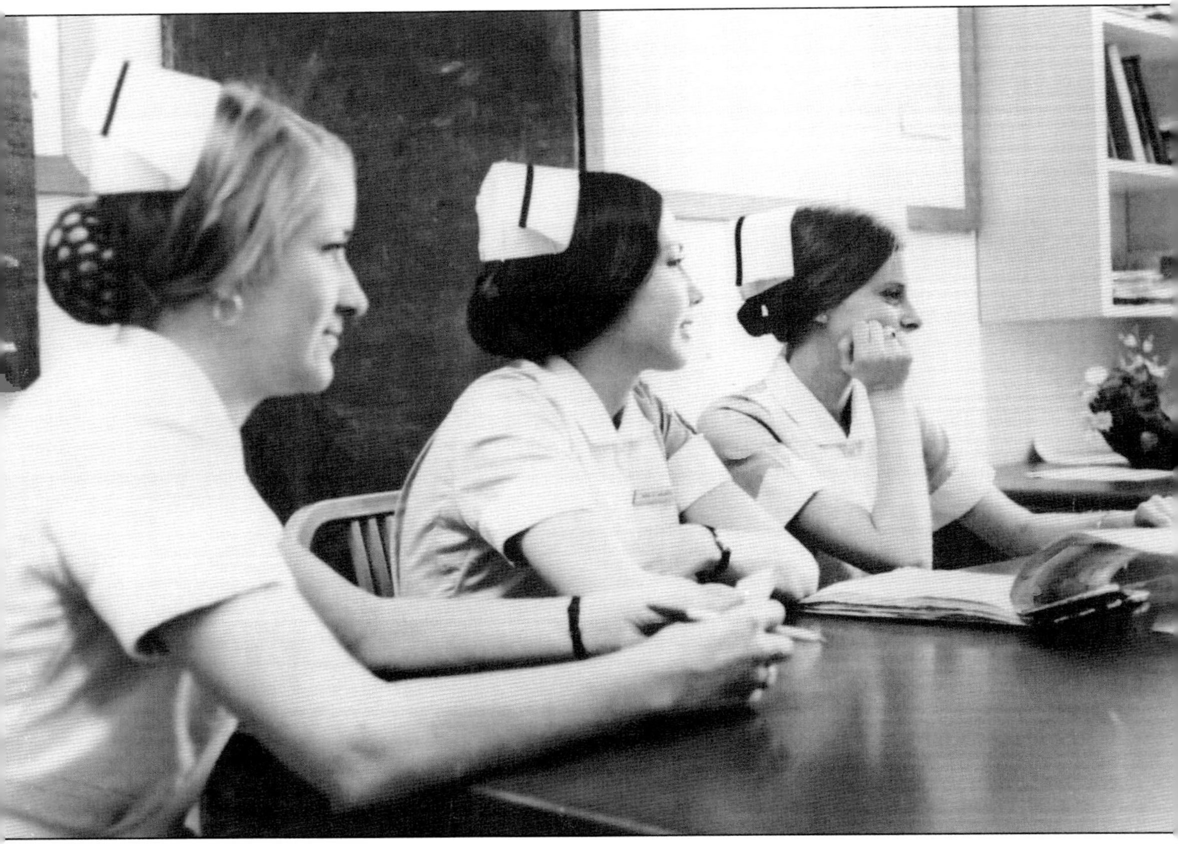

In 2008, the College of Nursing celebrated 125 years of nursing education, making it one of the oldest schools of nursing in the country. During its long history, the college's programs have grown and evolved to include, at various times, a Master of Science in Nursing program, a Doctor of Philosophy in Nursing in 2001, and a Doctor of Nursing Practice Degree in 2009. This photograph dates from around 1973.

Four

College of Graduate Studies

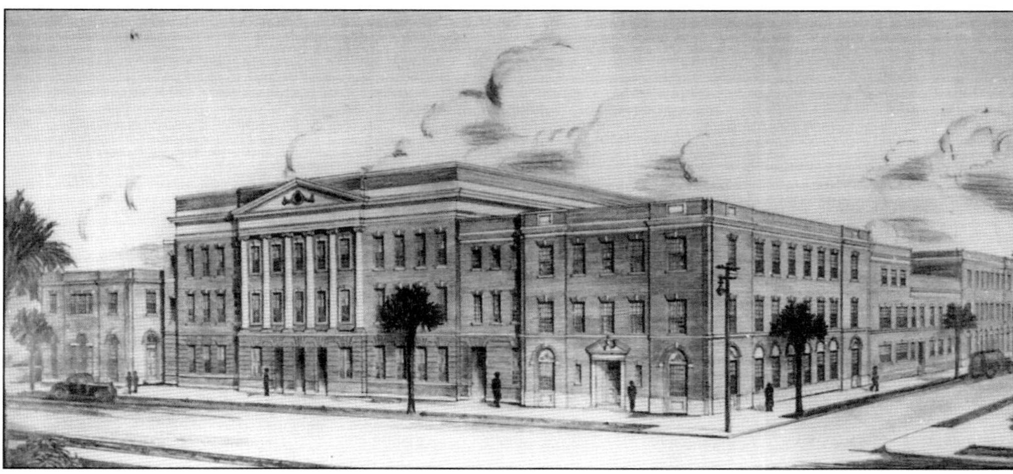

The College of Graduate Studies began as the Graduate Committee of the School of Medicine in 1949, with programs in anatomy, chemistry, pathology, pharmacology, and physiology. A program in microbiology was added, and the first students were admitted in 1950. The School of Graduate Studies was formally organized as the fourth branch of the Medical College in 1965. This is an architectural rendering of the Quadrangle, which served as the academic center for the Medical College.

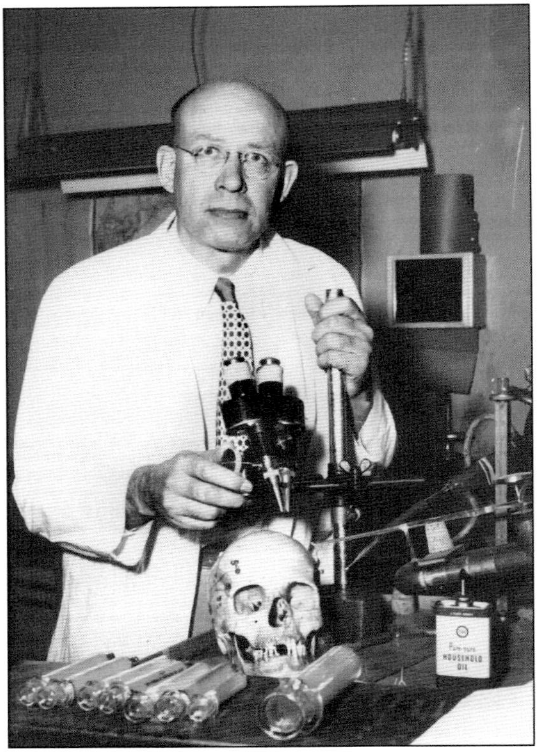

The foundation of the Graduate Studies program can be traced back to the work of Drs. Robert Wilson and Kenneth Lynch. In the wake of the 1910 Flexner Report, Wilson realized that standards for academic medical centers were only going to become more stringent. In order to address this, both men recruited four major figures in the basic science departments: Robert Walton (Pharmacology), T.G. Bernthal (Physiology), William McCord (Chemistry), and Melvin Knisely (Anatomy). With their arrival, the Medical College moved forward in the areas of research and clinical science. Dr. Melvin Henry Knisely (left) was appointed chairman of the department of anatomy for the Medical College in 1948 and served in that position for more than 20 years. Upon his retirement in 1969, he served in the department as a professor of anatomy until his death in 1975. Dr. Knisely was internationally known for his work in circulatory problems.

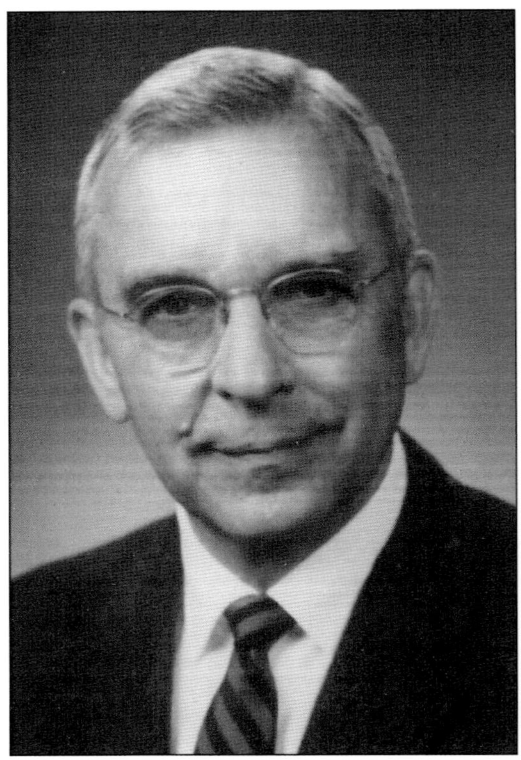

Dr. Theodor George Bernthal (right) came to the Medical College in 1946 and served as chair of the physiology department. Bernthal was a national leader in research in respiratory and circulatory physiology.

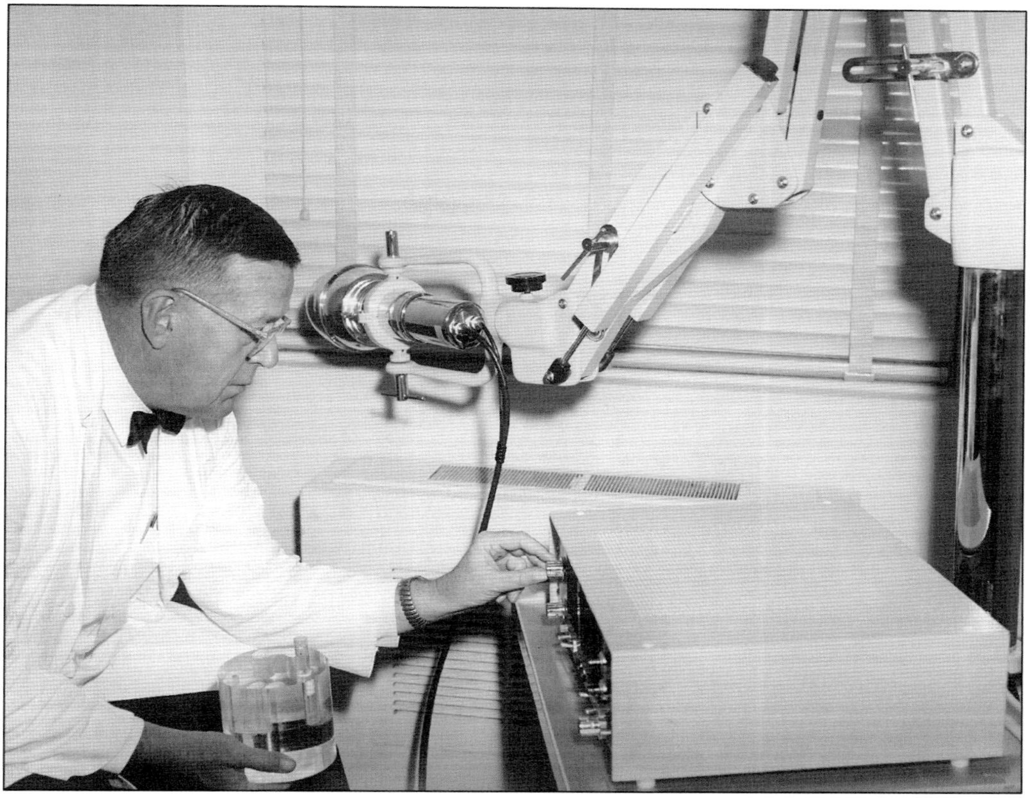

Dr. William M. McCord (above) joined the faculty of the Medical College as professor of chemistry and chairman of the department of chemistry on December 4, 1945. Upon the resignation of Dr. Harold Rawling Pratt-Thomas as president of the Medical College in 1964, McCord served as interim president until his appointment as president in November 1965. Dr. McCord served in this capacity until 1975.

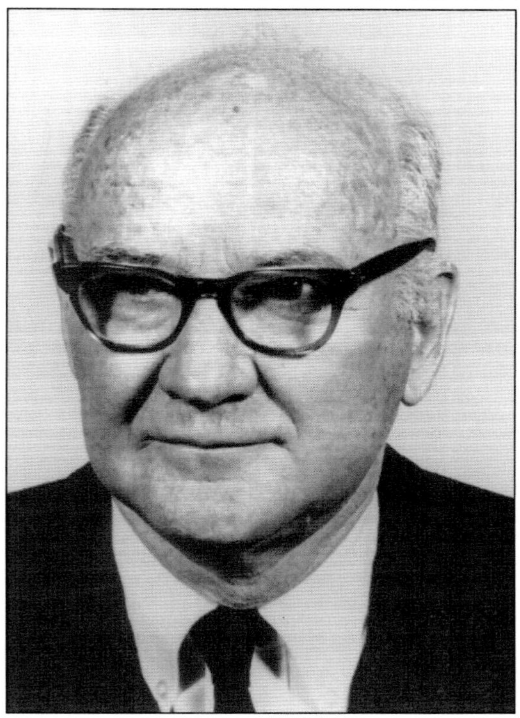

Dr. Robert Petrie Walton (right) was professor and chairman of the department of pharmacology from 1942 until his death in 1971 as well as a former coordinator of research. Among his innovations was the strain gauge arch for measuring the contractile force of the heart muscle. This strain gauge led to developments in the area of open-heart surgery. In 1982, the research building on the Quadrangle was renamed in his honor.

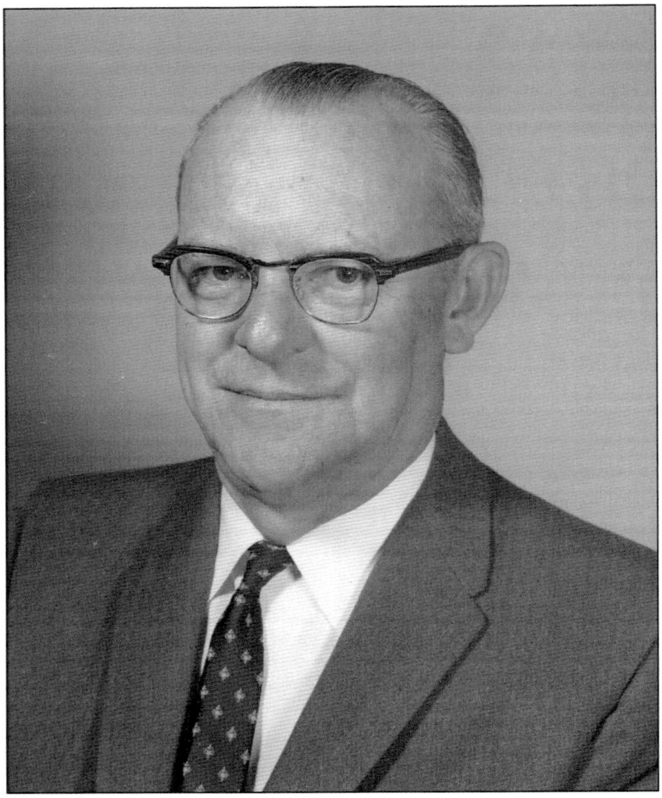

Dr. Fredrick W. Kinard arrived at the Medical College in 1927 as a member of the physiology department in the College of Medicine. In 1949, he was appointed chairman of the Graduate Committee of the College of Medicine, which developed the programs leading to the awarding of master of science and doctor of philosophy degrees. As chairman, Kinard worked to integrate the graduate programs into the overall mission of the college. When the School of Graduate Studies was established as the fifth school of the college, he was appointed the first dean in 1965.

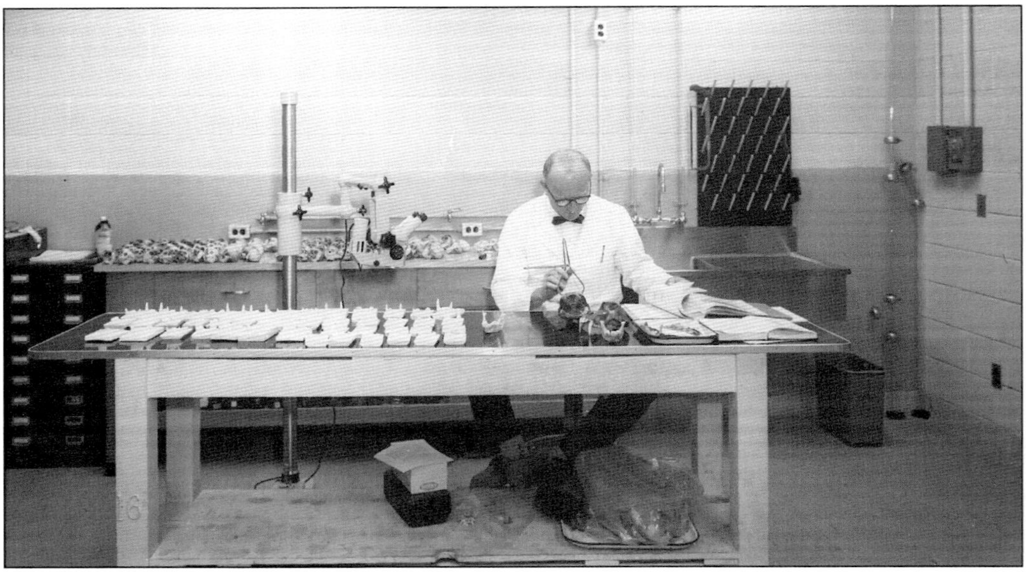

A graduate study is a full-time occupation in a protracted program. Applicants are not admitted if they are merely awaiting an opportunity to enter a school of medicine, nor may one simultaneously combine medical and graduate training," reads the 1950–1951 *Graduate Study in the Basic Medical Sciences Announcements*. This c. 1962 interior shot of the research building shows Dr. Daris Swindler studying the tooth development of monkeys.

The 1964–1965 announcement reports, "To meet a definite need in South Carolina a program of graduate studies in the basic medical sciences, leading to the M.S. or Ph.D. degree, was organized on March 31, 1949. In addition to those students who have chosen careers in medicine, dentistry, pharmacy or nursing, there are students who desire training in various branches of medical science to equip themselves for teaching and research in these fields." Seen in this 1962 photograph with a colleague is Dr. Hilda Debacker, who received both her masters and doctorate degrees from the School of Graduate Studies, where she later served as faculty until her retirement in 1990.

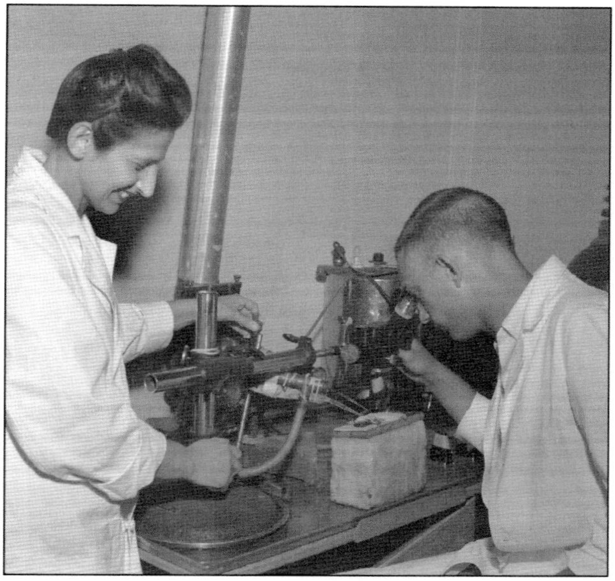

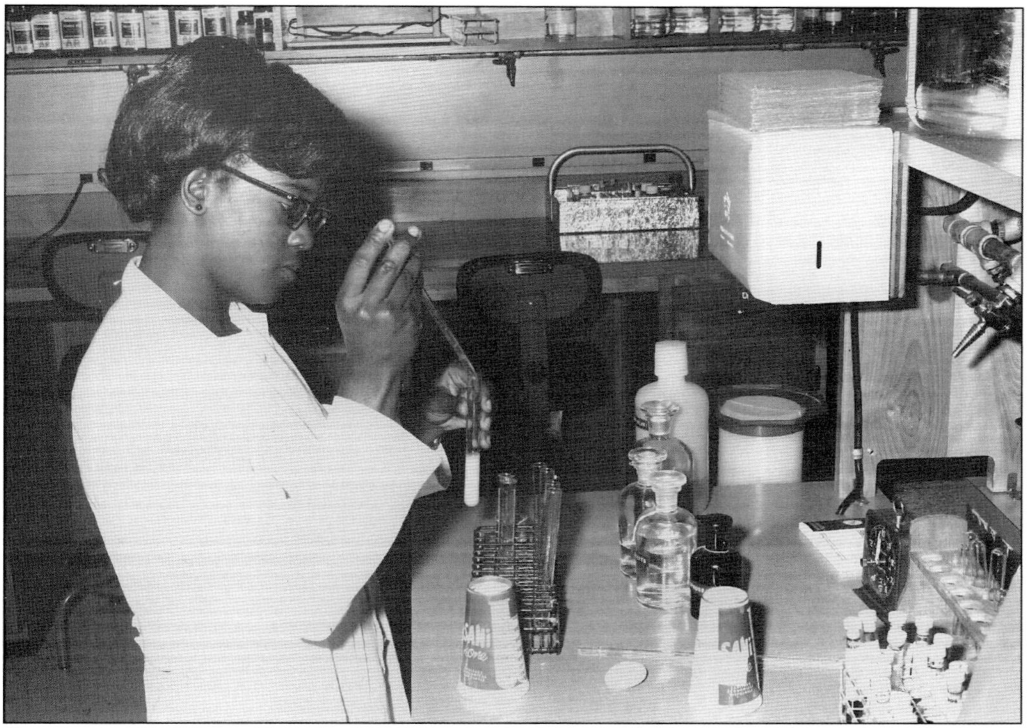

The 1950–1951 publication also states: "The Medical College of the State of South Carolina has both faculty and laboratories for this program of graduate study. The individual departments are carrying out investigations of fundamental importance in numerous fields of medical science. For this work to continue, and for it to expand, personnel must be trained and prepared for teaching and research. With these objectives in mind, the Medical College is offering integrated programs which include formal course work, teaching experience and investigation through experimentation, directed by instructors who are themselves actively engaged in both research and teaching."

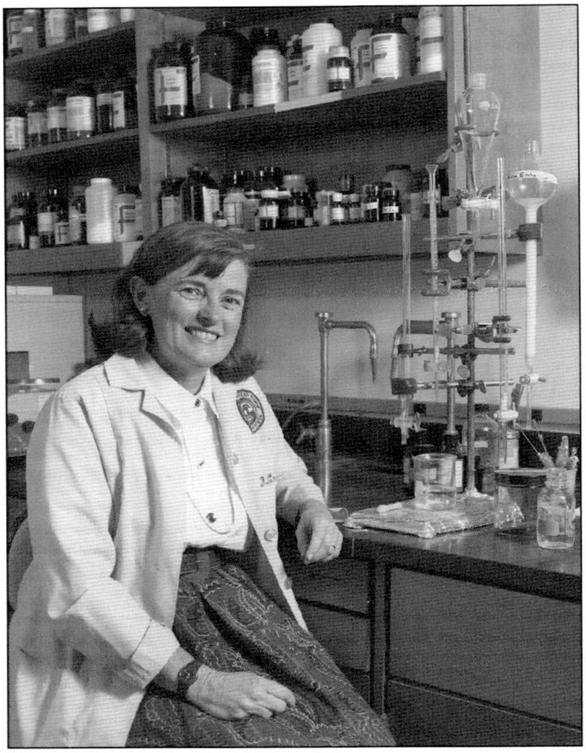

Dr. Rosalie Crouch joined MUSC in 1975 as a faculty member in the College of Medicine's departments of ophthalmology and biochemistry and by 1982 had earned the title of professor. In 1989, Crouch was appointed acting dean of the College of Graduate Studies and became its dean in 1991. She held the title of dean concurrently with her 1995 appointment as the College of Medicine's associate provost for research until 2000, at which time she became the Medical University's first female provost and vice president for academic affairs.

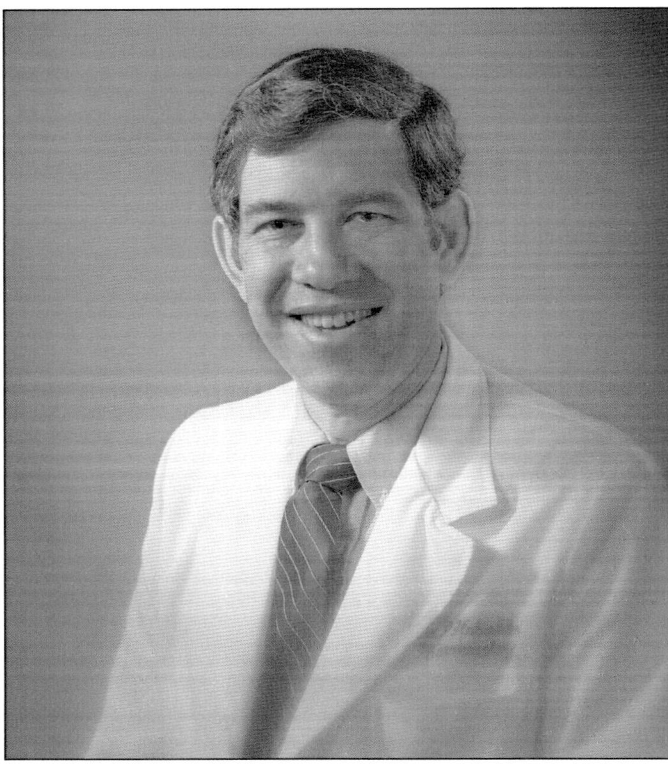

Dr. Perry V. Halushka joined MUSC in 1972 and in 2000 was named dean of the College of Graduate Studies. Currently, he is professor of pharmacology and medicine and director of the division of clinical pharmacology. Since 1987, Halushka has also been director of the Medical Scientist Training Program, which enables students to obtain both the doctor of medicine and doctorate degrees. He is perhaps most affectionately known for his skill at "Medical Jeopardy."

Five

College of Dental Medicine

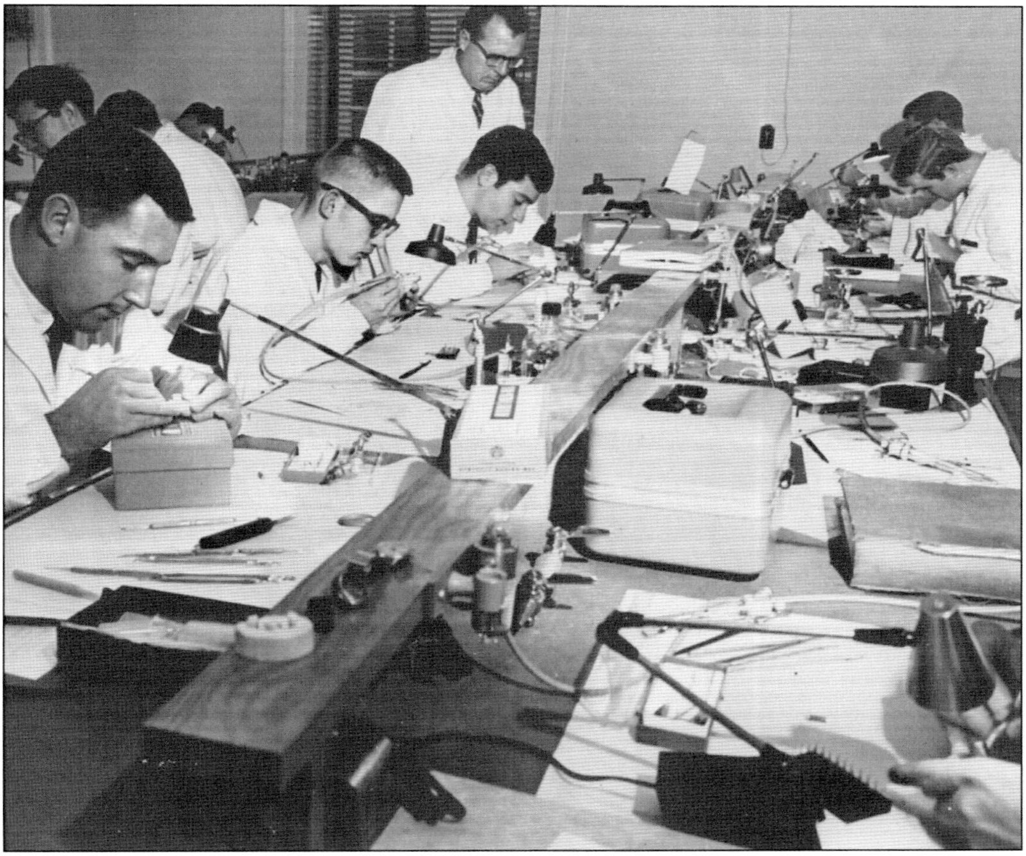

In 1952, the South Carolina Dental Association recommended that a school of dentistry be established as a unit of the Medical College of South Carolina. The state legislature authorized the development of the School of Dental Medicine the following year, but it was not until 1964 that legislators provided the funds to implement the 1953 authorization. This image, captioned "Future dentists at work in lab," appeared in the 1969 *Caducean*.

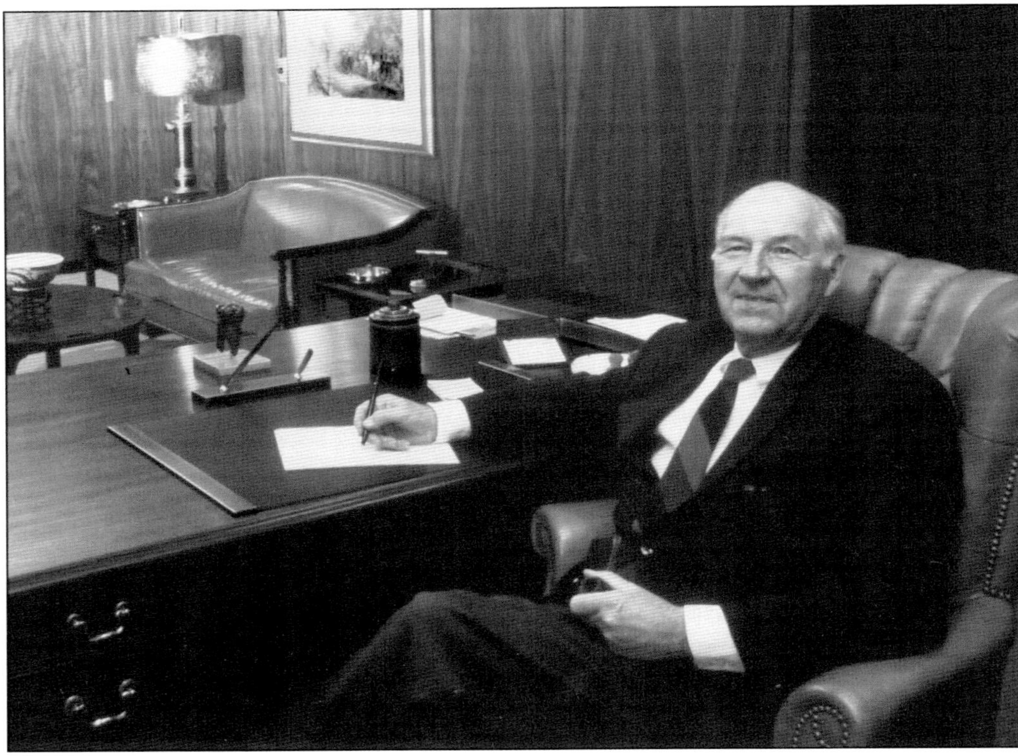

Dr. John E. Buhler was named dean of the proposed School of Dentistry in May 1964. Though it would not open for another three years, Medical College leadership appointed Buhler in order to meet federal agencies' application deadlines for assistance in implementing the new program. Buhler served as dean until 1971.

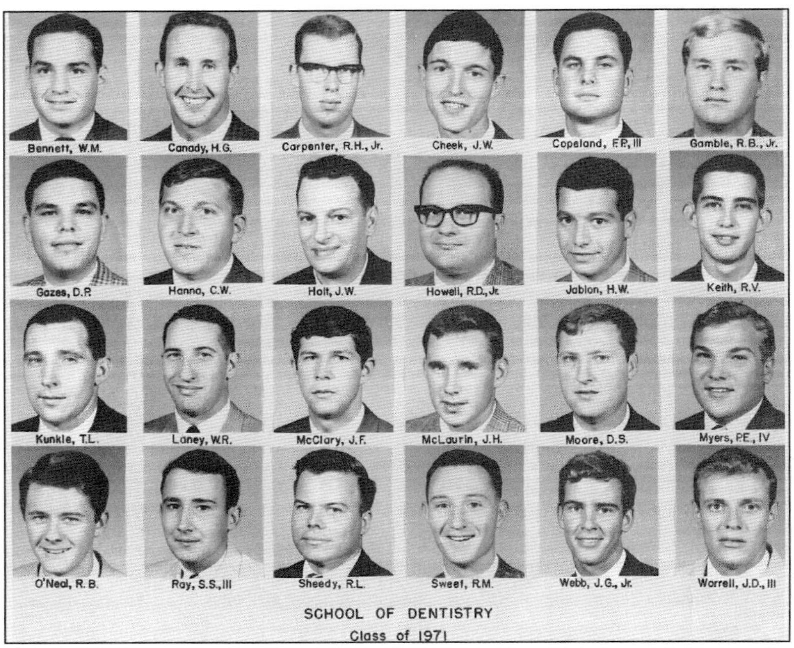

The school received 210 applications for its first class and ultimately selected 24 students, all South Carolinians. The first class enrolled in the Dental School in the fall of 1967, and 21 of the 24 matriculants were graduated with doctor of dental medicine degrees in June 1971.

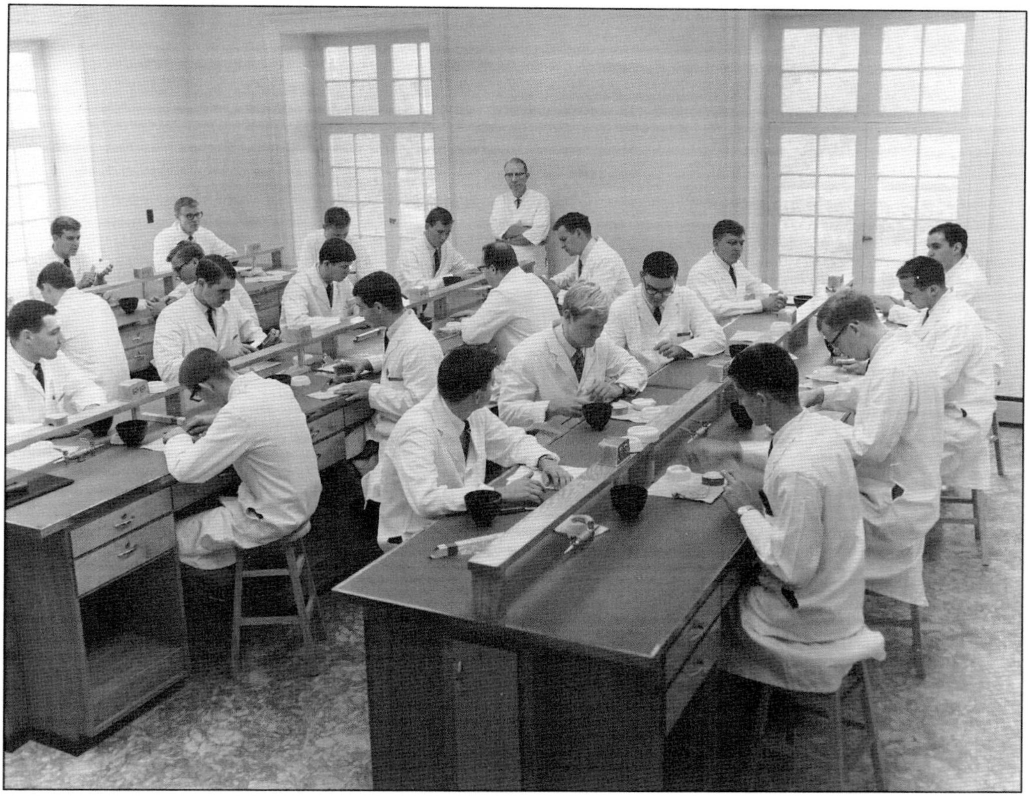

Before the completion of the Basic Sciences/College of Dental Medicine Building, dental students' classes and labs were held in Colcock Hall, seen above around 1967.

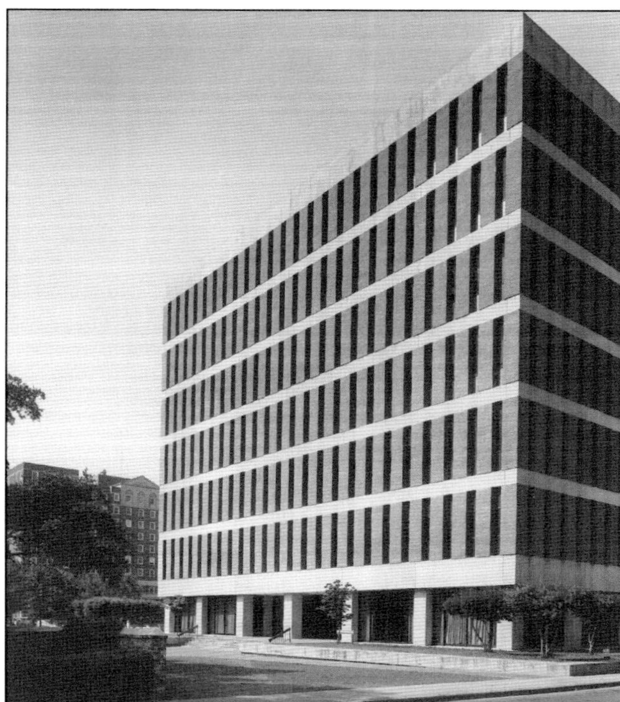

The school's new building, the Basic Sciences/College of Dental Medicine Building, was ready for occupancy in December 1970.

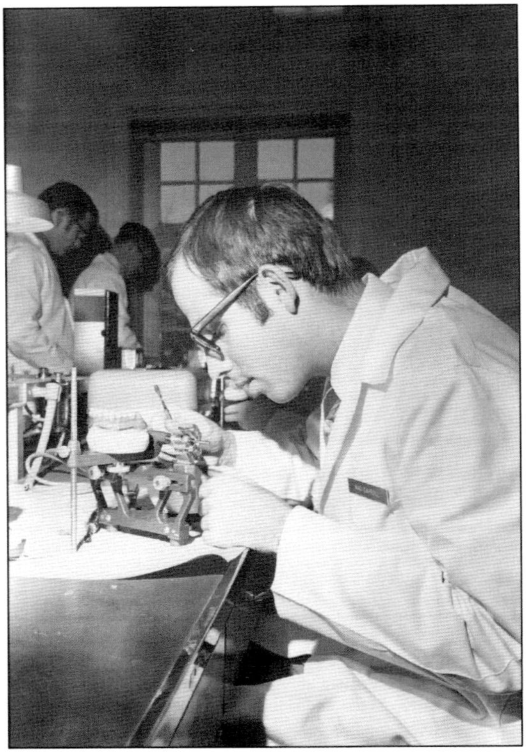

The *School of Dentistry Second Announcement* (1969–1970) states, "The School of Dentistry regards as its specific commitment and its mission to admit to dental study intellectually and morally qualified students and to prepare them for effective professional and community service in the technological and democratic society into which they will be graduated; to instill in them a sense of vocation, a solid foundation for professional and graduate education of a continuing nature, and the inspiration to pursue new ideas and to seek for new knowledge." Mac Carroll appears at left in preclinical lab in 1969.

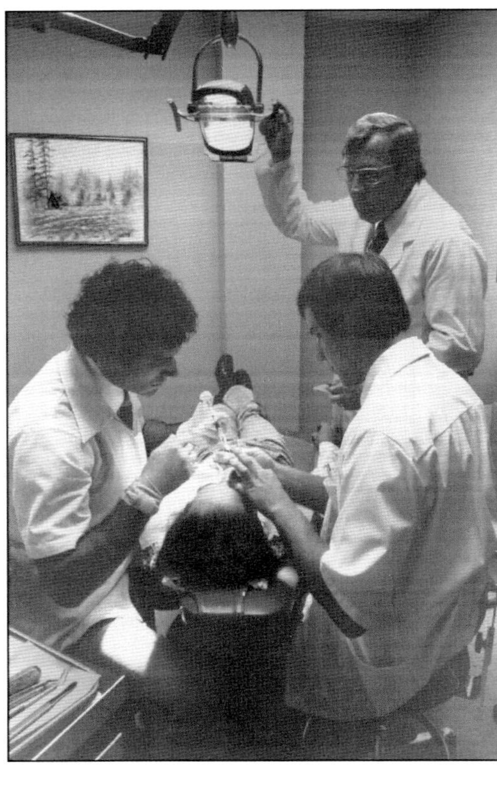

As explained in the 1973–1974 *University Bulletin*, "The treatment of patients and service to the public are practiced to the highest standards. The physical facilities, the clinical and technical procedures, the disposition of faculty and ancillary personnel are directed toward treating each patient as a whole person, completely and with understanding." Dr. James B. Edwards, standing, oversees the work of students in this undated photograph.

Cathy Moss, a native of Blacksburg, South Carolina, graduated from Clemson University in 1970 with a bachelor of science in zoology. She enrolled in the College of Dental Medicine as its first female student in 1970 and earned her doctor of dental medicine in 1974. Dr. Moss served on the MUSC faculty intermittently from 1974 until 1980.

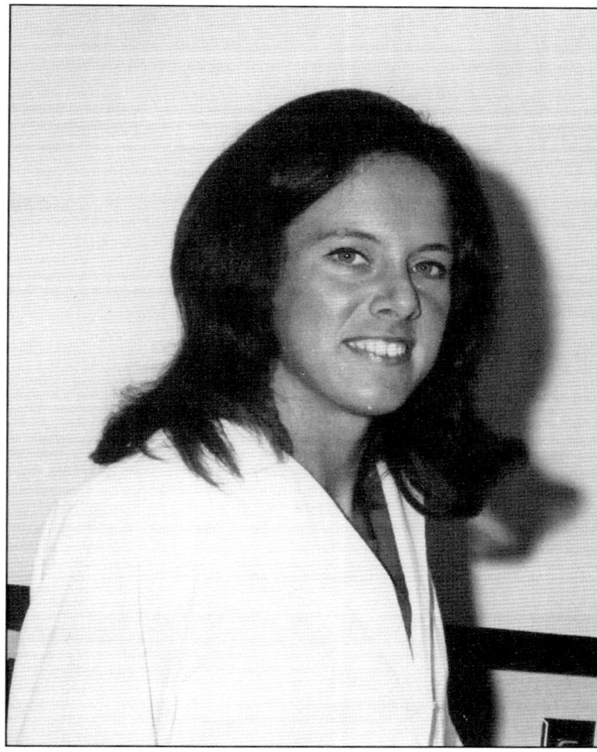

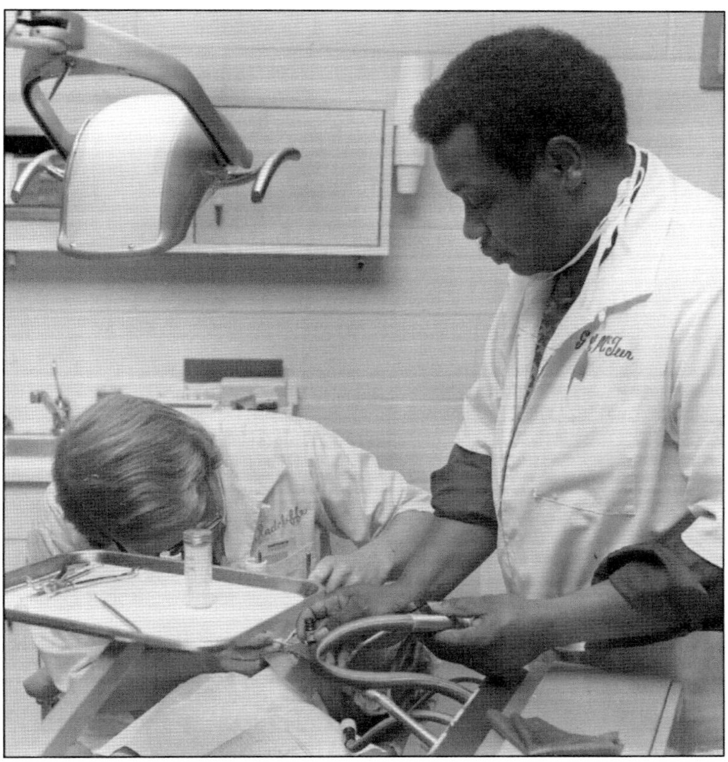

George Calvin McTeer (at right in the photograph) was the first African American to graduate from the College of Dental Medicine in 1974. Born in Barnwell, South Carolina, McTeer received his bachelor of science degree in 1960 and master of education degree in 1968 from South Carolina State University.

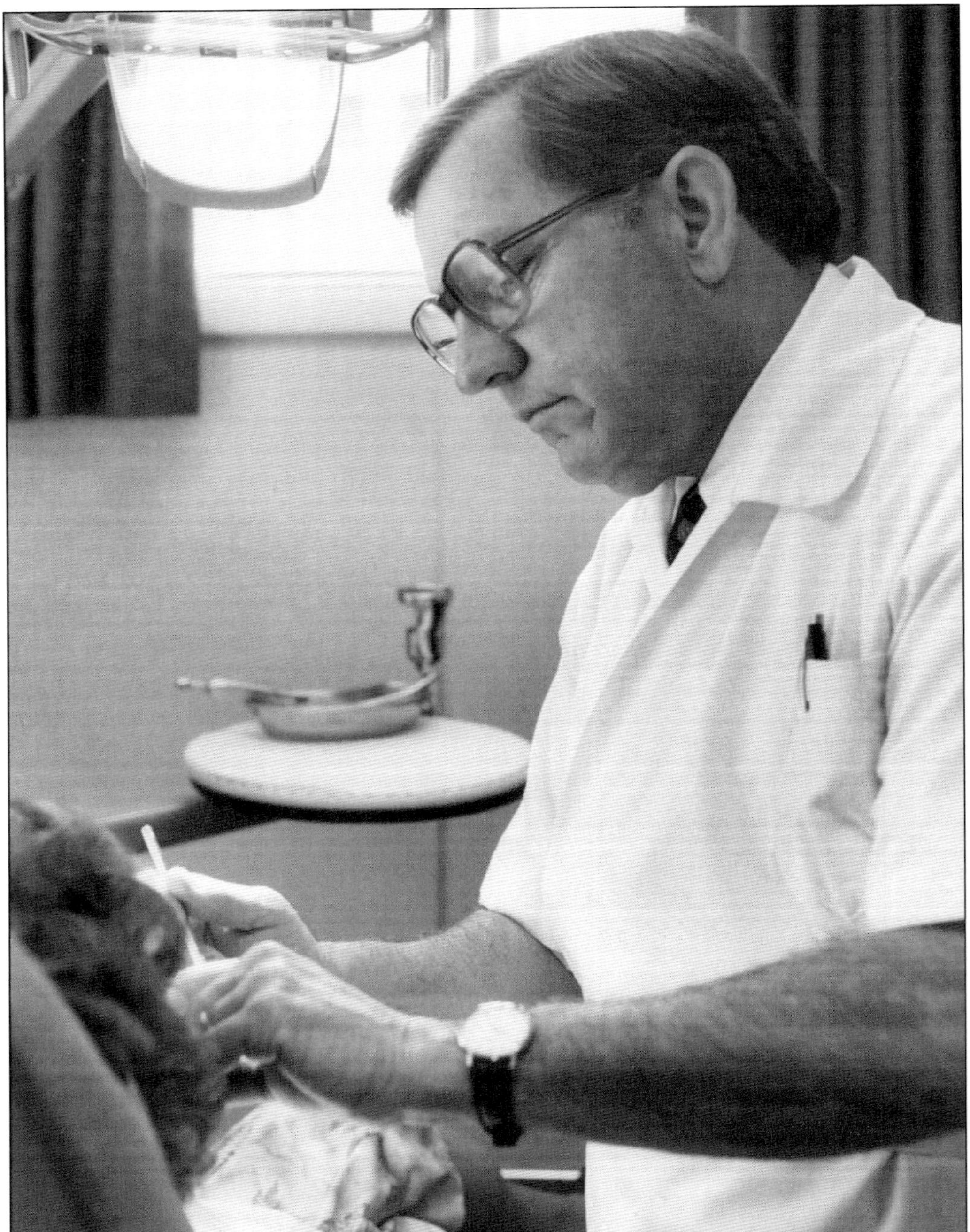

Dr. James B. Edwards may be the best-known oral surgeon in South Carolina, having served as both a state legislator and governor, South Carolina Republican Party chairman, US secretary of energy in President Reagan's administration, and president of the Medical University of South Carolina from 1982 to 1999. Starting out as one of only two board-certified oral surgeons in South Carolina, he treated patients from all over the state. Even while serving as a public official, Dr. Edwards continued seeing patients, working long hours to make up for the time he spent away from Charleston.

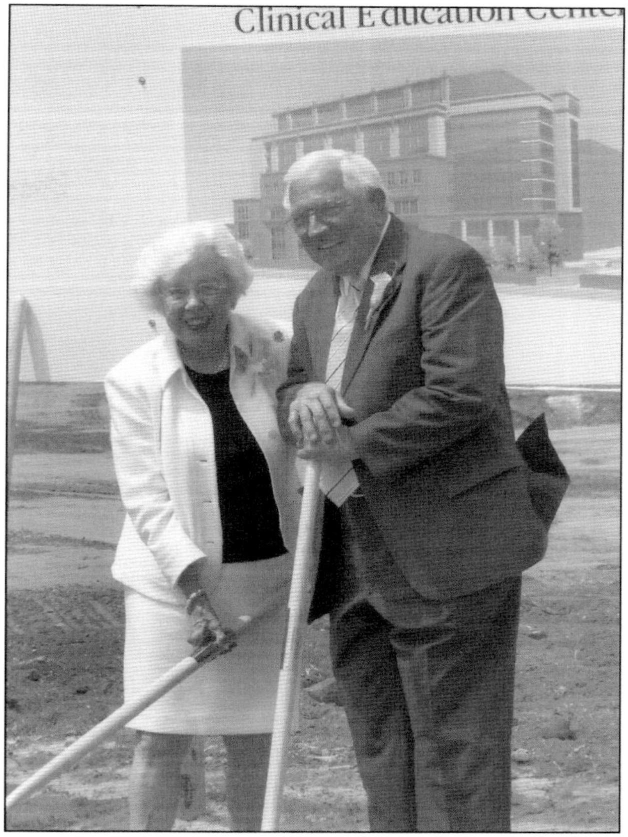

In 2009, the dental college was renamed in honor of James B. Edwards. The building seen below is a clinical-practice building with state-of-the-art equipment and facilities. It was dedicated in February 2010. Pictured at right are Dr. Edwards and his wife, Ann, at the ground-breaking on August 18, 2006. (Photograph by Dr. W. Eugene Atkinson II.)

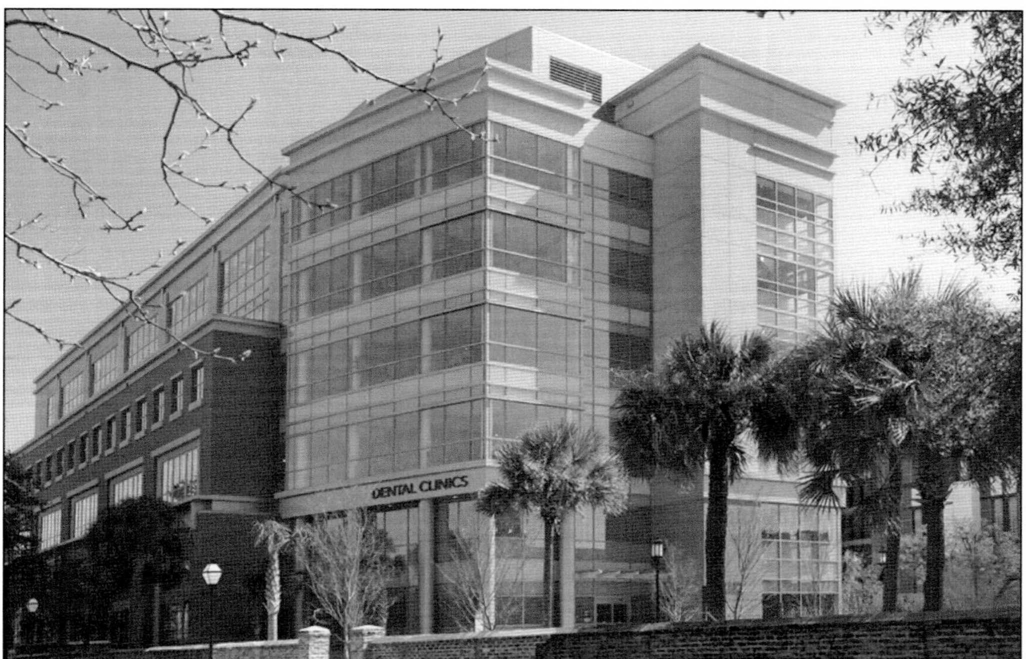

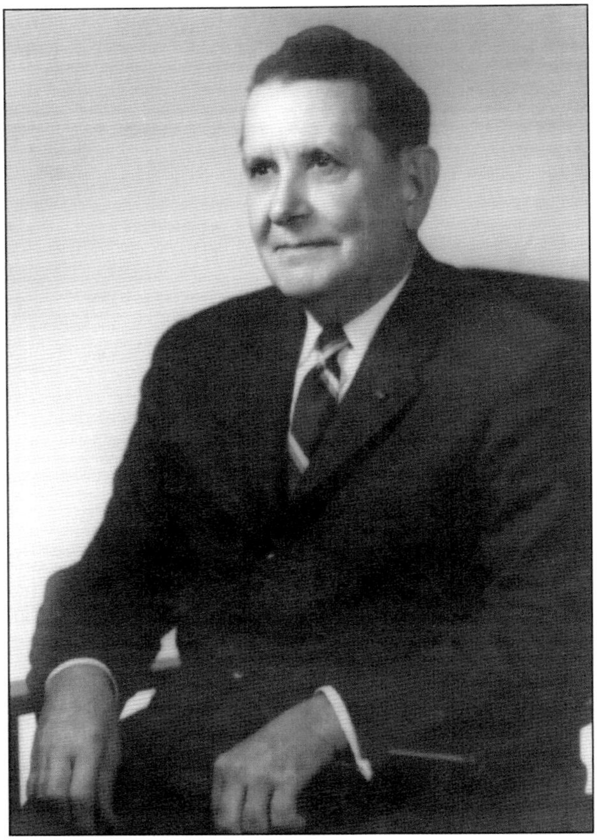

Neill W. Macaulay, DMD, (1904–1983) was an early advocate for the establishment of the dental school. He served as vice president of the South Carolina Dental Association during the period the school was being promoted. From 1968 to 1979, Dr. Macaulay served as a trustee for the Medical College/University. In 1973, the university trustees accepted the donation of Dr. Macaulay's dental history museum, and the collection was dedicated in 1976.

The Macaulay Museum of Dental History houses an impressive collection of dental memorabilia, including a dental office from approximately 1900; a series of dental chairs spanning many years, including a child's chair; an instrument belonging to Dr. Josiah Flagg, the first American-born full-time dentist; and an itinerant dentist's chest from the Civil War era.

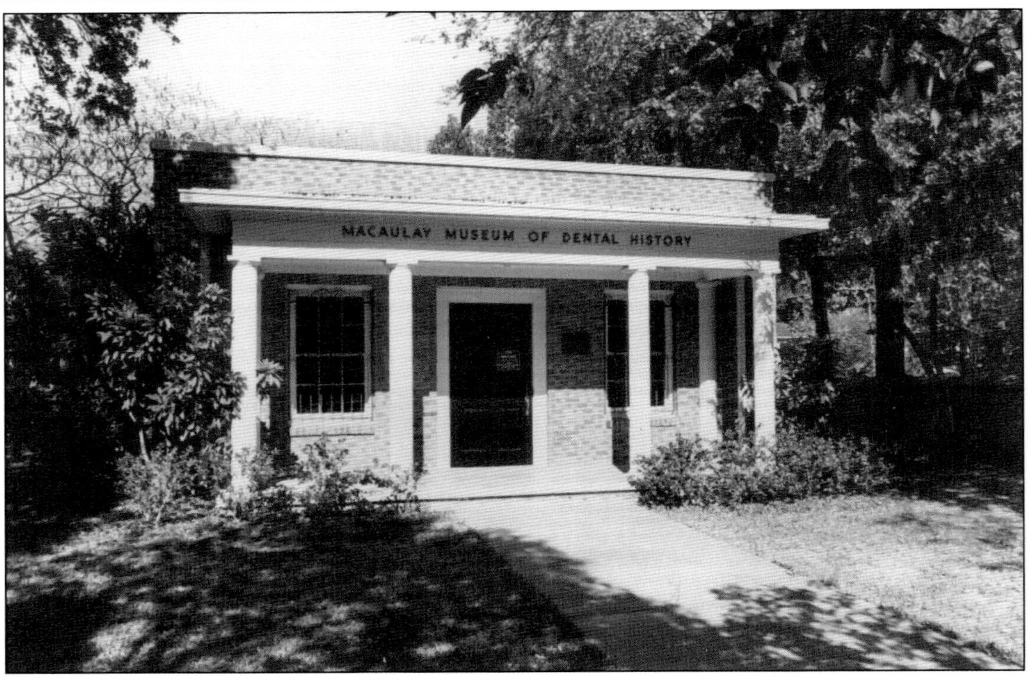

Six

College of Health Professions

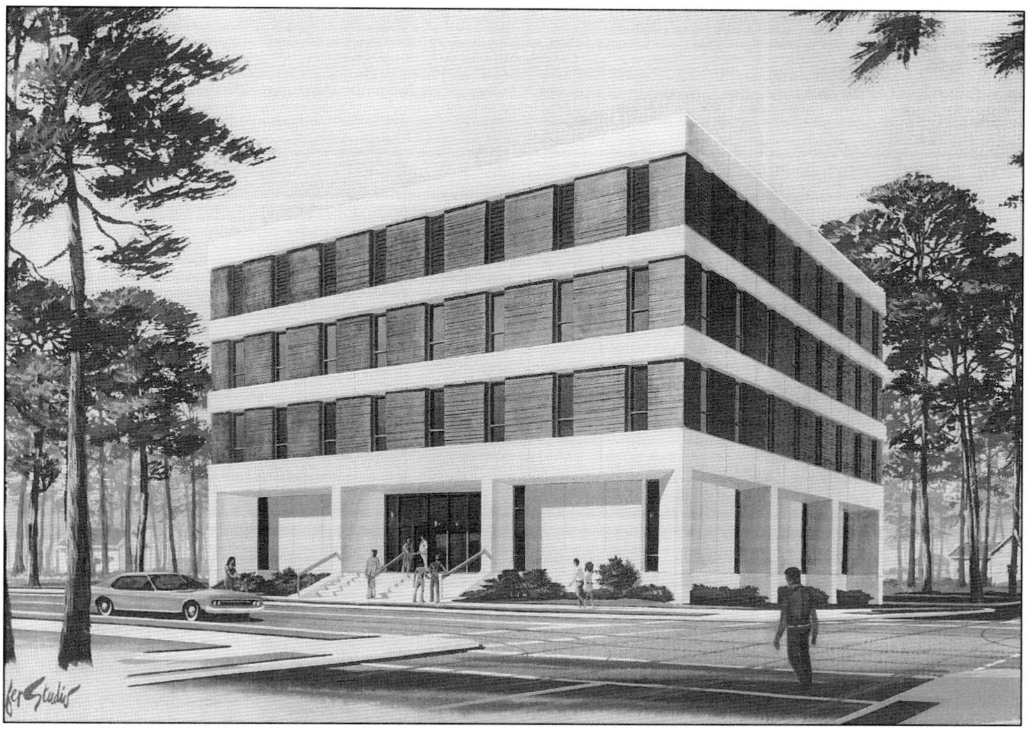

Established in 1966, the School of Allied Health Sciences was formally organized from the Medical College's Division of Technical Training to prepare allied health professionals for careers in the growing health-care industry. In 1986, the name of the school was changed to the College of Health Related Professions, and in 1993, the name changed again to the College of Health Professions (CHP). This is an architectural rendering of the school's first building, located at the corner of President and Bee Streets.

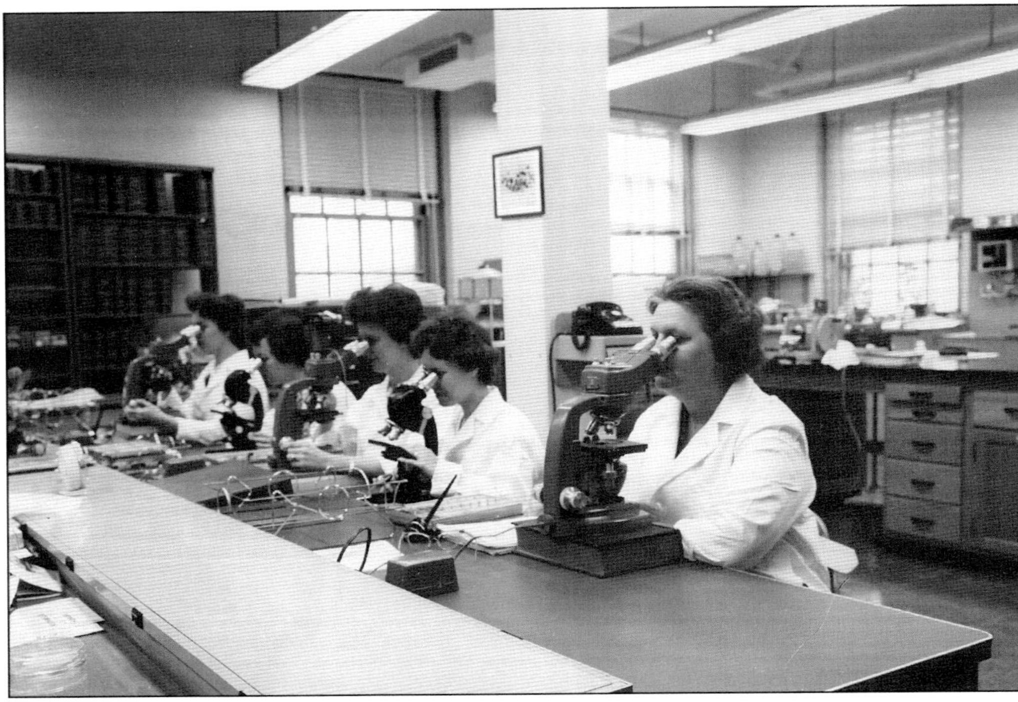

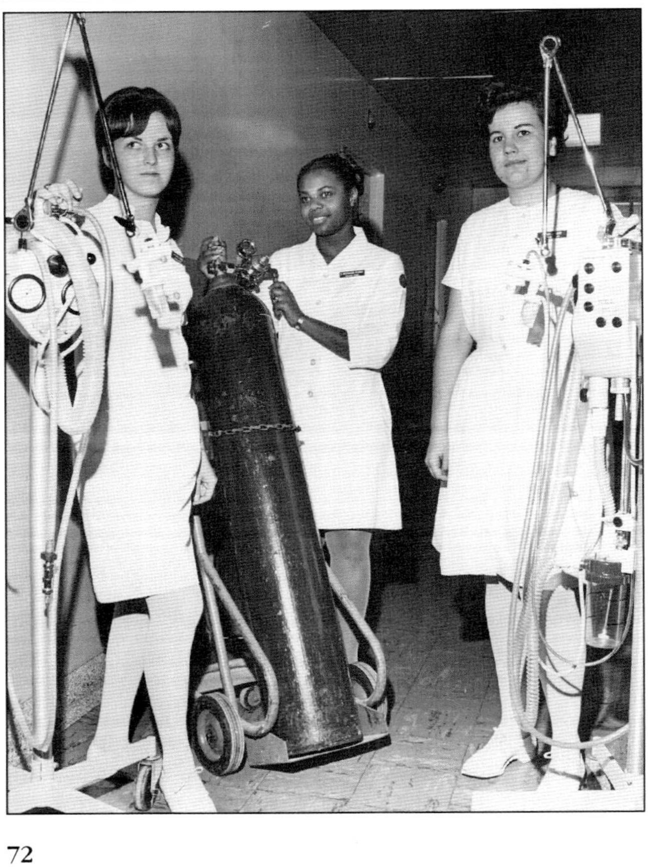

In 1968, the new school awarded its first bachelor of science degrees to one cytotechnologist and four medical technologists. Established around the fields of medical technology, radiologic technology, cytotechnology, inhalation therapy and a nurse anesthetist program, the curriculum expanded to offer over 20 different training options in the paramedical field. Above, cytotechnology students observe specimens under their microscopes, as depicted in the 1970 *Caducean*. At left are inhalation therapy students Jean McLoud (left), Rita Oestricher (center), and Linda Cart, from that same year.

The nurse anesthetist program was among the first five in the School of Allied Health Sciences.

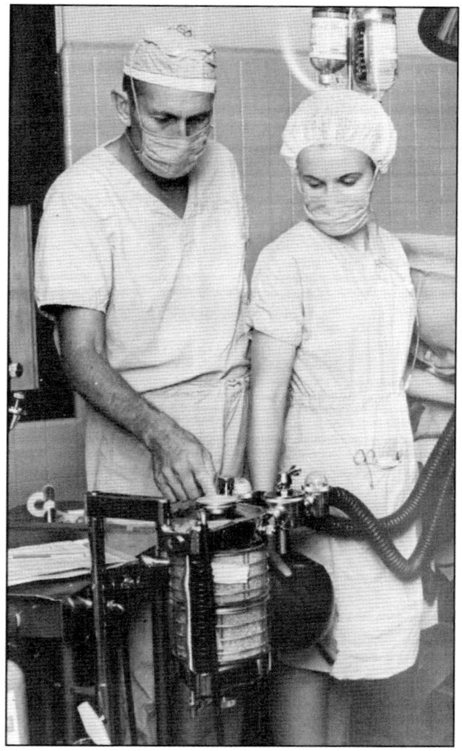

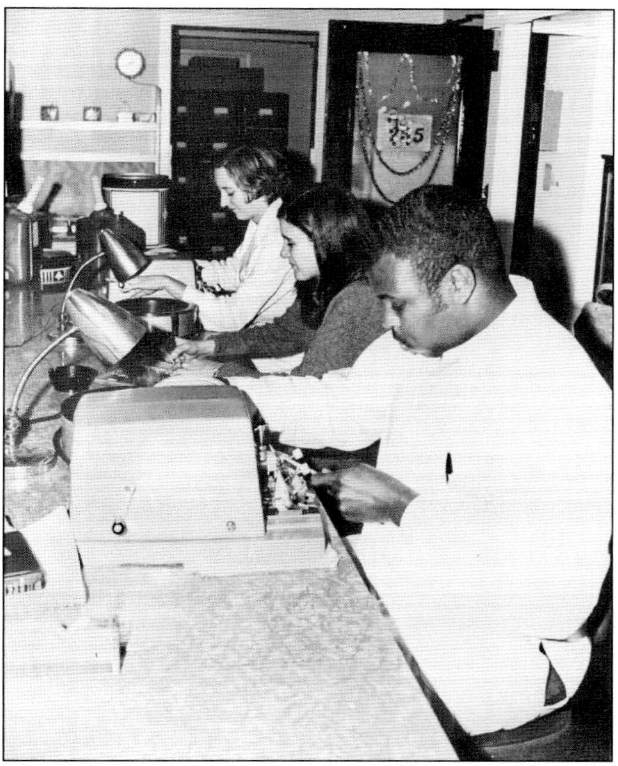

The histologic technique program began in September 1965. From left to right, Nancy Mahoney, Peggy Umphlett, and Christopher Walker, students in the program, prepare specimens for microscopy in a photograph from 1970.

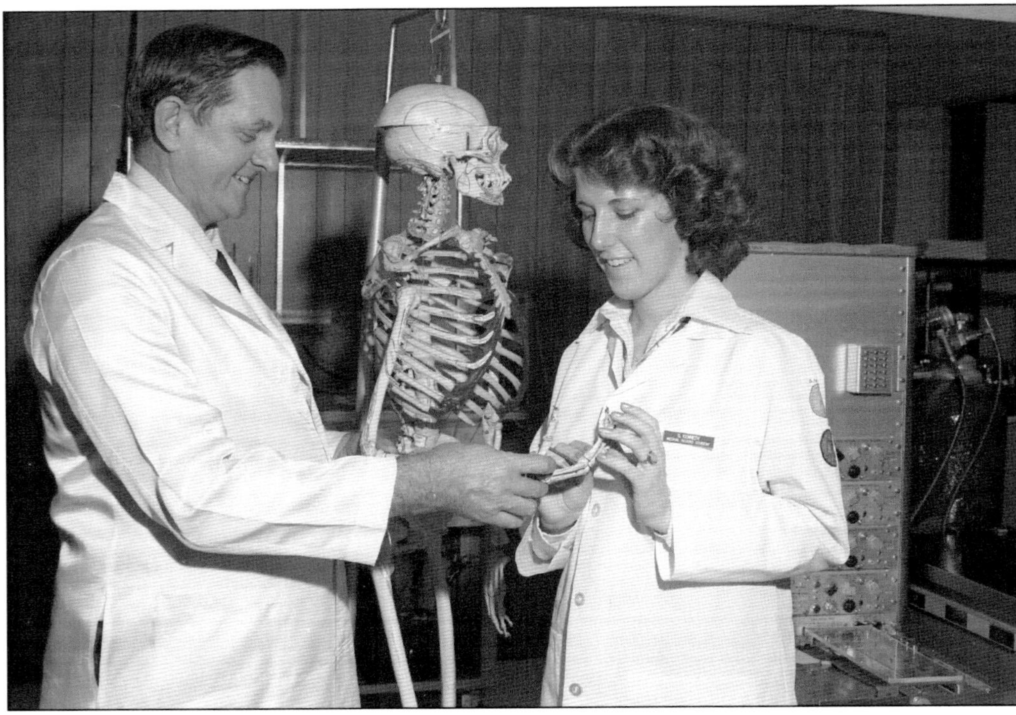

The Medical Records Administration program was established in 1969. Shannon Kennedy, a 1981 graduate of that program, is seen above with a faculty member. Below is the newly renovated CHP Building A. MUSC acquired the structure, formerly the site of Charleston High School, in 1987, and, after much public debate and input about design, the completely renovated building complex was dedicated on April 7, 2006. The facades from the high school were retained during the renovation. The exterior pediment reads, "enter to learn, leave to serve." (Below, courtesy of the College of Health Professions, MUSC.)

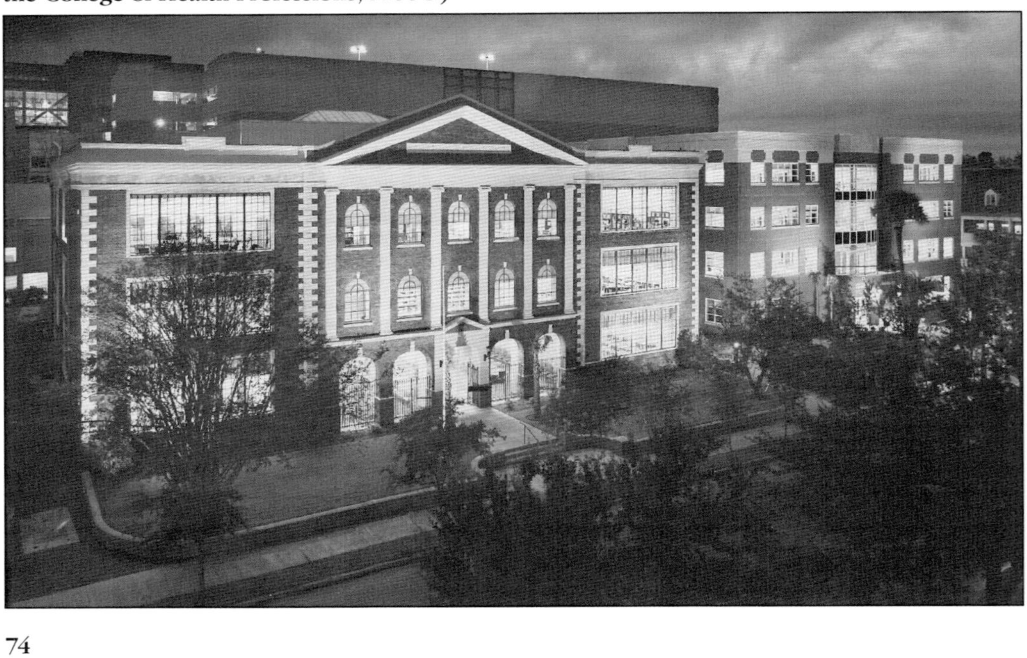

Seven

Student Life

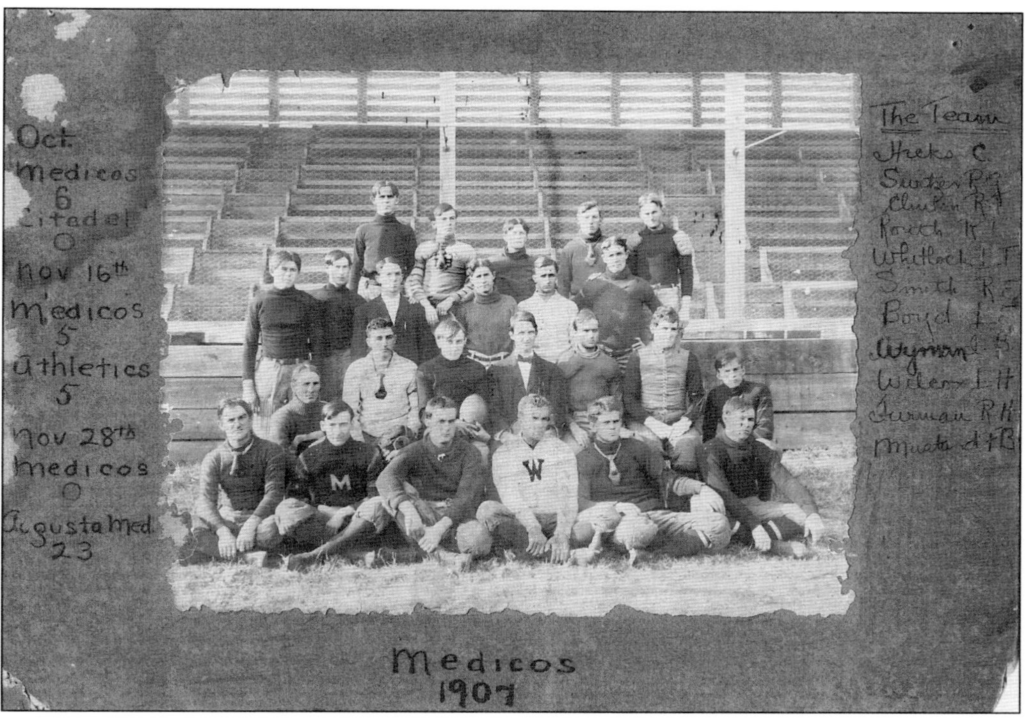

Students at the Medical University of South Carolina endure long hours and demanding course work, spending much of their time in classrooms, clinics, labs, and the library. But they also make time for fun. Over the years, the students have let off steam and showed their school pride in many ways. In the early 1900s, students fielded an intercollegiate football team, the Medicos, which in 1907 beat The Citadel 6-0.

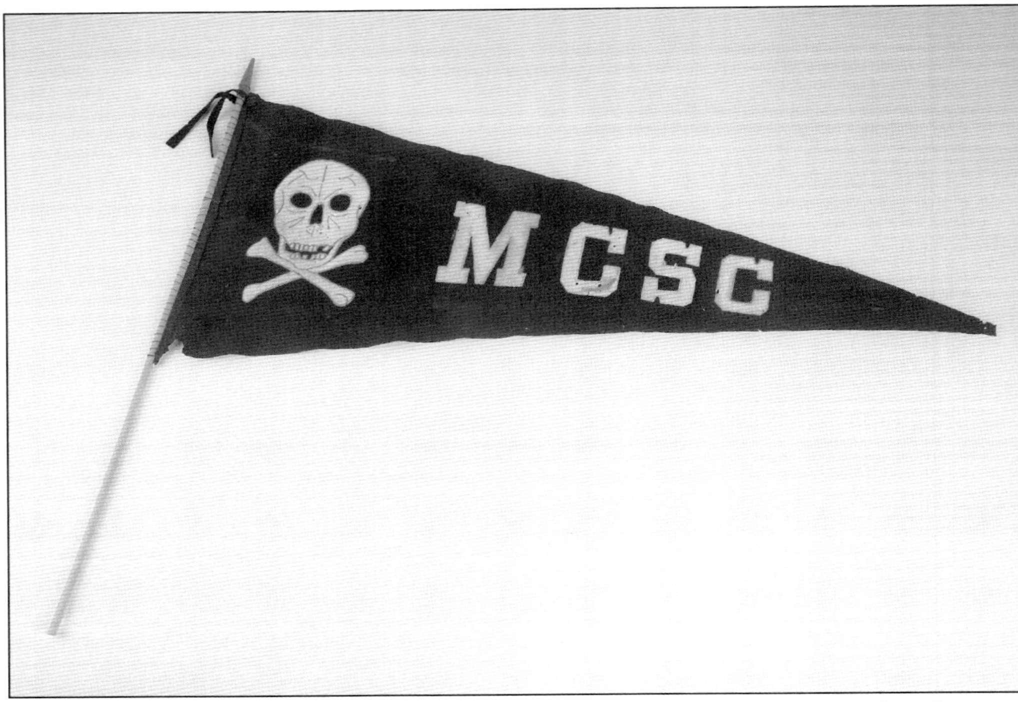

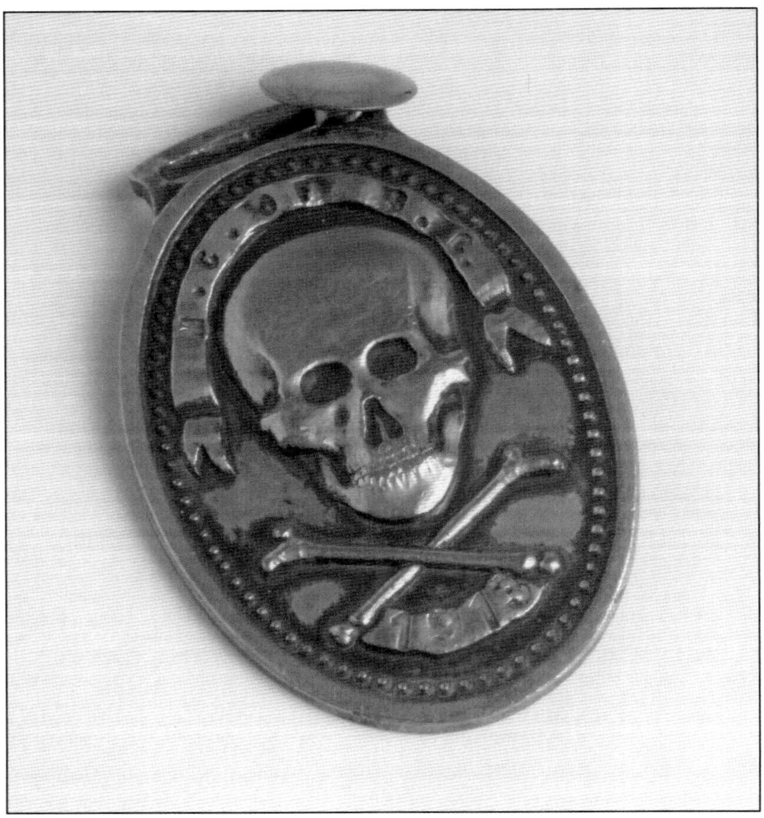

The skull and crossbones reflects the school spirit of the Medical College students and features prominently in memorabilia from the late 19th and early 20th centuries. The pennant above was a gift to the Waring Historical Library from Dr. Alan H. Rosen in 1982. At left is a silver pin from 1913 donated to the Waring Historical Library by Dr. Thomas A. Pitts II.

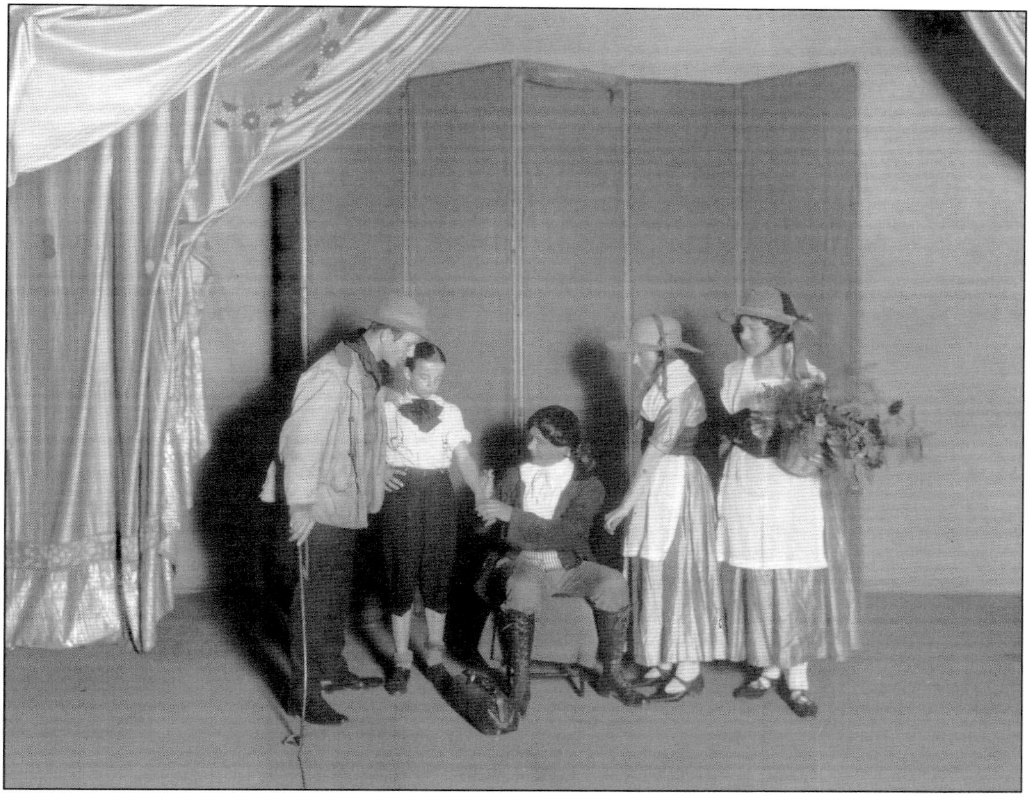

In 1924, for the 100th anniversary of the founding of the Medical College, students and faculty staged a "Centennial Celebration," a theatrical performance that re-created great moments in medicine, including Edward Jenner's smallpox vaccination (above) and the establishment of the nursing corps by Florence Nightingale (below).

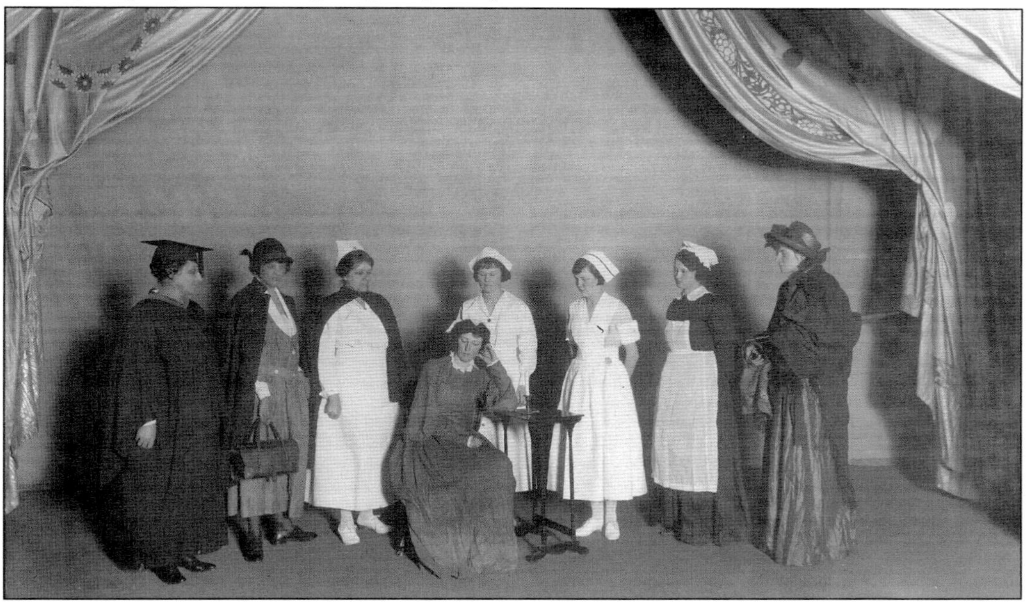

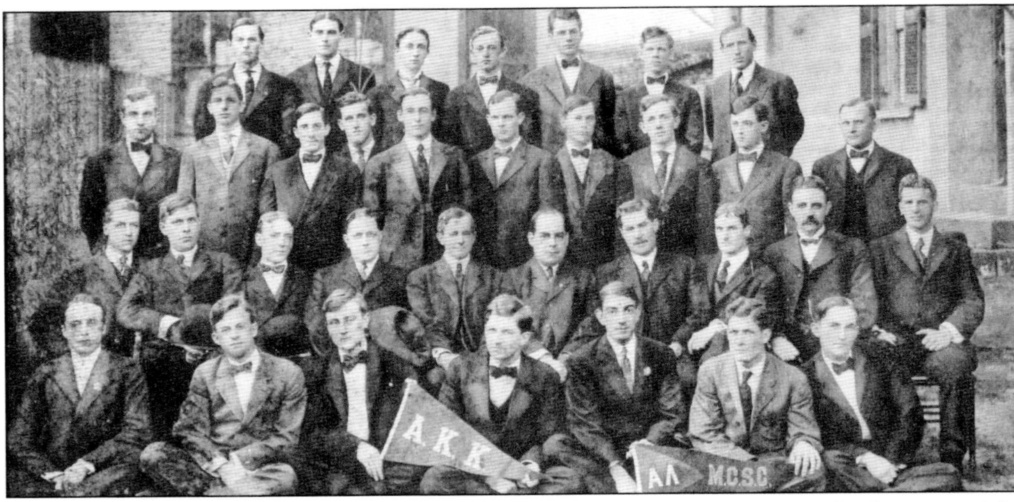

Fraternal organizations served to bring students together around common medical interests. The Alpha Lambda chapter of Alpha Kappa Kappa was instituted in Charleston on January 4, 1908. The picture above dates from around 1908. Members are, from left to right, (first row) Charles Lietsgi, W. Atmar Smith, Marion H. Wyman, Floyd McDaniel, Harold Osborne, Theo Croft, and L.S. Hay; (second row) Avery Finger, C. O'Driscoll, R.S. Cathcart, E.F. Parker, T.P. Whaley, C.M. Reese, A.E. Baker, Henry W. deSaussure, C.P. Aimar, and F.B. Johnson; (third row) Paul Switzer, L.A. Wilson, S.R. Lucas, Harry S. Mustard, William Buck Sparkman, Ralph K. Foster, F.M. Billy Routh, Phil Hunter, Theo M. DuBose, and R. B. Blackburn; (fourth row) Floyd D. Rodgers, Fitzhugh Salley, Hiram Green, W.L. Zimmerman, Jeter Glenn, George A. Hennies, and Huger Richardson. Below is a detail from the 1933 membership certificate of Dr. David B. Gregg.

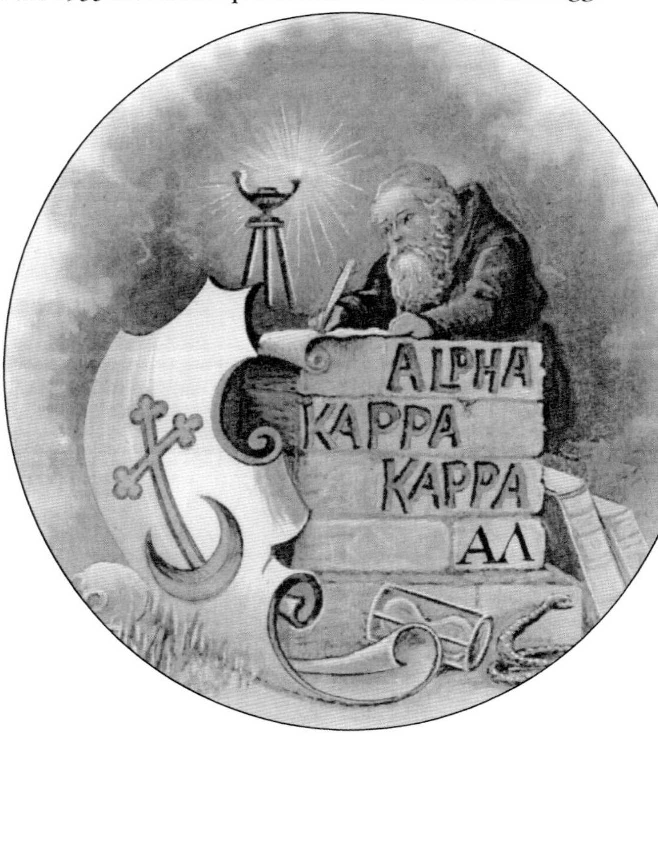

The Soro Club was organized on November 19, 1945, by a group of female pharmacy students. On April 24, 1948, this club was installed as the Omega chapter (the first in the South) of the Lambda Kappa Sigma sorority. The stated mission of the club is "to promote the happiness and usefulness of its members and to create a center of enjoyment, friendship, and culture."

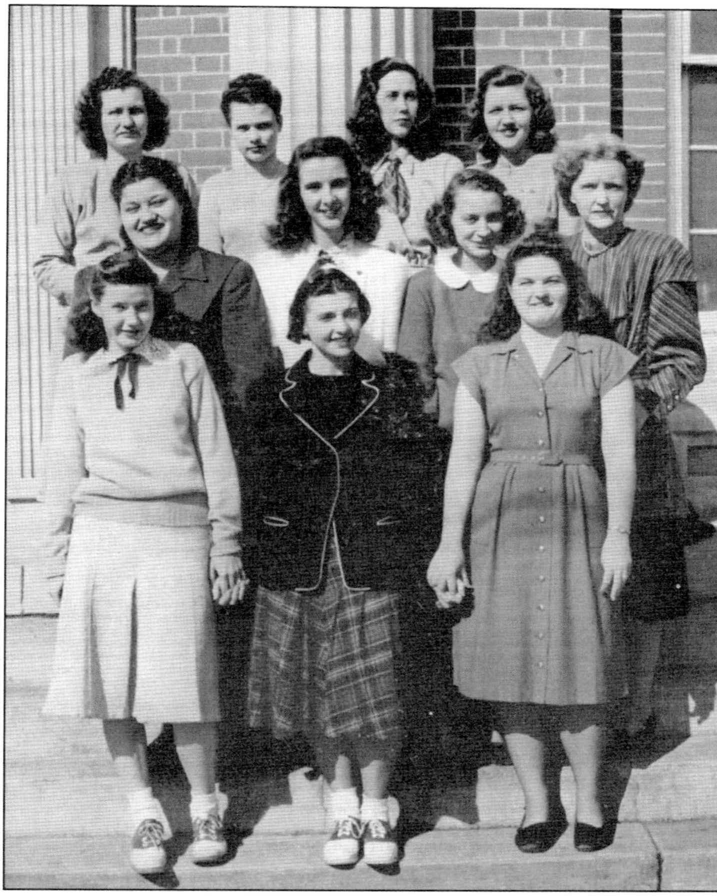

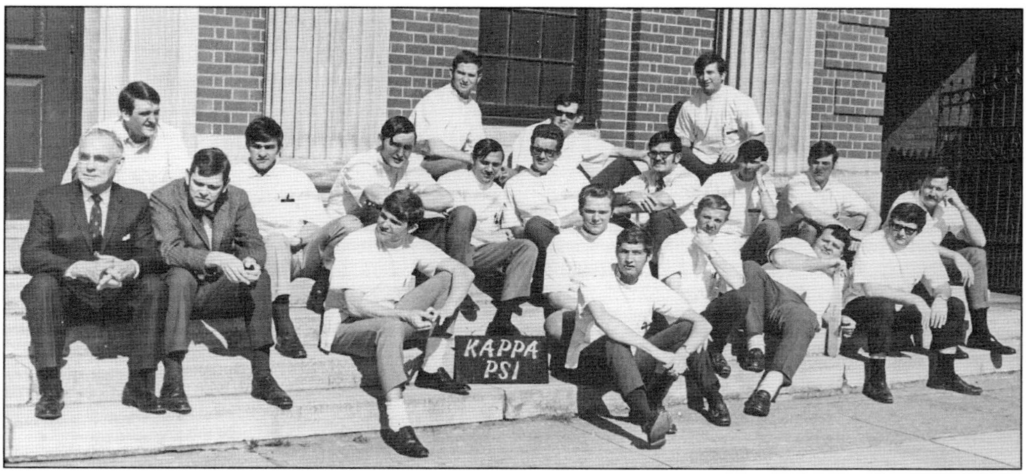

The national pharmacy fraternity Kappa Psi was founded in 1879. The Medical College chapter (Nu) was originally established in 1907 but was discontinued when the college was taken over by the state in 1913. In 1927, the chapter was reinstituted with a new chapter name, Iota. Kappa Psi continues to be an active fraternity for members of the College of Pharmacy. This photograph dates from around 1955.

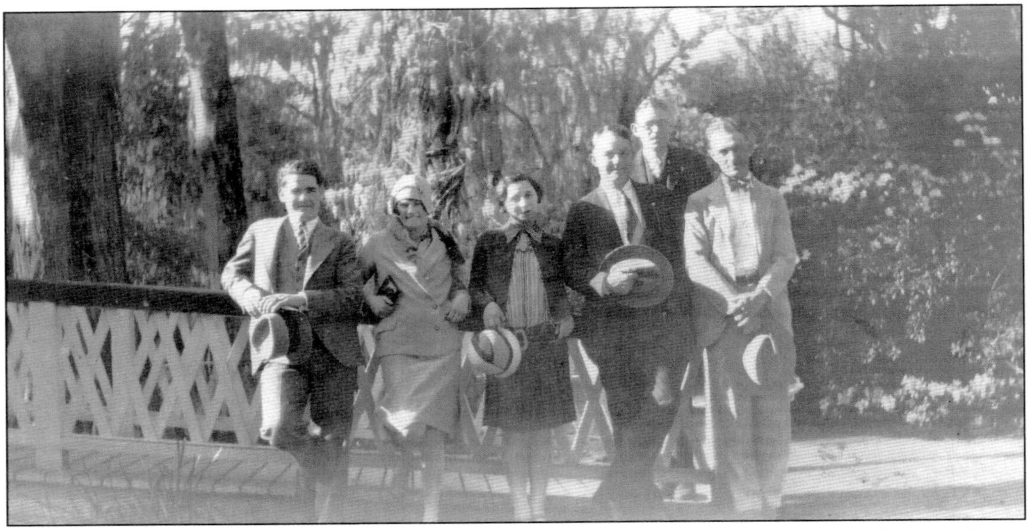

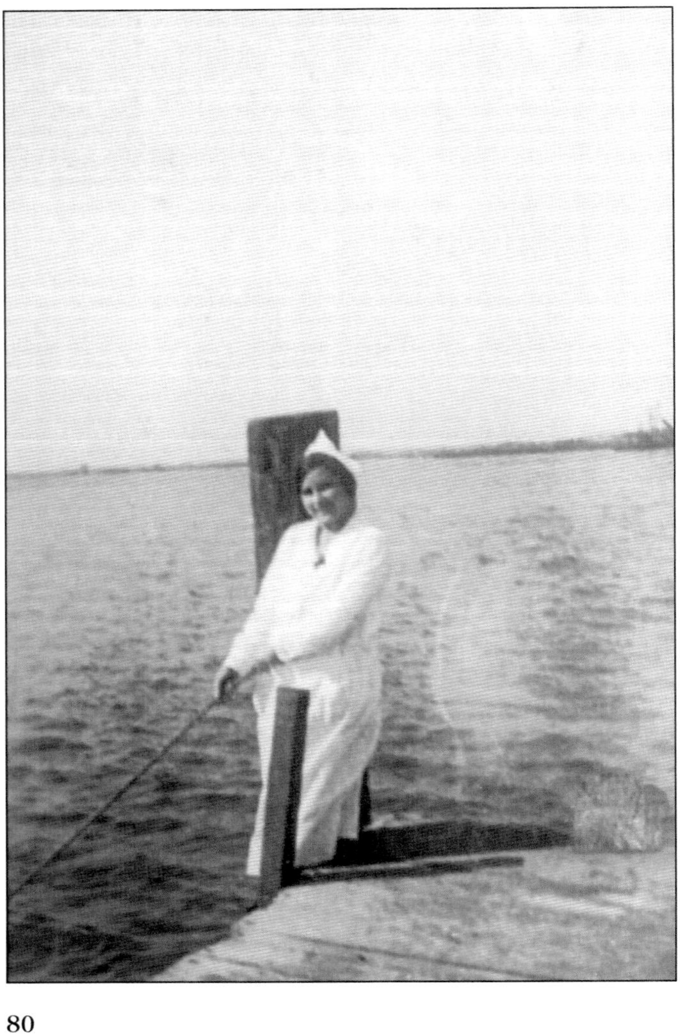

In this c. 1925 photograph, pharmacy students take part in an outing to Magnolia Gardens, a plantation turned public garden west of the city on the Ashley River.

Bertie Lee Starnes, College of Nursing class of 1924, is seen here crabbing at West Point Rice Mill on the Ashley River.

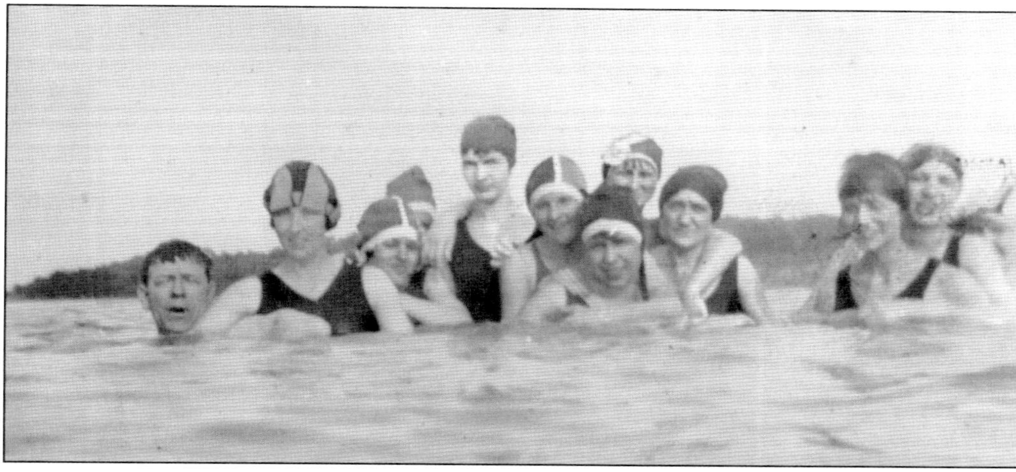

School of Nursing students explored Charleston and surrounding areas. Their excursions included hiking in Maryville, swimming near the quarantine station (above), picnicking at James Island (right), and camping at the Andell family cottage at Seabrook Island. Among those pictured above are Effie Banks, Mamie Hall, Ruth T. Smith, Sewanee Trammell, Ina Smith, Ida Edwins, and Estell Edwins. Both images date from 1924.

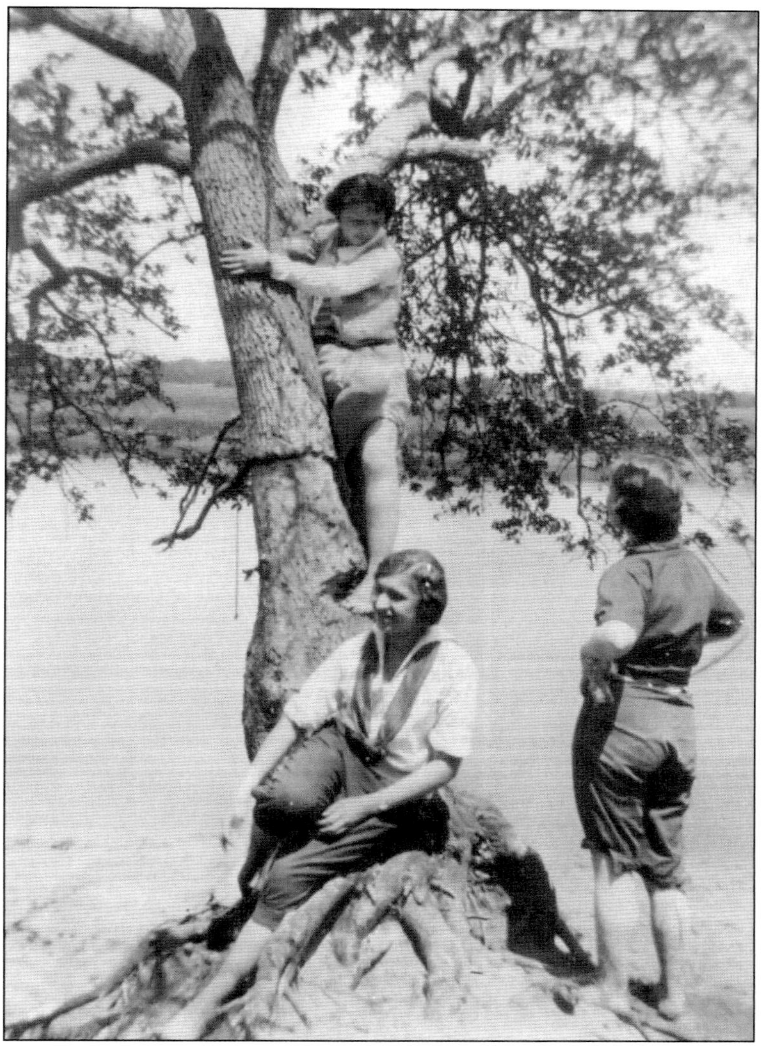

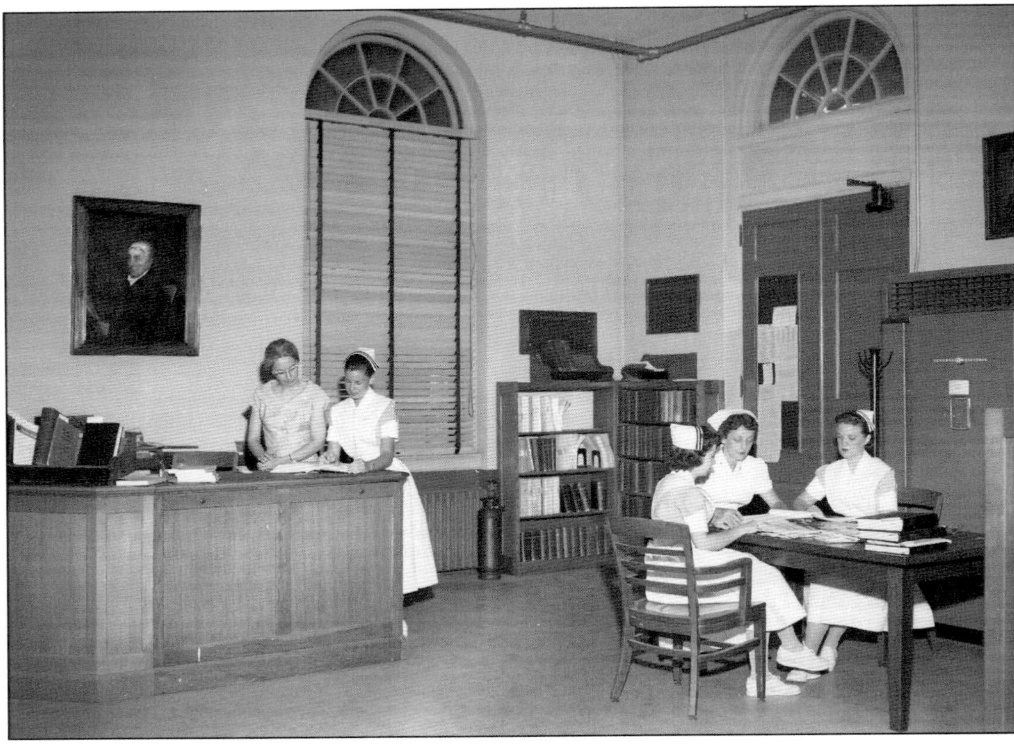

In 1930, the college library was opened on the ground floor of the building at the corner of Calhoun and Lucas Streets. Then, as now, it served as a gathering place for students to study and socialize. In 1971, a new library and administrative building was opened at the head of the MUSC horseshoe. The old library building was torn down to make room for the Hollings Cancer Center. The image above is from 1958; the image below dates from around 1968.

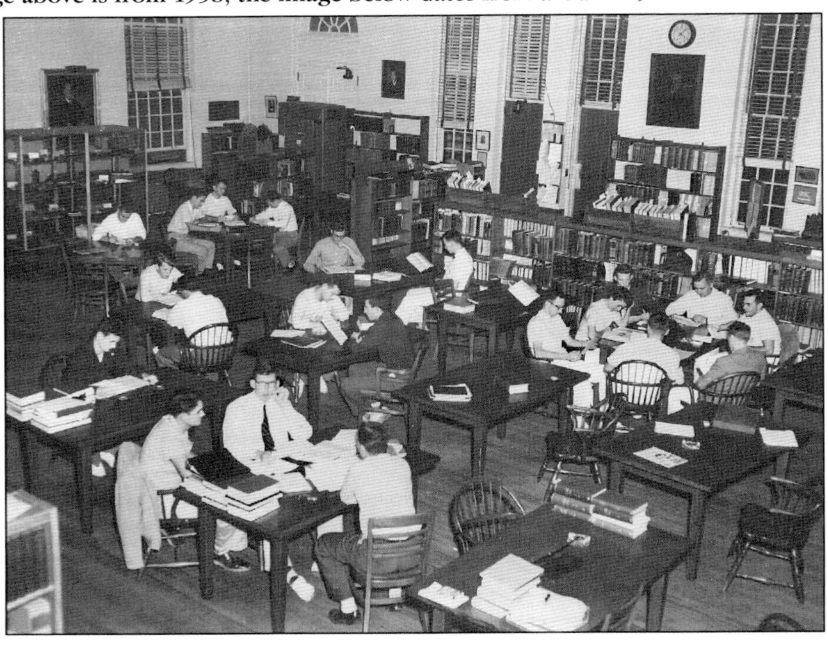

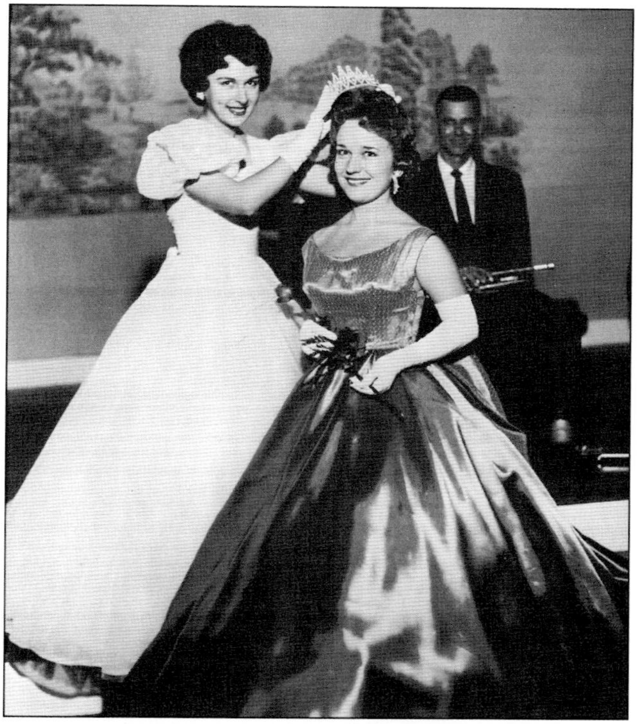

In the 1950s and 1960s, students at the colleges of medicine and nursing held various pageants and socials. At right, Gail Whitfield is crowned Miss Christmas Belle by Bonnie Bloom at the 1962 Christmas Ball. Below is the 1953 Christmas Dance.

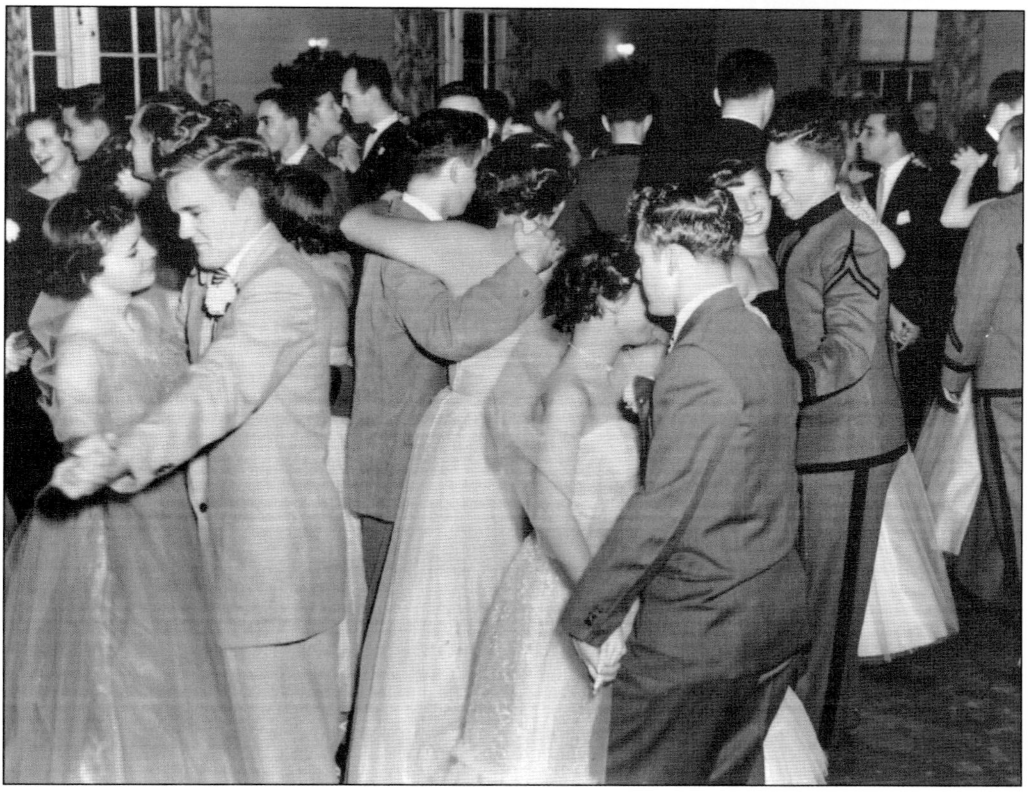

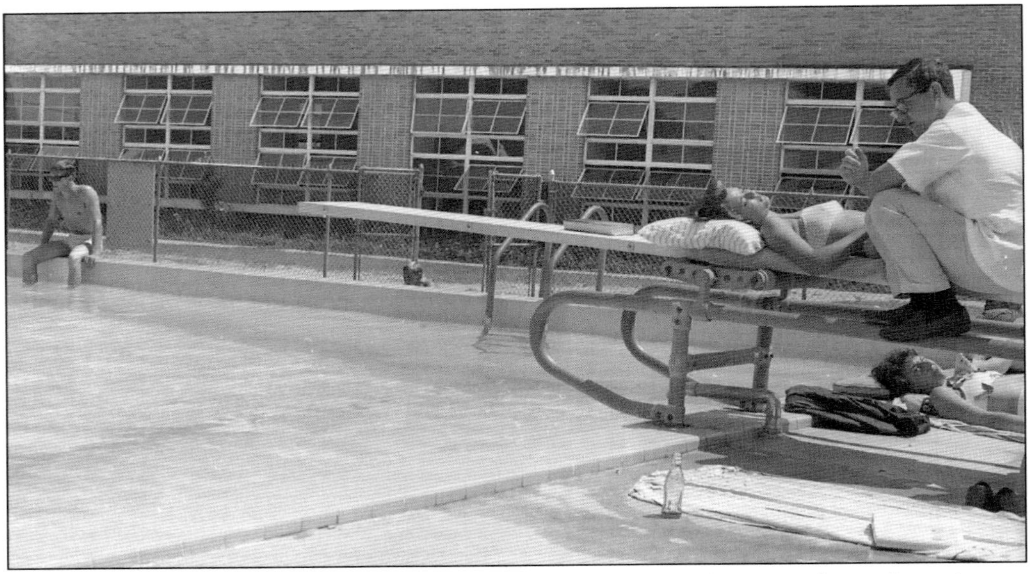

On January 1, 1955, the Alumni Memorial House was opened as a dormitory for students. Among its amenities were tennis and basketball courts and a swimming pool. "It is indeed a pleasure to have an abundance of feminine pulchritude surrounding our swimming pool during these very warm days and we are very anxious that they continue to make their appearances at the pool," wrote business manager L.W. Michaelis to Dean Chamberlin in 1963. The alumni house was closed and the building incorporated into the Stiles and Virginia Harper Student Center, officially dedicated in 1993 (ground-breaking 1988). Part of the dorm remains at the south end of the building and serves as MUSC administrative offices.

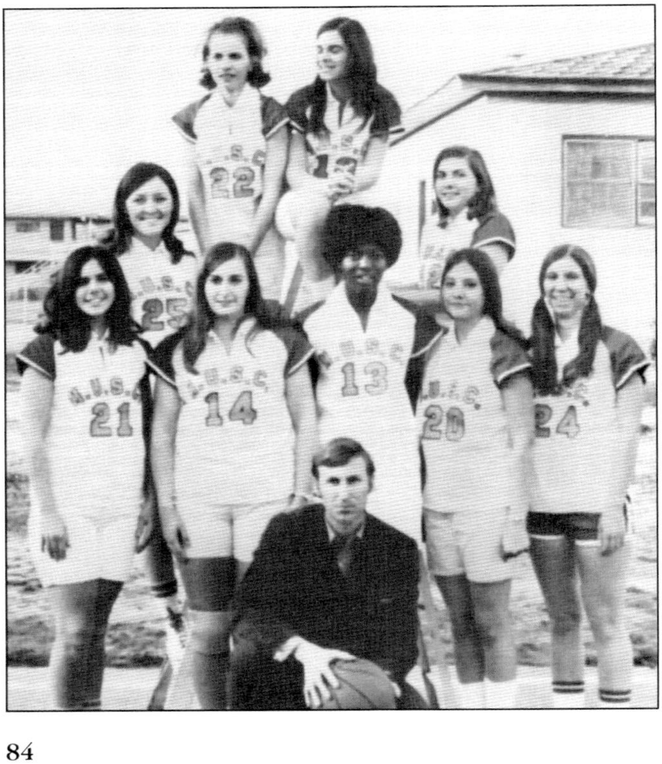

Sports have long played a role in the lives of students at MUSC, in some years as intramural and in other years as intercollegiate teams. The 1971 *Caducean* proclaims, "One of the more attractive additions to MUSC this year is the Girls' Basketball Team. Although the girls' season was not a winning one, their laughs and enjoyment more than made up for it." Team members were, from left to right, (first row) Elaine Morris, Ann Hardy, Lois Pressley, Rosemary Griggs, and Lorna Bagwell; (second row) Ann Wall and Juanita DeLoach; (third row) Wanda Cain and Starr Johnson. Wesley Smith, kneeling, was the coach.

Eight

DISASTERS

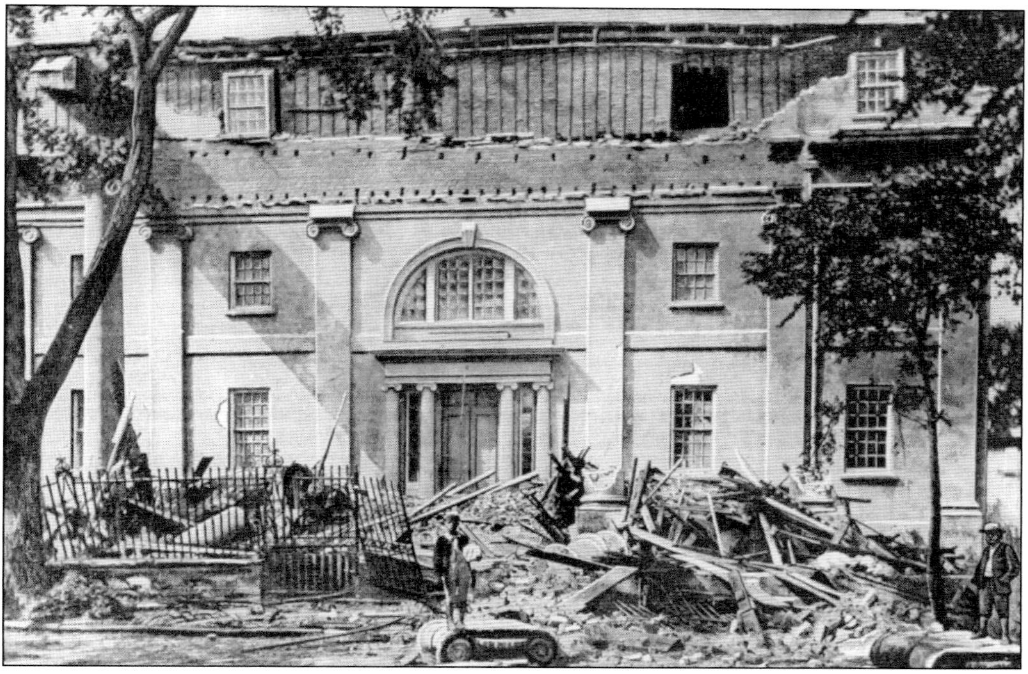

Since its founding, the Medical University of South Carolina has experienced its share of catastrophes, ranging from war to earthquakes to hurricanes to epidemic diseases. Through it all, the faculty and students persevered. The 1886 earthquake damaged the original college building on Queen Street, seen here.

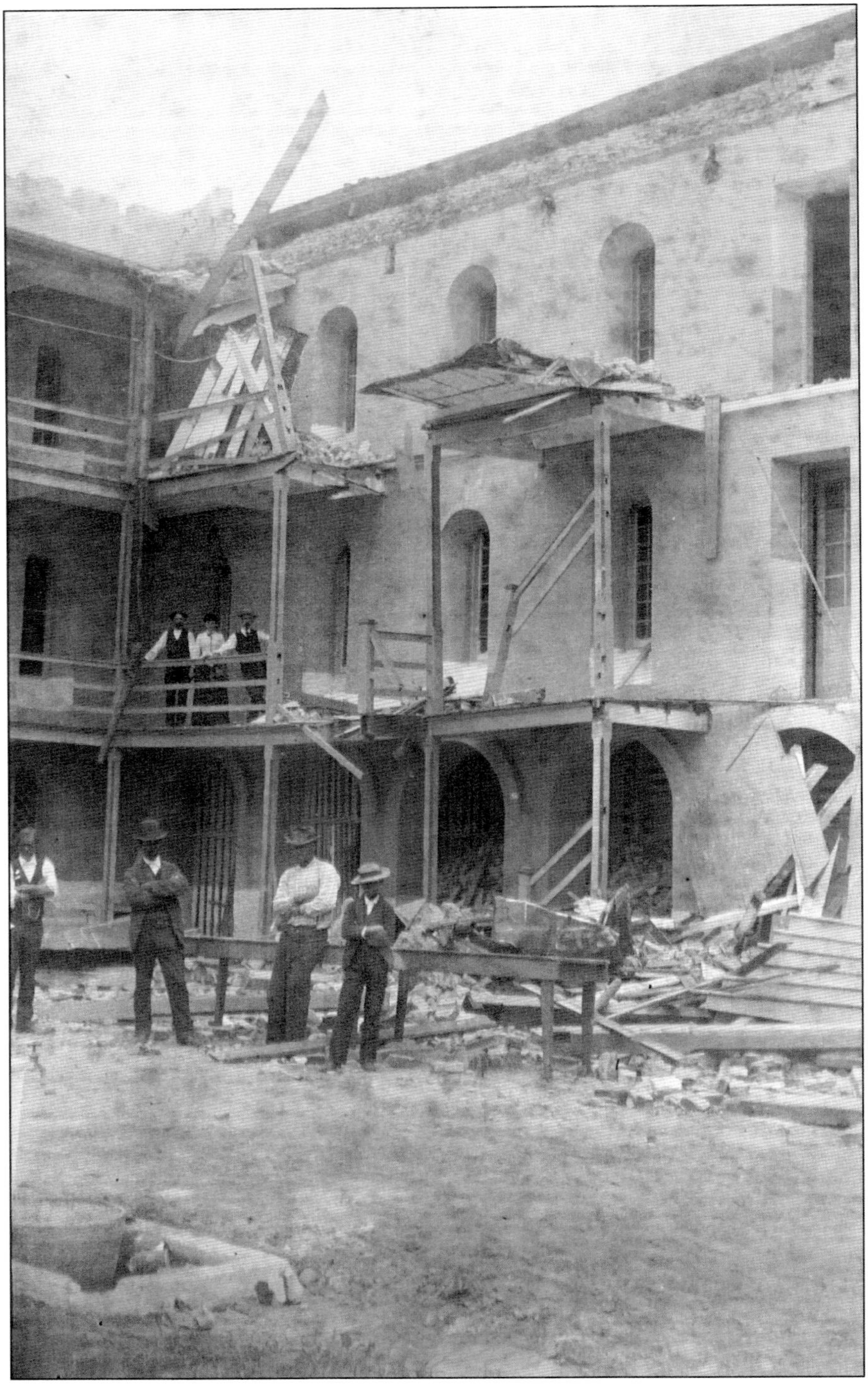

Roper Hospital was so badly damaged by the earthquake that it was closed for several years, during which time the city built a new hospital, Memorial (City) Hospital on Lucas Street. In 1906, a new Roper Hospital was opened on Lucas Street by the Medical Society, replacing the Memorial (City) Hospital.

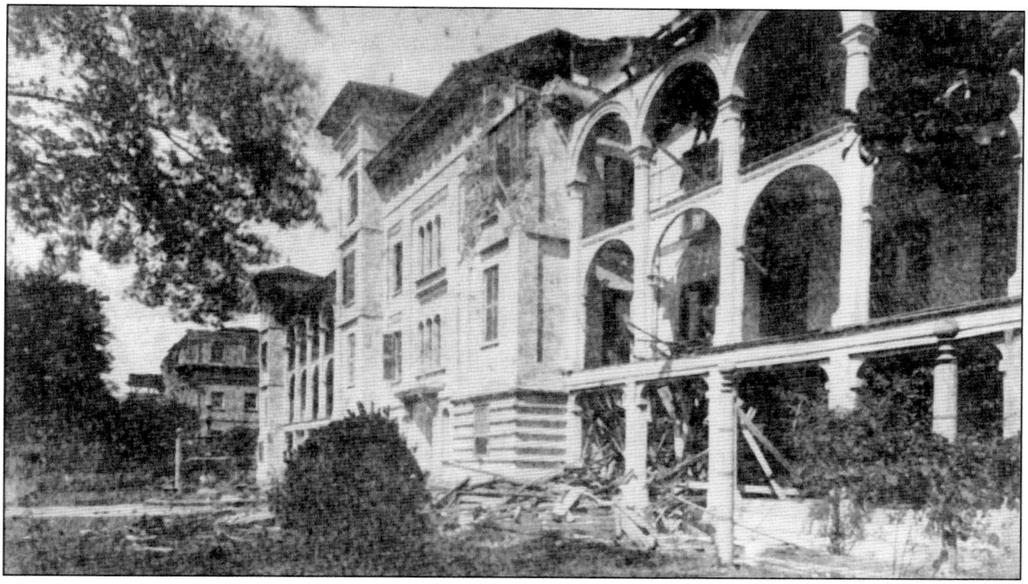

The view above pairs Roper Hospital in the right foreground with the Medical College Building in the left background. These buildings, both now gone, used to occupy the entire block of Queen Street between Franklin and Mazyck (now Logan) Streets. Below is the front of the Medical College Building with its front portico demolished.

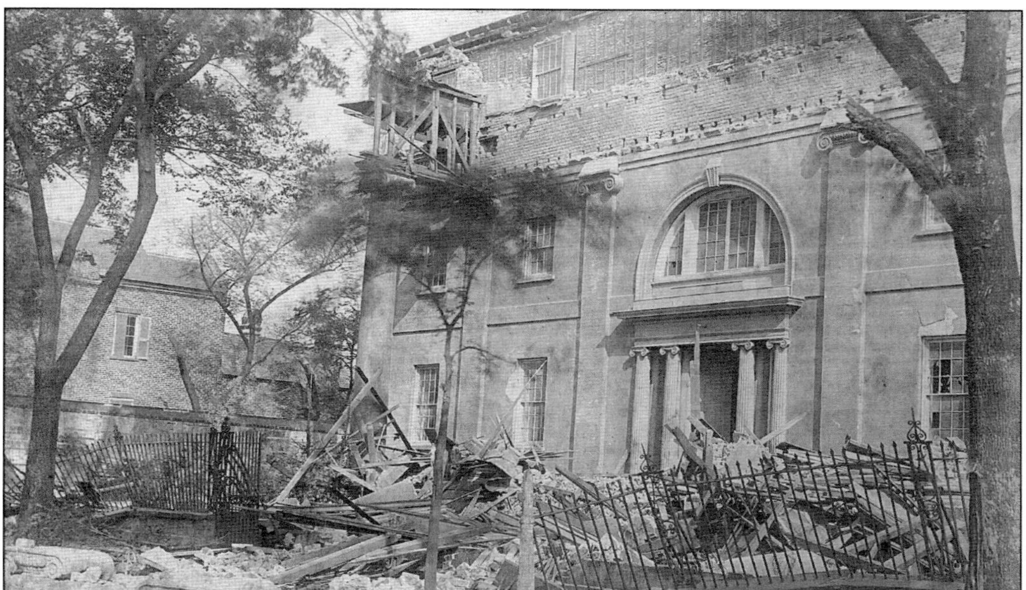

84 *Mayor Courtenay's Annual Review.*

MORTUARY STATISTICS.

REPORT OF THE NUMBER OF DEATHS IN THE CITY OF CHARLESTON IN EACH MONTH, FOR THE YEAR 1884.

WHITES.

CAUSES OF DEATH.	January.	February.	March.	April.	May.	June.	July.	August.	September.	October.	November.	December.	TOTAL.
Abscess	..	..	..	1	..	..	..	..	..	..	..	..	1
Albuminuria	..	1	..	..	..	..	..	..	..	..	..	..	1
Alcoholism	..	..	..	..	1	..	..	..	..	..	..	..	1
Anæmia	..	..	..	..	..	..	..	..	..	..	..	1	1
Anasarca	..	..	1	..	..	..	..	..	..	..	..	..	1
Aneurism Aorta	..	..	..	..	..	1	..	..	..	..	1	..	2
Angina Pectoris	..	..	..	..	..	..	1	..	..	..	..	..	1
Apoplexy	2	7	3	..	2	1	1	3	2	2	3	4	30
Ascites	1	..	..	..	..	..	..	..	..	..	..	1	2
Atheroma	1	..	..	..	..	..	..	..	..	..	..	..	1
Asthma	..	..	..	..	1	..	..	..	..	..	..	..	1
Atrophy	..	..	..	..	..	1	..	..	..	..	..	..	1
Bowels, Inflammation of	..	..	..	..	3	..	..	1	..	..	..	..	4
Brain, Anæmia of	..	..	..	..	..	..	..	..	..	1	..	..	1
Brain, Congestion of	1	1	..	2	1	2	1	4	1	3	1	..	17
Brain, Effusion on	..	1	1	..	..	..	..	..	1	..	..	..	3
Brain, Inflammation of	..	..	..	..	1	..	..	..	..	..	..	..	1
Brain, Sclerosis of	..	..	..	..	..	..	..	..	..	..	1	..	1
Brain, Softening of	1	..	..	..	1	1	2	..	1	..	..	..	6
Bronchitis	..	..	2	2	..	..	2	1	2	1	1	1	12
Bronchitis, Capillary	2	..	..	..	..	..	..	..	..	..	..	..	2
Cancer	3	..	..	..	..	..	..	1	2	1	..	..	7
Cancer Œsophagus	..	..	1	..	..	..	..	..	..	..	..	..	1
Cancer Uteri	..	..	..	..	1	..	1	..	..	..	..	1	3
Carditis	..	..	..	..	..	..	..	..	..	1	..	..	1
Catarrh	..	..	..	1	..	..	..	..	..	..	..	..	1
Cellulitis	..	..	..	..	1	..	..	..	..	..	..	..	1
Cerebro-Spinal Meningitis	..	1	1	..	1	..	1	1	..	2	..	..	7
Cholera Infantum	..	..	..	1	10	2	4	1	2	2	..	1	23
Cholera Morbus	..	..	..	..	..	1	..	1	1	1	..	..	4
Consumption	6	7	8	4	5	5	3	5	5	2	5	3	58
Convulsions	..	..	1	..	2	..	..	..	2	..	1	..	6
Convulsions, Puerperal	1	..	..	1	..	1	..	..	..	..	..	1	4
Croup	..	..	..	..	..	..	..	..	..	..	..	1	1
Croup, Membranous	..	..	..	..	..	..	..	..	..	..	..	2	2
Cystitis	..	..	..	..	..	..	..	..	..	1	..	..	1
Debility	..	..	..	1	1	..	..	..	..	..	..	..	2
Dentition	..	..	1	..	1	3	2	5	..	3	2	..	17
Diabetes Insipidus	..	..	..	..	..	..	..	..	..	..	..	1	1
Diarrhœa	1	..	..	2	..	..	5	2	..	1	..	1	12
Diphtheria	5	..	1	..	..	1	..	2	1	4	4	4	22
Dropsy	1	1	2	..	..	1	1	..	1	1	..	1	9
Dropsy, Cardiac	..	..	..	..	..	..	1	1	..	..	..	..	2
Dysentery	..	..	..	1	..	1	1	1	..	1	..	1	6
Endocarditis	..	1	..	..	..	..	..	..	..	..	..	..	1

Charleston's position as a major East Coast port resulted in frequent outbreaks of smallpox, yellow fever, malaria, plague, cholera, dengue fever, typhoid, typhus, tuberculosis, diarrhea, dysentery, tetanus, whooping cough, and more. These diseases often brought high mortality to a city also struggling against fire, hurricanes, and earthquakes.

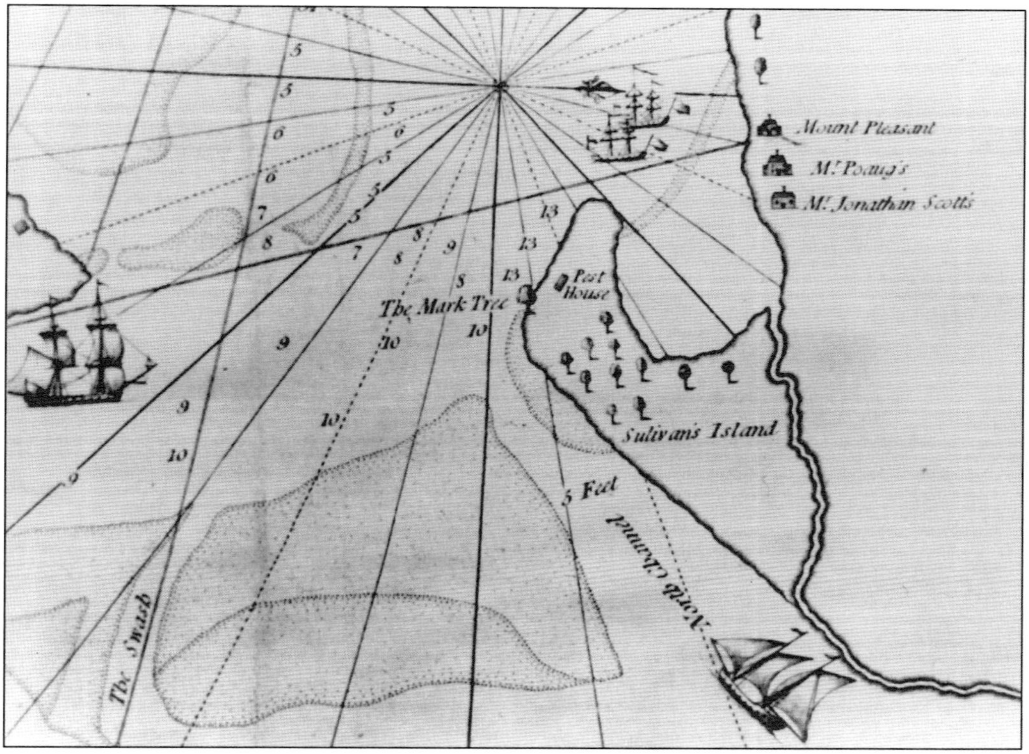

For many years, quarantine was employed to protect Charleston from disease imported by ships from foreign ports. The map above shows the location of the first "Pest House" or quarantine station on Sullivan's Island, built around 1707. Historian Peter H. Wood has called Sullivan's Island the "Ellis Island of black Americans" because of its use as a quarantine station for incoming slave ships. Fort Johnson, seen below around 1935, traces its roots as a quarantine station to 1756, when the colonial government required all incoming vessels to stop at the fort for medical inspection. South Carolina operated a maritime quarantine station at Fort Johnson from 1872 to 1906, when the US Public Health Service (USPHS) took over the station. The USPHS continued operations at Fort Johnson until 1948, when the station was closed. (Above is a detail from "An Exact Plan of Charles-Town-Bar and Harbour," printed in London by Robert Sayer and John Bennett, July 17, 1776, and based on an actual survey.)

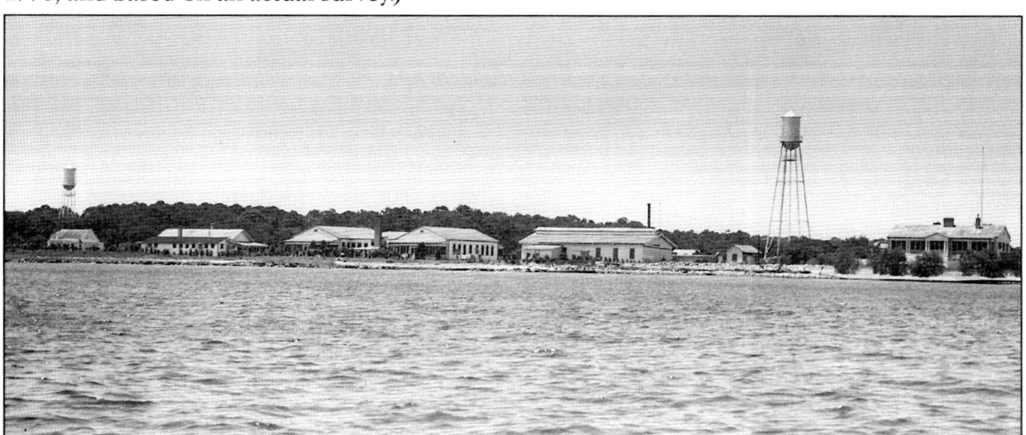

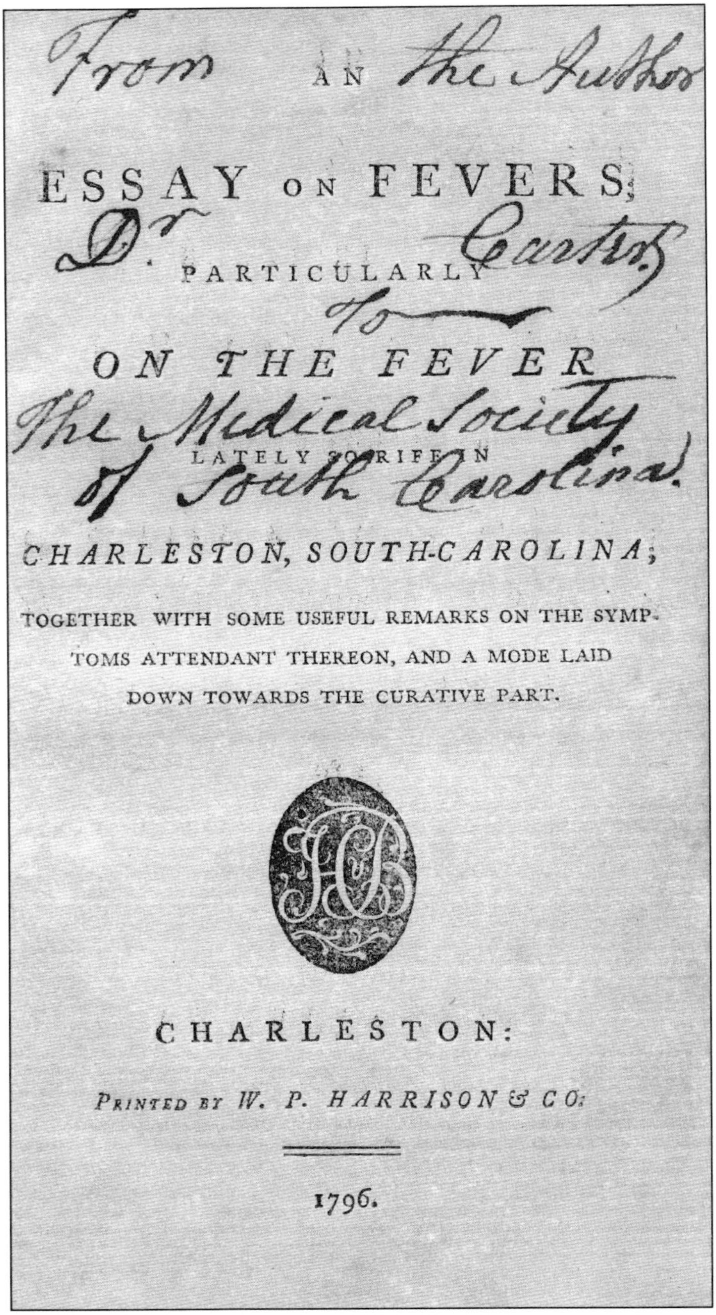

AN

ESSAY ON FEVERS;

PARTICULARLY

ON THE FEVER

LATELY SO RIFE IN

CHARLESTON, SOUTH-CAROLINA;

TOGETHER WITH SOME USEFUL REMARKS ON THE SYMPTOMS ATTENDANT THEREON, AND A MODE LAID DOWN TOWARDS THE CURATIVE PART.

CHARLESTON:

PRINTED BY W. P. HARRISON & CO.

1796.

After tuberculosis, the most devastating disease of 19th-century Charleston was yellow fever, which caused twice as many deaths as all other fevers combined between 1821 and 1858. Miasmas (or pockets of unhealthy air) were generally thought to be the cause of yellow fever and malaria. At the time, medicine had not identified the mosquito as the vector of these diseases. These mosquitoes thrived in stagnant ponds and other standing waters, which were common in South Carolina due to the increased development of rice fields and the large reserves of standing water that they required.

The last official epidemic outbreak of yellow fever occurred in Memphis in 1878. Charleston physician and 1867 Medical College graduate Dr. T. Grange Simons was awarded this medal by the Howard Association "for services during the Yellow fever epidemic in Memphis 1878. A.D. Langstaff, Pres Howard Assoc R.W. Mitchell Medical Director."

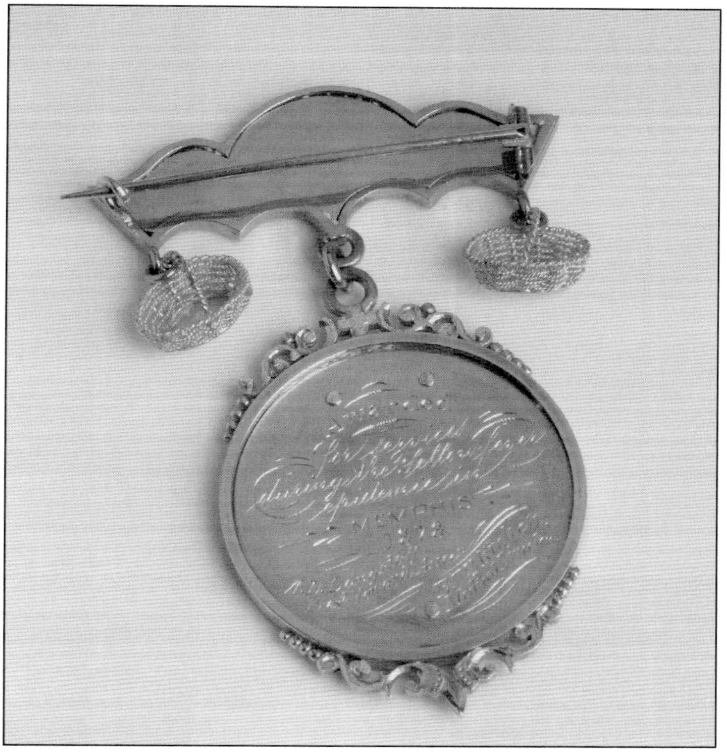

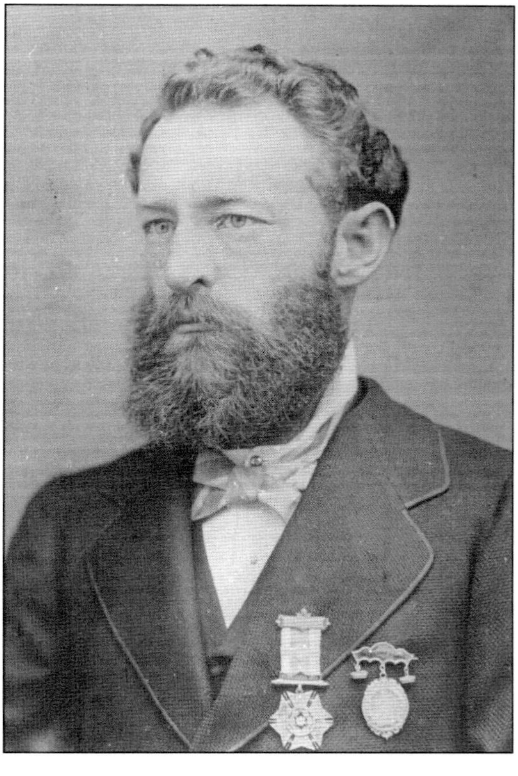

Dr. Simons served as president of the Medical Society of South Carolina and the South Carolina Medical Association and was chairman of the State Board of Health. He was a demonstrator in anatomy, assistant professor of pathology and practice of medicine, and, ultimately, chair of materia medica at the Medical College.

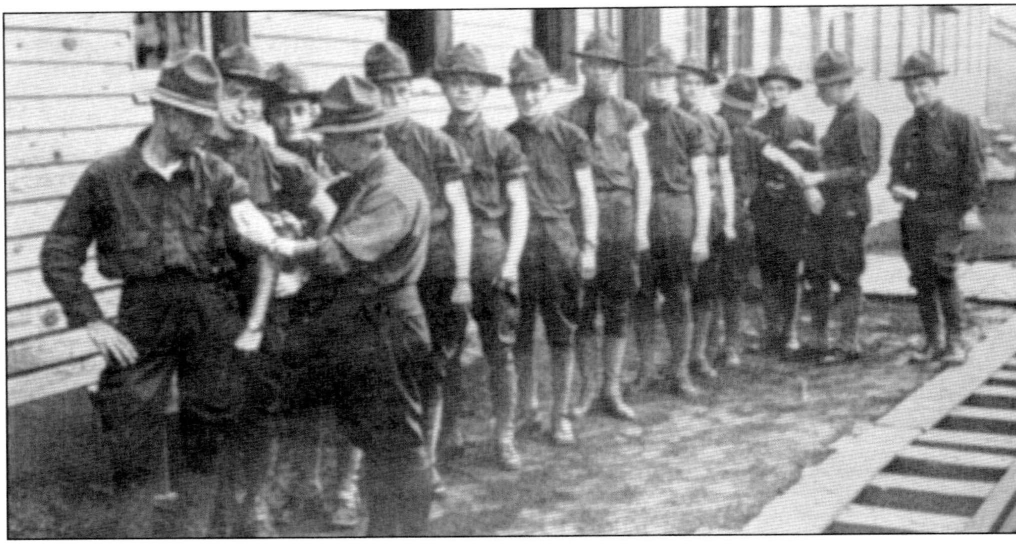

Influenza arrived in South Carolina in September 1918, peaked in mid-October, and abated by November. In his annual report to the city, Charleston board of health officer J. Merceir Green wrote, "There has never been any disease in the history of the city which has equaled the death toll taken by this disease and its complications during the present epidemic." In this photograph, soldiers at Fort Jackson, near Columbia, are getting inoculated against influenza. (Courtesy of the South Caroliniana Library, University of South Carolina, Columbia, South Carolina.)

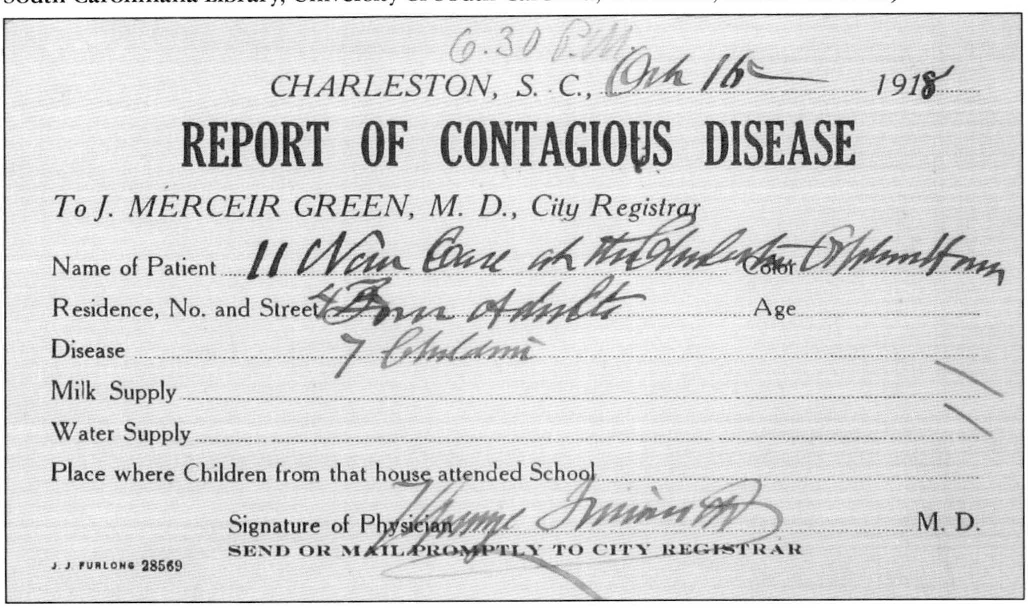

CHARLESTON, S. C., ... 1918

REPORT OF CONTAGIOUS DISEASE

To J. MERCEIR GREEN, M. D., City Registrar

Name of Patient .... Color ....

Residence, No. and Street .... Age ....

Disease ....

Milk Supply ....

Water Supply ....

Place where Children from that house attended School ....

Signature of Physician .... M. D.

SEND OR MAIL PROMPTLY TO CITY REGISTRAR

J. J. FURLONG 28569

Green continues, "Notices were then sent out to all physicians requesting the report of all cases of Influenza occurring within their practice, and in a few days great numbers of cases began to pour in and were recorded, a watchful eye was kept on the situation, as it was becoming alarming." The city responded by initiating quarantine, organizing relief, and taking possession of contraband whiskey to be distributed by physician prescription only. One of hundreds of notices completed by physicians to report influenza in Charleston, this report announces "11 new cases at the Charleston Orphan House" and is signed by T. Grange Simons.

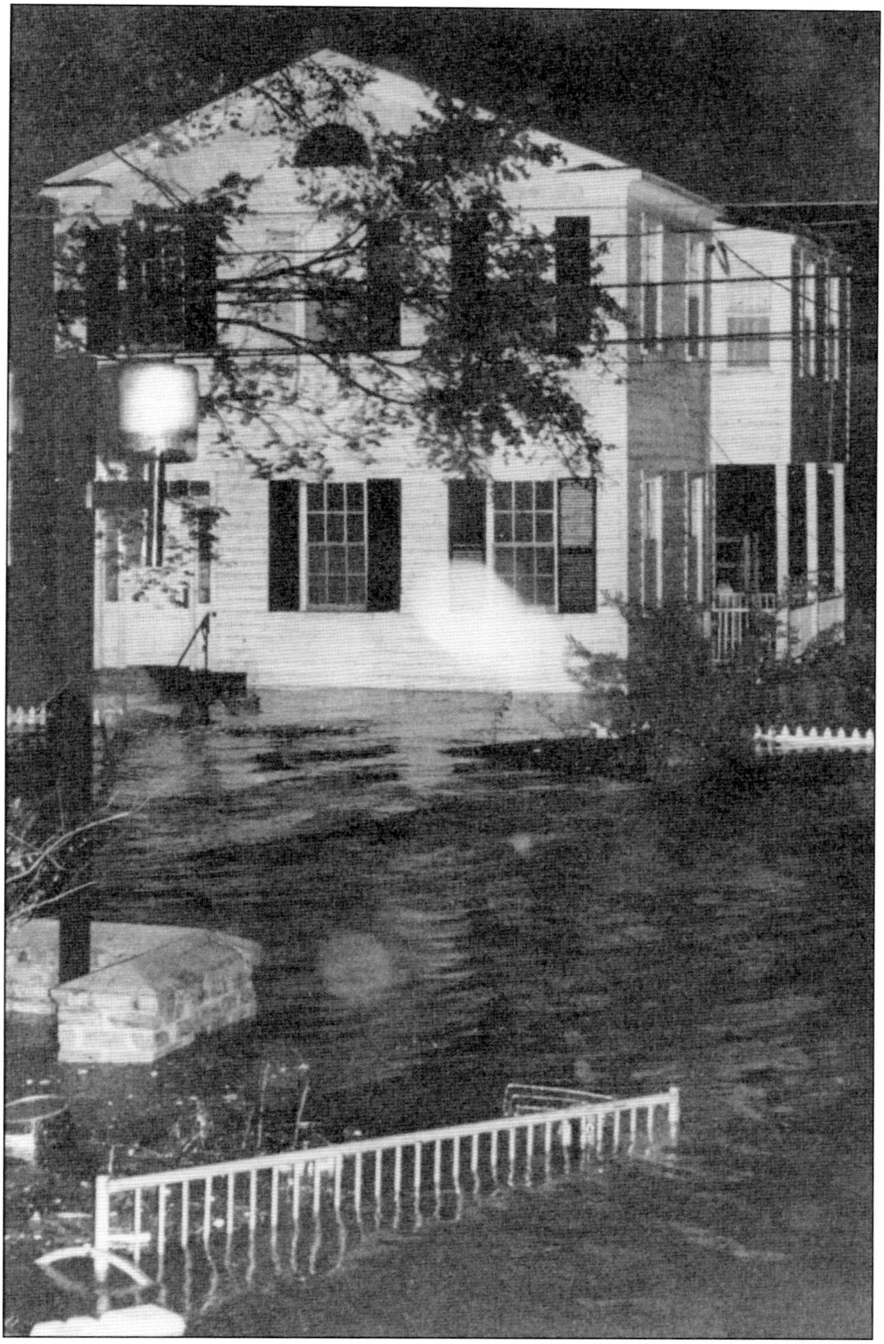

In addition to disease and earthquakes, Charleston has suffered greatly from hurricanes, including those of 1885, 1893, and 1959. Perhaps none caused greater havoc than Hugo in 1989. On the night of September 21, Hurricane Hugo, a Category 4 hurricane, struck Charleston with a vengeance and battered the region with heavy rains and 140-mile-per-hour winds. Seen above is a view of Ashley Avenue taken from in front of the Basic Sciences Building during the eye of the storm. The six-foot brick wall to the left shows the high-water mark above street level.

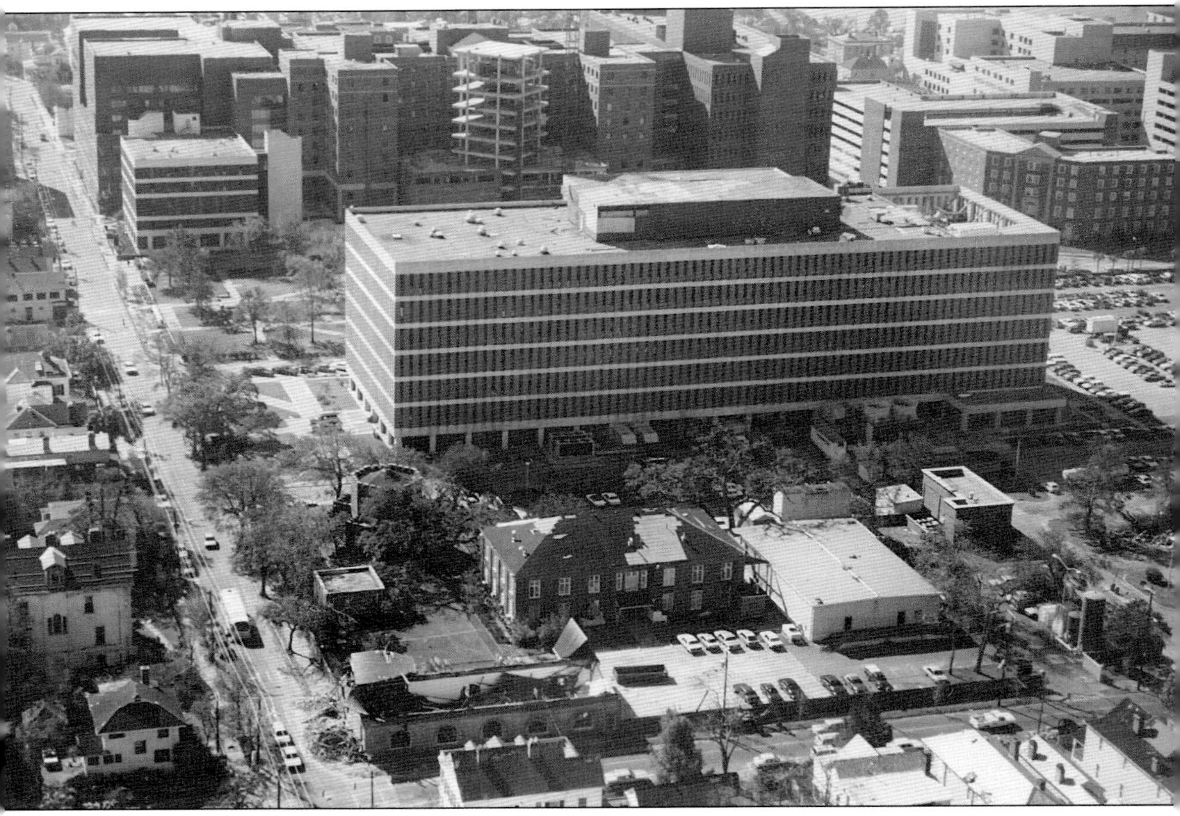

During the storm, medical staff was reduced to only those absolutely required to meet the needs of the patients. With the primary goal of ensuring safety and security, hospital management continually evaluated strategies regarding patient care and the allocation of resources. MUSC administration established two shifts of workers in all departments: those who remained on campus and those who went home or evacuated. This morning-after aerial view shows the scene greeting those who stayed on or returned to campus. In the foreground are St. Luke's Chapel and Colcock Hall, both of which suffered heavy damage.

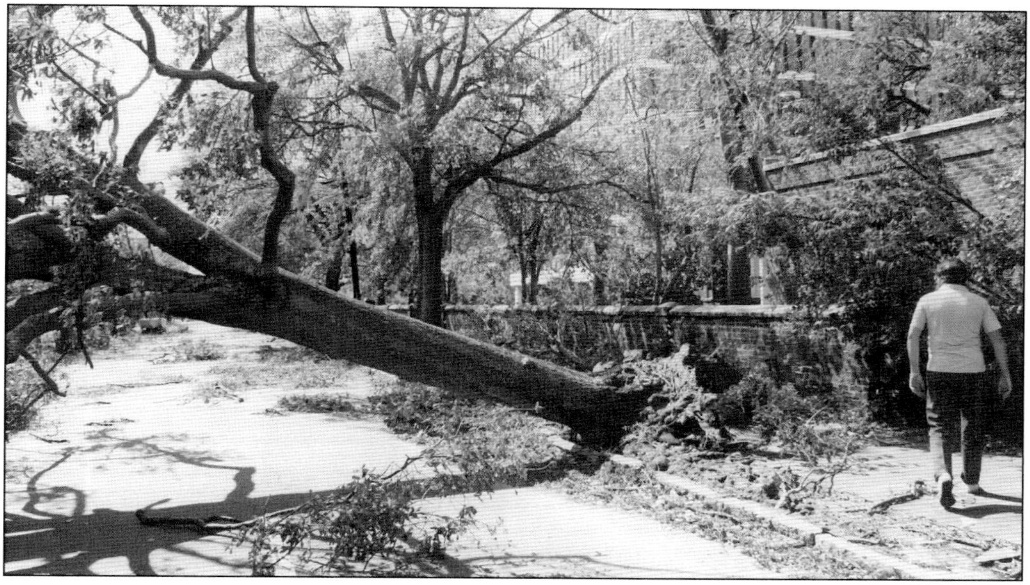

Hurricane Hugo proved to be the most expensive storm in Charleston's history, with damages exceeding $6 billion—$33 million at MUSC alone. Here is a view of Ashley Avenue looking south from Bee Street. The MUSC campus is immediately to the right of the brick wall. The Basic Sciences Building can be seen in the right background.

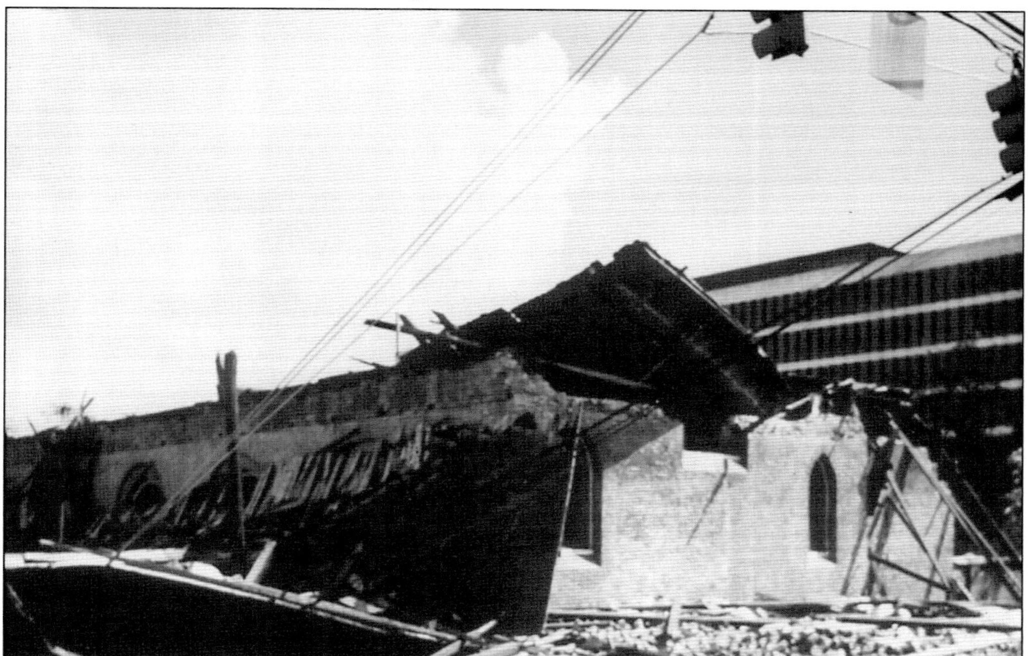

One of the most heavily damaged buildings at MUSC was St. Luke's Chapel. The high winds of Hugo ripped the roof off the chapel, blew out the windows, and collapsed multiple walls. The devastation was near total. The Bee Street corner of campus where St. Luke's Chapel and Colcock Hall are located is thought to have been hit by one of the more than 200 tornadoes that blasted through Charleston County.

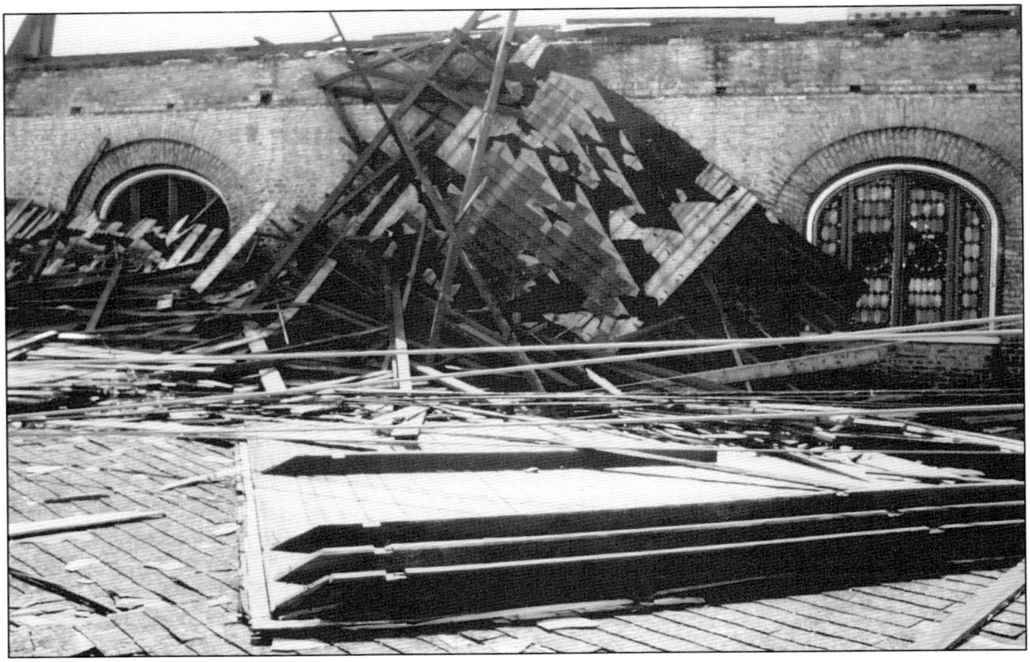

Dr. W. Curtis Worthington Jr., on the chapel restoration committee, said, "The chapel looked like it [had] been in an air raid. The roof had caved in, the south side of the roof fell into the main body, the church nave, and the other side, the northern side, had fallen into Bee Street, and the Toomer Porter window had fallen more or less into Ashley Avenue."

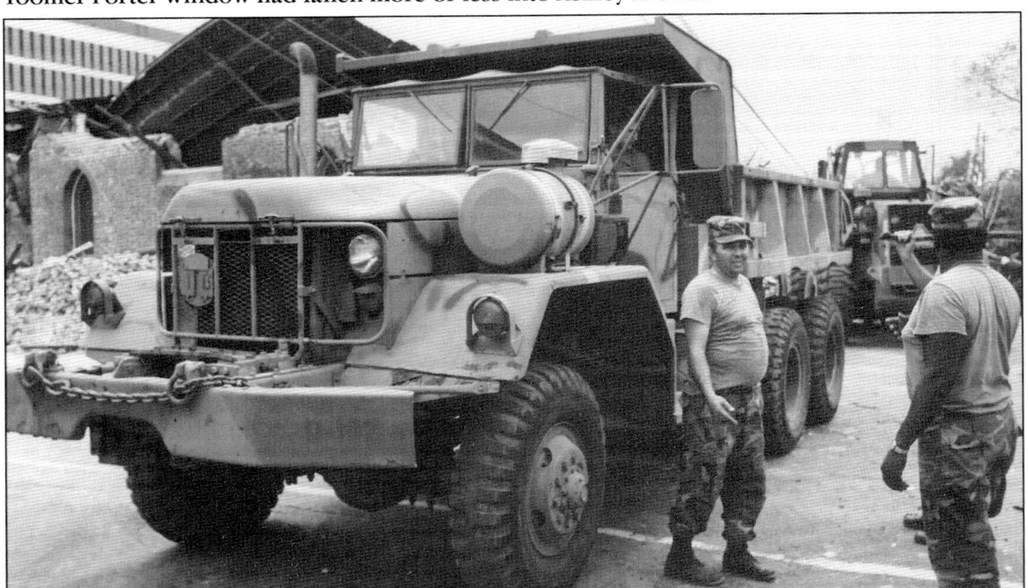

The National Guard cleared debris from the St. Luke's Chapel, in the background. Troops were deployed throughout Charleston for cleanup and security. Across campus, offices, laboratories, and clinical spaces suffered extreme damage from rising water, blown-out windows, and leaking roofs. Even amid destruction, however, staff and students resumed normal routines within two weeks.

Nine

MILITARY MEDICINE

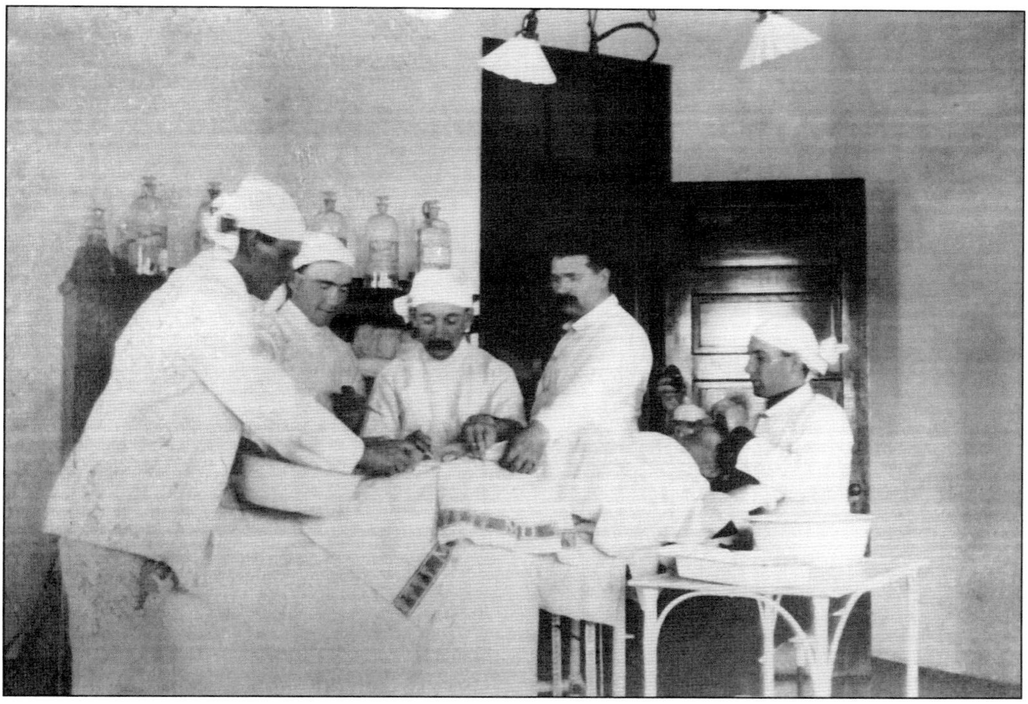

From the earliest years of the country's history, MUSC alumni, faculty, and staff have fought and healed in times of war. Beyond providing basic medical care, these practitioners also advanced the course of treatment of wartime injuries through innovation and invention. Above is a c. 1895 image of the station surgeons at Fort Moultrie.

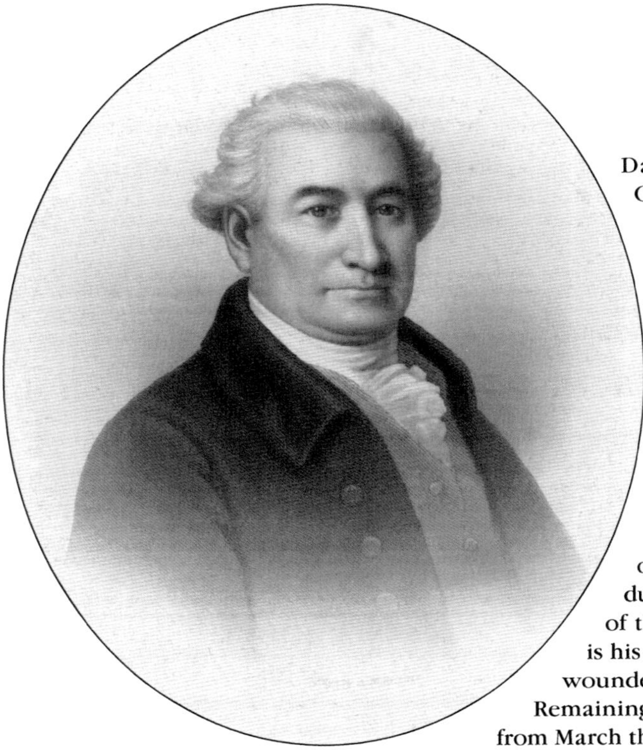

David Olyphant (left) arrived in Charleston from his native Scotland around 1749. In 1755, he settled in Dorchester and practiced medicine, serving also as a port physician for Charlestown. An ardent patriot, Olyphant was appointed director-general of the hospitals of the Southern Department in 1776. He was made a prisoner of war during the British siege of Charlestown in 1780, after which he was appointed director of American hospitals and later deputy director of the hospital of the Southern Army. Among his duties as director-general was a survey of the hospital in Charlestown. Below is his "Monthly Report of all the Sick and wounded Received, Dead, Dismissed and Remaining in the Continental Gen. Hospital from March the 1st to April 1st 1780."

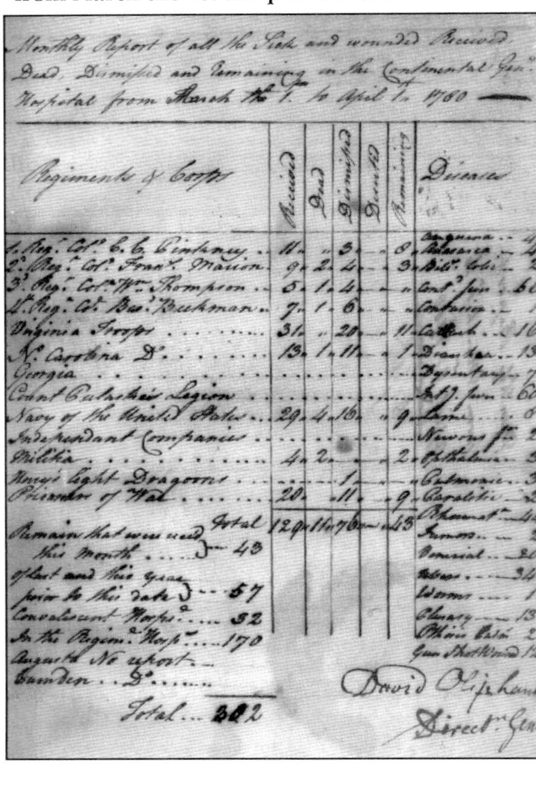

Monthly Report of all the Sick and wounded Received, Dead, Dismissed and Remaining in the Continental Genl. Hospital from March the 1st to April 1st 1780

Regiments & Corps	Received	Dead	Dismissed	Deserted	Remaining
1. Regt. Col. C. C. Pinckney	11	–	3	–	8
2. Regt. Col. Franc. Marion	9	2	4	–	3
3. Regt. Col. Wm. Thompson	5	1	4	–	–
4. Regt. Col. Barn. Beekman	7	1	6	–	–
Virginia Troops	31	–	20	–	11
N. Carolina Do.	13	1	11	–	1
Georgia					
Count Pulaski's Legion					
Navy of the United States	29	4	16	–	9
Independant Companies					
Militia	4	2	–	–	2
Horry's Light Dragoons	–	–	1	–	–
Prisoners of War	20	–	11	–	9
Total	129	11	76	–	43

Diseases	
Angina	4
[illegible]	4
Bilious Colic	2
Cont. fever	66
Contusion	1
Catarrh	16
Diarrhoea	13
Dysentery	7
Int. fever	60
Lame	8
Nervous fever	2
Opthalmia	3
Pulmonic	3
Paralitic	2
Rheumatism	44
Tumors	2
Venereal	20
Ulcers	34
Worms	1
Pleurisy	13
[illegible]	2
Gun Shot Wound	12

Remain that were recd. this month ... 43
of last and this year prior to this date ... 57
Convalescent Hospl. ... 32
In the Regiml. Hospl. ... 170
Augusta No report
Camden ... Do.

Total ... 302

David Olyphant
Direct. Genl.

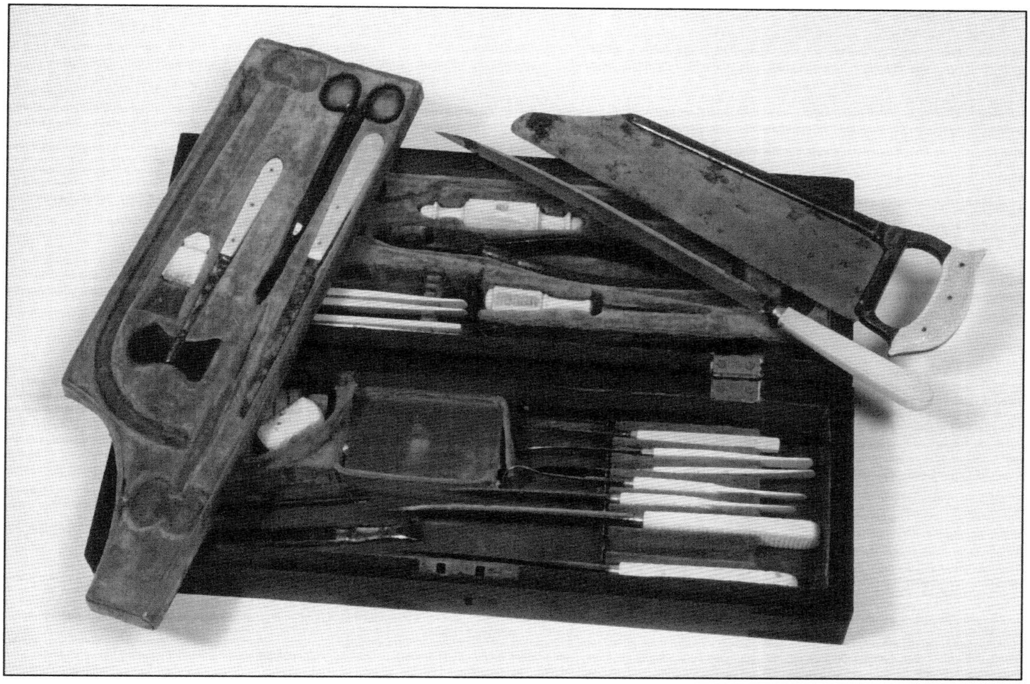

The Civil War forced the medical profession in Charleston, and elsewhere, to innovate and improve, particularly in trauma management. Officially, 257 South Carolinians served in the Confederate Medical Department, mostly general practitioners with no experience with war wounds. This c. 1850 amputation kit was used by Dr. Isaac Waight Angel, Medical College class of 1855.

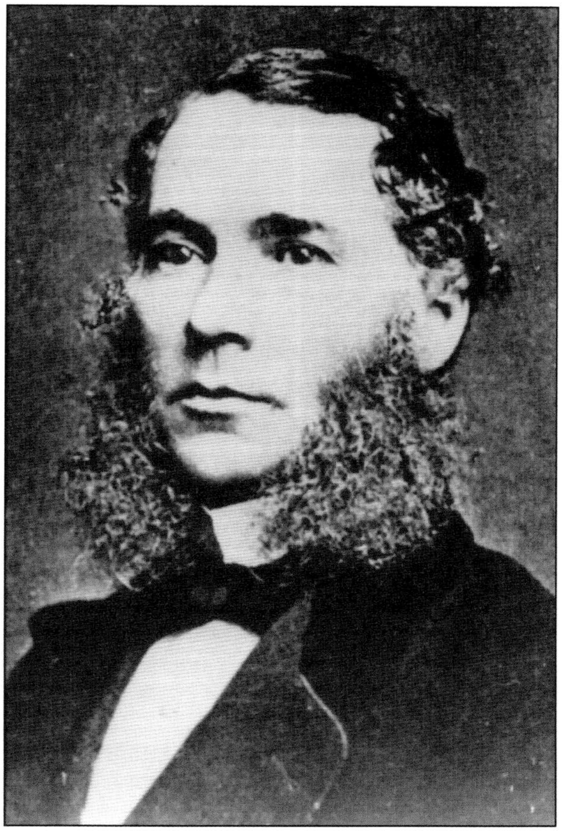

Hundreds of alumni, faculty, and students took their medical bags to war. Among them was class of 1834 alumnus Samuel Preston Moore (right), surgeon general of the Confederacy. Born in 1813 in Charleston, Moore moved to Little Rock, Arkansas, where he practiced briefly before being appointed assistant surgeon in the US Army. He became surgeon general of the Confederate army on July 30, 1861. Moore commissioned fellow Medical College alumni to write two bibles of Confederate military medicine: John Julian Chisolm's *Manual of Military Surgery* and F. Peyre Porcher's *Resources of the Southern Fields and Forests.*

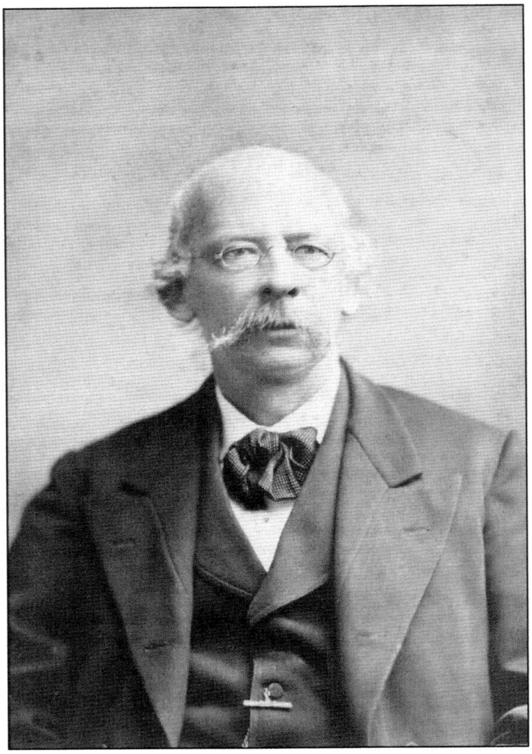

Dr. Francis Peyre Porcher, class of 1847, hailed from a long line of botanists, including his maternal ancestor, Thomas Walter, author of *Flora Caroliniana*, which was the first catalog of the flora of the state, published in 1788. Porcher served as professor of materia medica at the Medical College before and after the war. He served as president of both the South Carolina Medical Association (1871) and Medical Society of South Carolina (1874) and as vice president of the American Medical Association (1880). Porcher was also a founding member of the American College of Physicians, then called the Association of American Physicians.

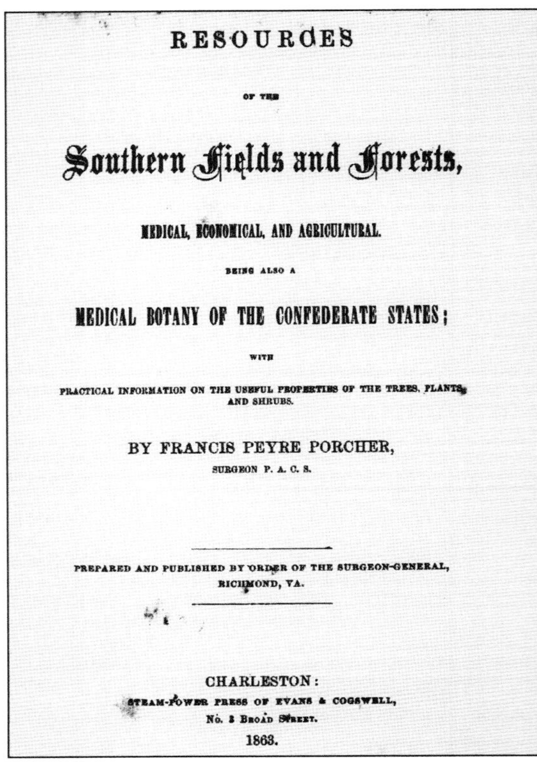

RESOURCES

OF THE

Southern Fields and Forests,

MEDICAL, ECONOMICAL, AND AGRICULTURAL.

BEING ALSO A

MEDICAL BOTANY OF THE CONFEDERATE STATES;

WITH

PRACTICAL INFORMATION ON THE USEFUL PROPERTIES OF THE TREES, PLANTS, AND SHRUBS.

BY FRANCIS PEYRE PORCHER,

SURGEON P. A. C. S.

PREPARED AND PUBLISHED BY ORDER OF THE SURGEON-GENERAL, RICHMOND, VA.

CHARLESTON:

STEAM-POWER PRESS OF EVANS & COGSWELL,

No. 3 BROAD STREET.

1863.

Infections and disease were made worse by lack of drugs due to the Union blockade of Southern ports and a scarcity of Southern pharmaceutical laboratories. In response to Dr. Samuel Preston Moore's request, Dr. Porcher wrote *Resources of the Southern Fields and Forests*, which identified native plants with therapeutic qualities that could be used in place of imported manufactured drugs.

John Julian Chisolm was born in Charleston in 1830 and graduated from the Medical College in the class of 1850. After postgraduate study abroad, Chisolm returned to Charleston and served as professor of surgery. As such, he was among those attending to the wounded after the attack on Fort Sumter in April 1861. After the war, Chisolm returned to Charleston and served as dean of the Medical College from 1866 to 1867.

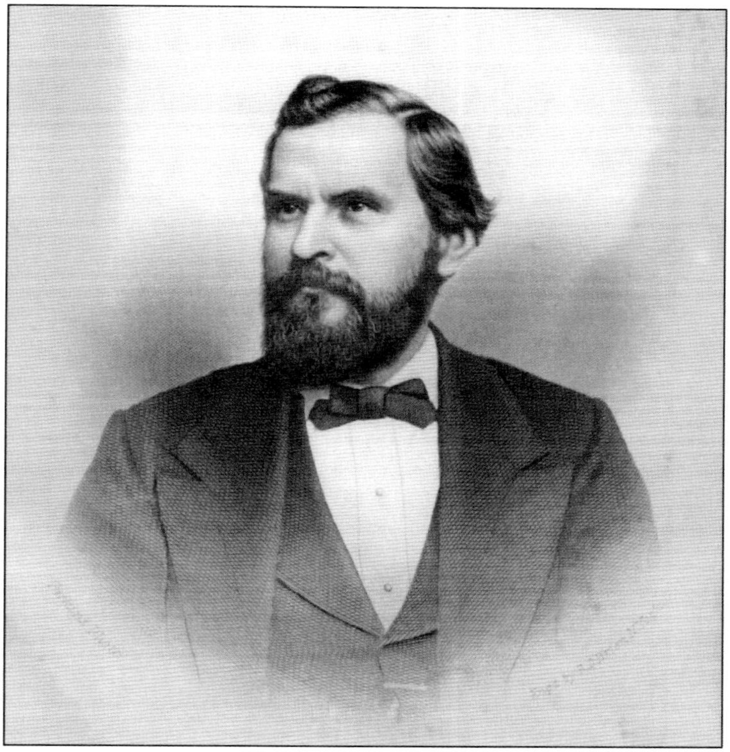

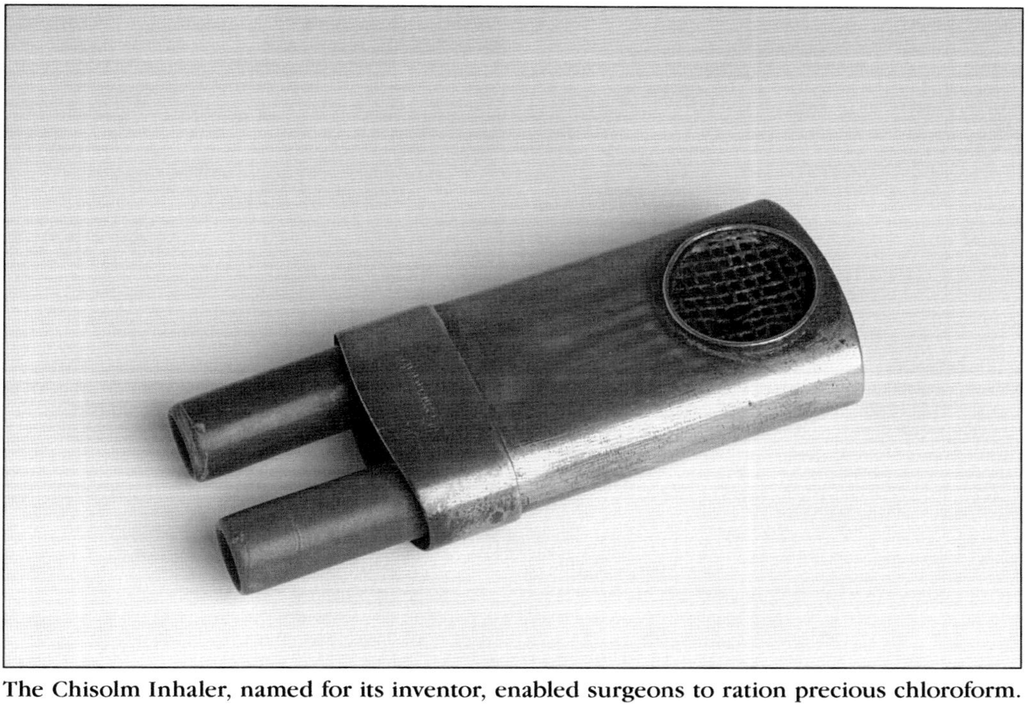

The Chisolm Inhaler, named for its inventor, enabled surgeons to ration precious chloroform. This advancement established John Julian Chisolm as one of the most innovative physicians of the Confederacy. This inhaler is among the collections of the Waring Historical Library.

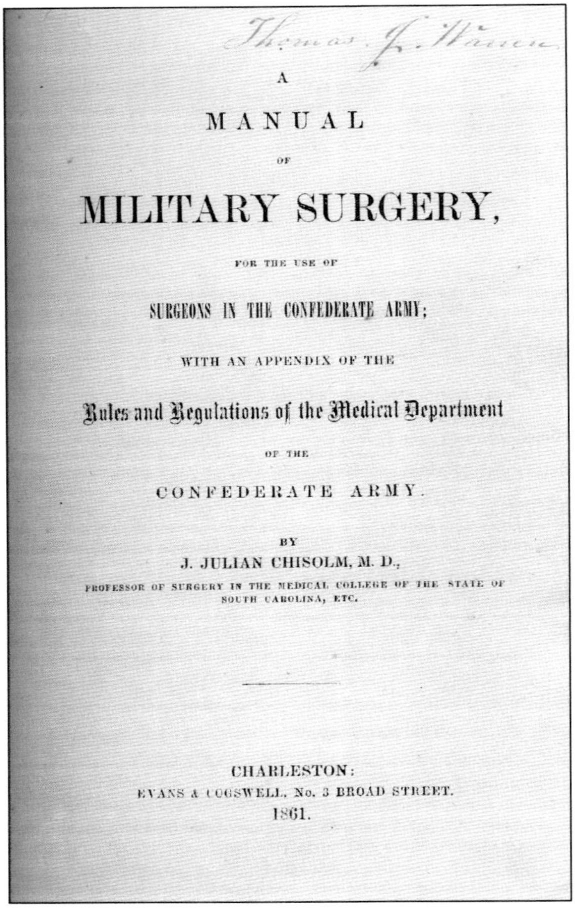

A

MANUAL

OF

MILITARY SURGERY,

FOR THE USE OF

SURGEONS IN THE CONFEDERATE ARMY;

WITH AN APPENDIX OF THE

Rules and Regulations of the Medical Department

OF THE

CONFEDERATE ARMY.

BY

J. JULIAN CHISOLM, M. D.,

PROFESSOR OF SURGERY IN THE MEDICAL COLLEGE OF THE STATE OF SOUTH CAROLINA, ETC.

CHARLESTON:

EVANS & COGSWELL, No. 3 BROAD STREET.

1861.

In 1863, Dr. Chisolm published his groundbreaking *A Manual of Military Surgery*, which illustrated in words and images how to treat specific types of wounds, construct field hospitals, and manage food, clothing, hygiene, and nonsurgical diseases. This detailed information was desperately needed by physicians whose training and experience was largely confined to general practice. Below is a detail from the manual illustrating the construction of a field stretcher and ambulance.

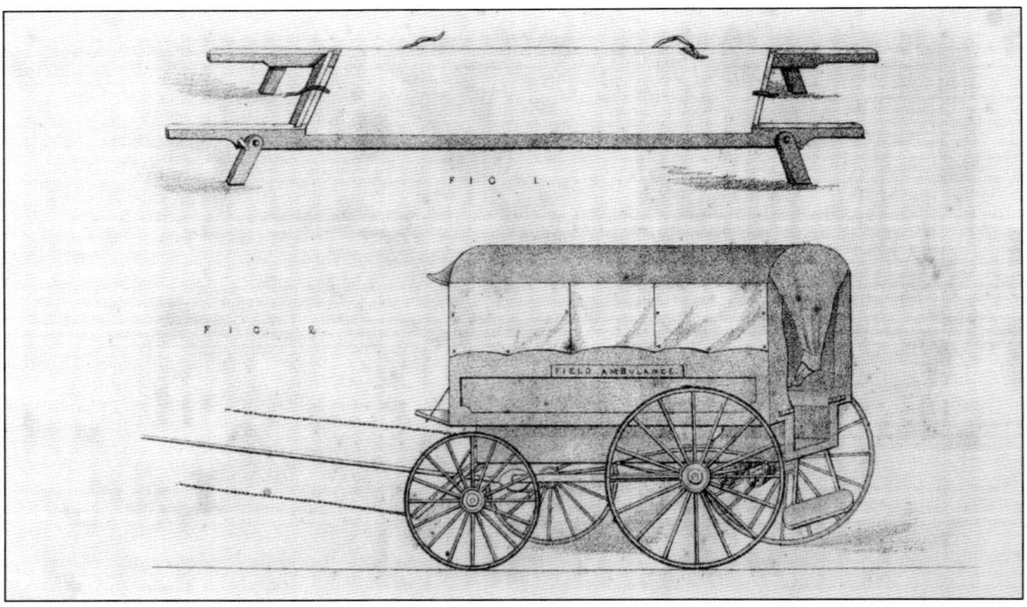

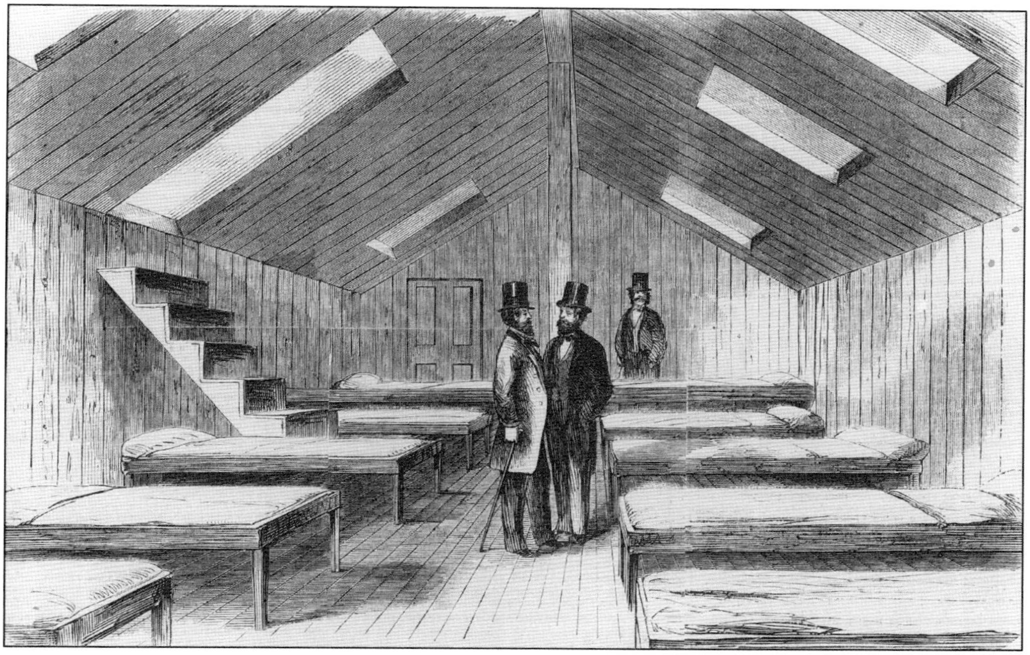

Another Medical College alumnus prominent in the Civil War was Dr. Columbus DaVega, who was born in Charleston on December 23, 1830, to a local Jewish family. After graduating in 1852, he traveled to Europe, where he was recruited to serve as a field surgeon with the Russian Army in the Crimean War (1853–1856). When the Civil War erupted, DaVega was one of the few physicians in South Carolina who had actual battlefield experience. He designed and served as surgeon on a hospital attached to a floating battery built to attack Fort Sumter from the water. The hospital, a one-story wooden structure attached to the battery (as seen in the image below), was outfitted with 10 beds and medical supplies to treat soldiers wounded aboard the battery. These images appeared in an 1861 issue of *Frank Leslie's Illustrated Magazine.*

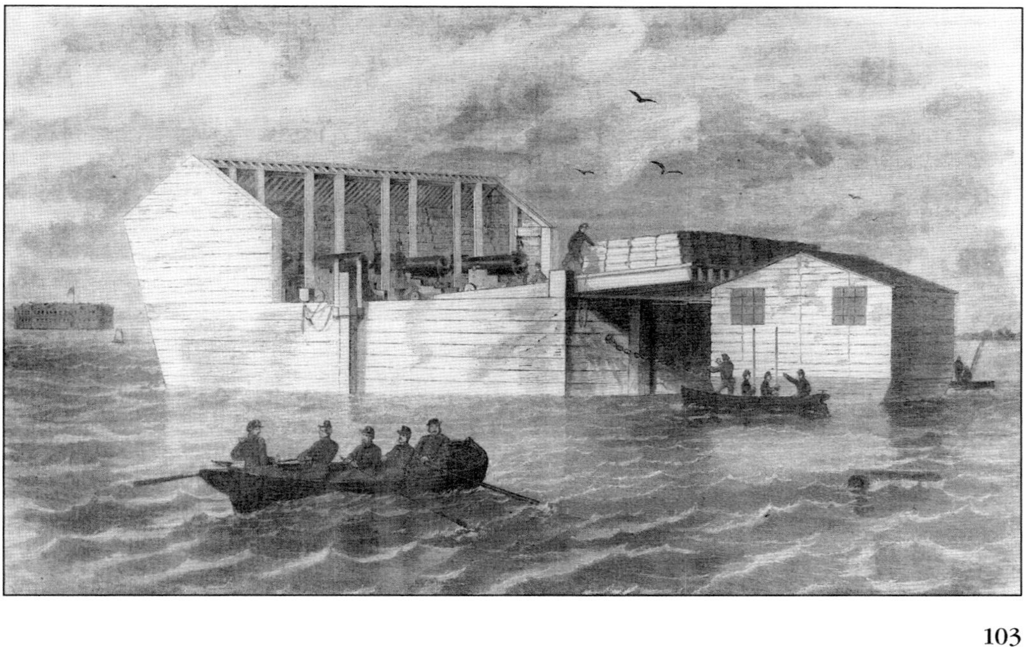

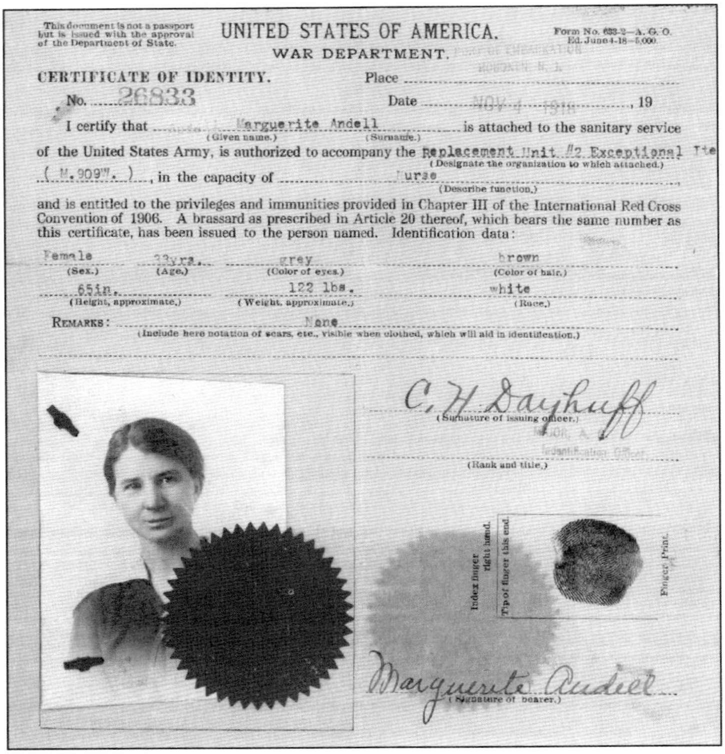

This document is not a passport but is issued with the approval of the Department of State.

UNITED STATES OF AMERICA.

WAR DEPARTMENT.

Form No. 633-2—A. G. O. Ed. June 4-18—5,000.

CERTIFICATE OF IDENTITY.

No. 26833

Place

Date NOV 4 1918, 19

I certify that Marguerite Andell (Given name.) (Surname.) is attached to the sanitary service of the United States Army, is authorized to accompany the Replacement Unit #2 Exceptional Ite (M.909W.) (Designate the organization to which attached.), in the capacity of Nurse (Describe function.)

and is entitled to the privileges and immunities provided in Chapter III of the International Red Cross Convention of 1906. A brassard as prescribed in Article 20 thereof, which bears the same number as this certificate, has been issued to the person named. Identification data:

Female (Sex.) 33yrs. (Age.) grey (Color of eyes.) brown (Color of hair.)

65in. (Height, approximate.) 122 lbs. (Weight, approximate.) white (Race.)

REMARKS: None (Include here notation of scars, etc., visible when clothed, which will aid in identification.)

C. H. Dayhuff (Signature of issuing officer.)

(Rank and title.)

Index finger right hand. Tip of finger this end. Finger Print.

Marguerite Andell (Signature of bearer.)

After the Civil War, America's next major military engagement was in World War I. Florence Nightingale's work in the Crimean War and Clara Barton's work in the American Civil War changed the role of women in military medicine. Marguerite Andell, a graduate of Roper Hospital School of Nursing in 1914, was commissioned in the sanitary service of the US Army as a nurse in November 1918.

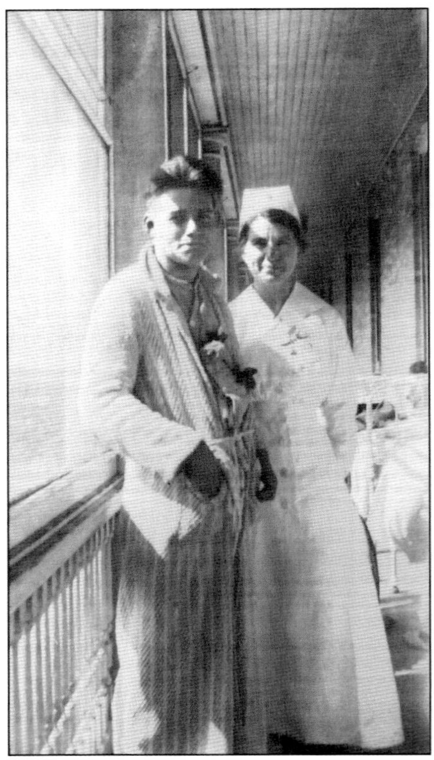

Marguerite Andell poses with a soldier in a hospital in France. She served as a nurse in the US Sanitary Service for one year before returning to Charleston and assuming the role of superintendent of nursing at Roper Hospital School for Nurses. She held that position for 24 years, longer than anyone else.

The College of Nursing's Ruth Chamberlin, seen here in her military uniform, served three years, from 1942 to 1945, in the Army Nurse Corps during World War II. Major Chamberlin was stationed in North Africa, Italy, and France.

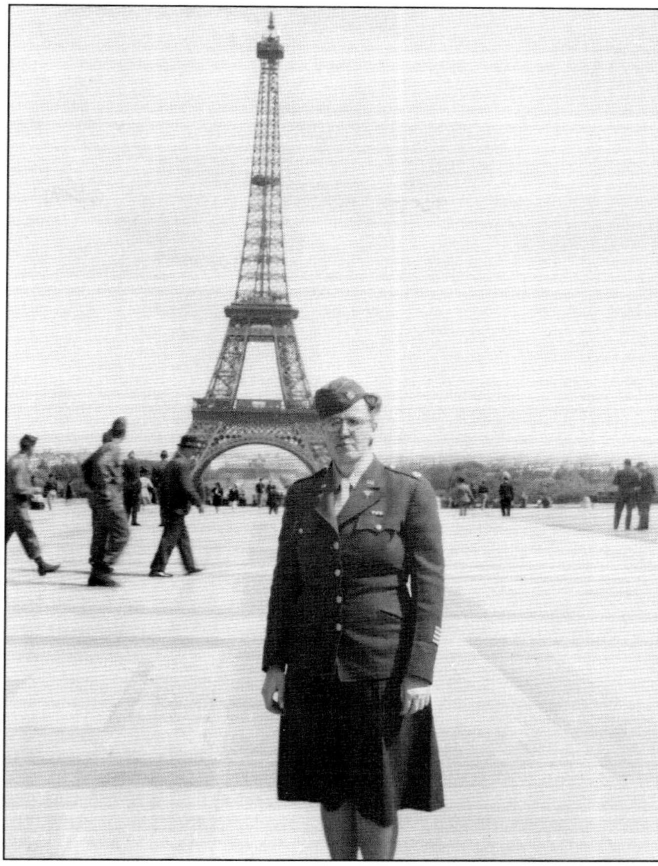

In 1942, Pres. Franklin Roosevelt created the War Manpower Commission (WMC) to identify and recruit labor needed for the war effort. The Physicians Procurement and Assignment Service of the WMC was responsible for classifying civilian physicians as available for service, essential for limited or unlimited duration of service, or unavailable for service. Below is a 1942 report from Greenville County.

September, 1942

POPULATION OF GREENVILLE COUNTY 136,580

PHYSICIANS IN GREENVILLE COUNTY

IN ACTIVE PRACTICE

	NAME	AGE		STATUS	CITY
1.	J. L. Anderson	59	Gen. Prac.	Active	Greenville
2.	C. C. Ariail	52	Gen. Prac.	"	"
3.	H. P. Bailey	44	Gen. Prac.	"	"
4.	I. S. Barksdale	45		City Health Dept. Full Time.	"
5.	C. O. Bates	56	Surgery	Active	"
6.	W. L. Bates	51	Gen. Prac.	"	"
7.	B. C. Bishop	44	Gen. Prac.	"	"
8.	R. A. Blakey	42	Gen.&Surgery	"	"

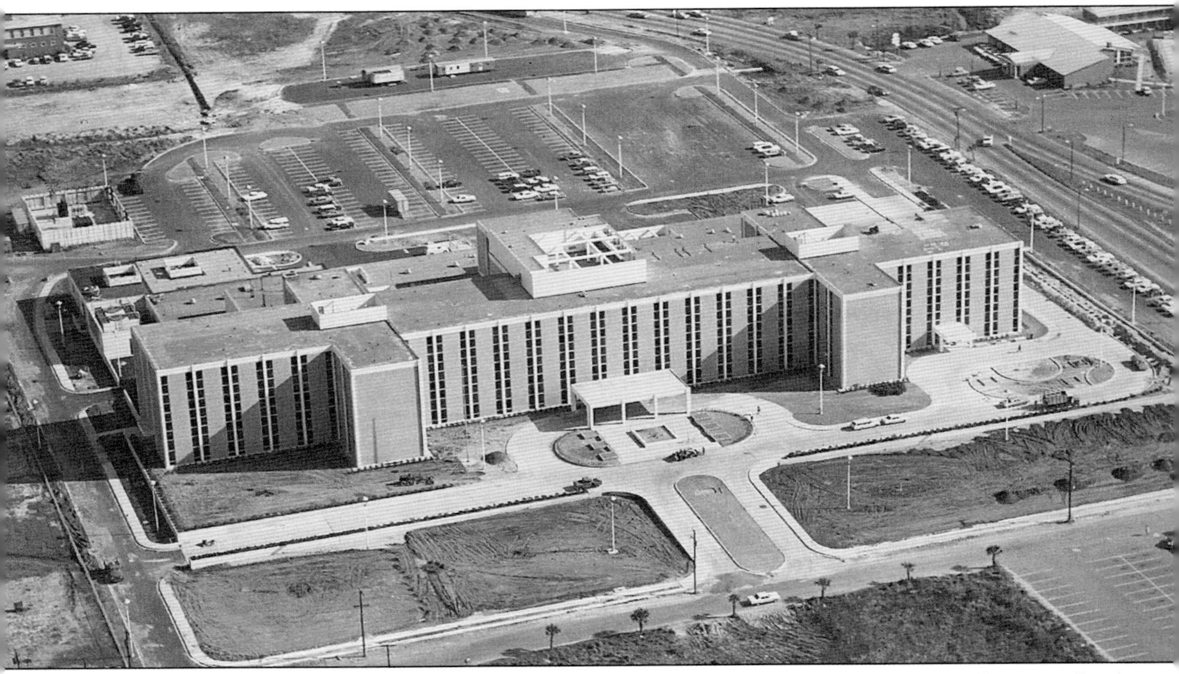

In 1966, the Veterans Administration hospital was opened on the west edge of the Medical College campus. The 117-bed facility continues to serve US veterans from 15 counties along the South Carolina and Georgia coasts. On September 5, 1991, it was named for Pfc. Ralph H. Johnson, US Marine Corps, who was born in Charleston and died in 1968 protecting the lives of his comrades during a skirmish in Vietnam. He was posthumously awarded the Medal of Honor for his heroism.

Ten

Community Health

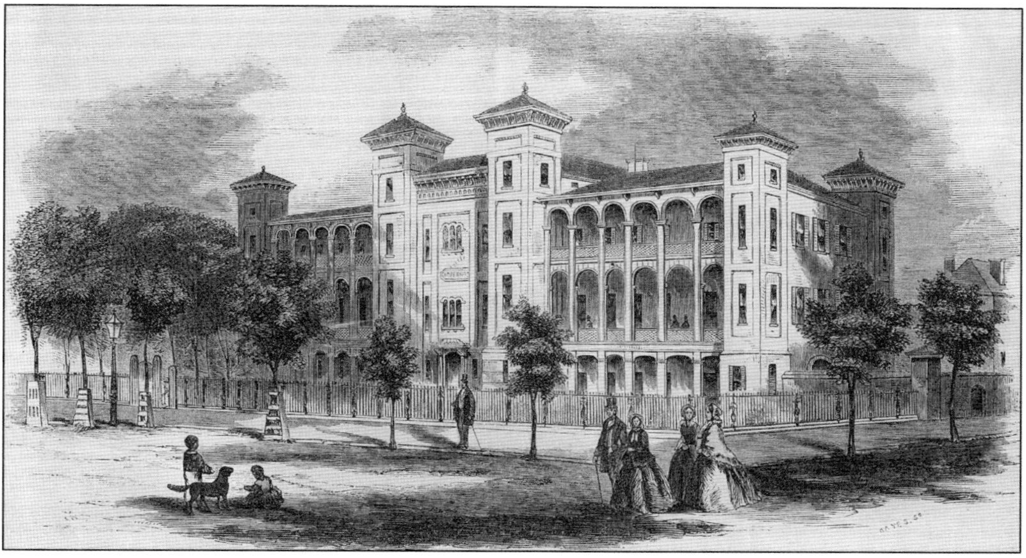

Charleston has had hospitals of various kinds for more than 300 years. During the 1700s, a combination of private and temporary hospitals, often run by churches, met the needs of the city during times of disease and war. As the population of Charleston grew, so did the need for hospitals. Above is the first of three hospitals named Roper Hospital, seen at its original Queen Street location. It opened for regular use in 1856, at which time the cost for patients was 25¢ per day.

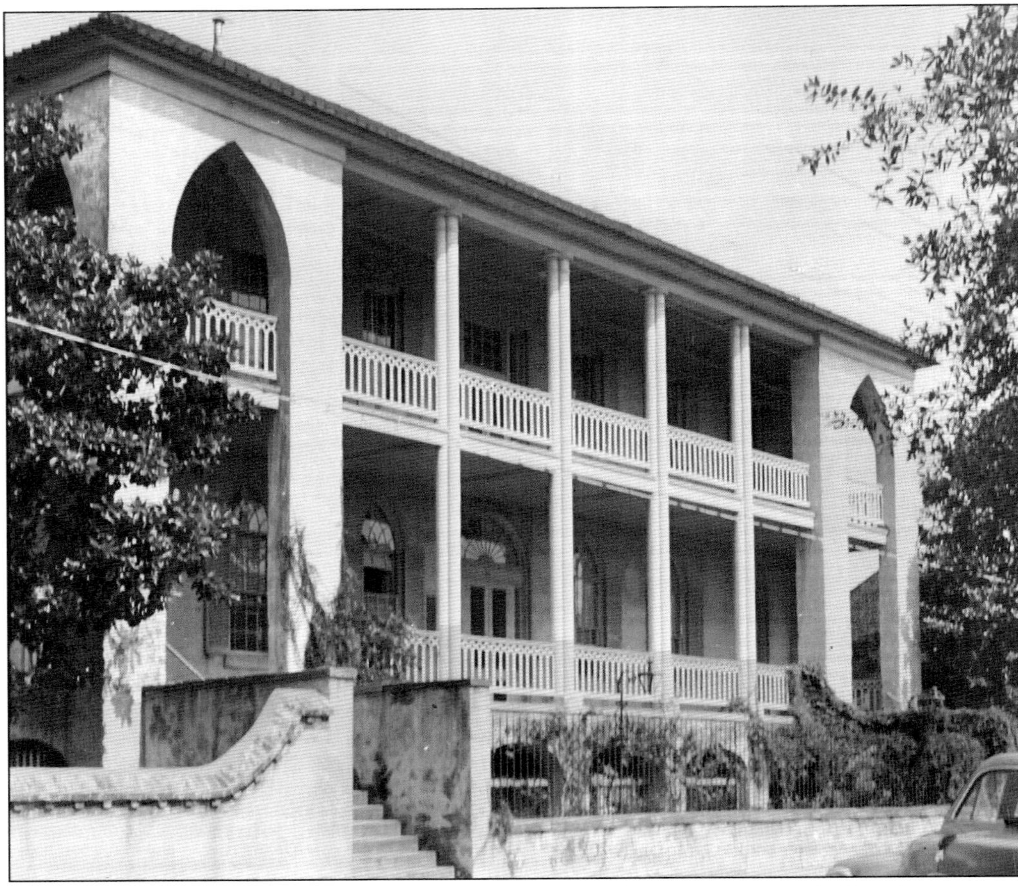

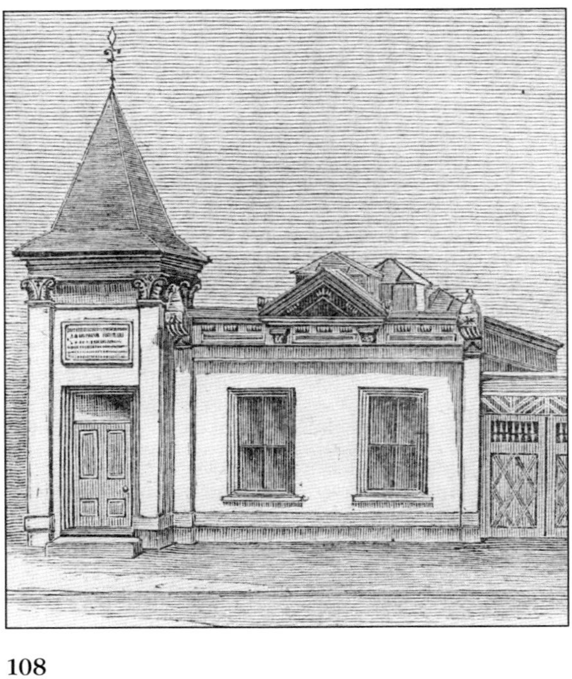

The Marine Hospital (above) was designed by Robert Mills and built on Back (now Franklin) Street in 1834. It was exclusively for American and foreign seamen who became ill while in port. During the Civil War, it was a military hospital and was successively a school for black children, the Jenkins Orphanage until 1938, and offices for the city's public housing authority. Now the upper two floors house Clemson Architecture Center classrooms and faculty offices.

Beginning in 1801, the Medical Society operated a dispensary for the poor. Without city support, the effort languished until 1810, when Alexander Shirras donated this building (left) on the northwest corner of Society and Meeting Streets to be used as a public dispensary, named for him in 1813.

In 1845, Thomas Roper's bequest of $30,000 for the first community hospital in Charleston was transferred to the Medical Society of South Carolina and the City of Charleston jointly. It was Roper's wish that the hospital be "for the permanent reception or occasional relief of all such sick, maimed and diseased paupers as need surgical or medical aid . . . without regard to complexion, religion or nation." The Medical Society of South Carolina, trustees of the Roper Fund, built the Roper Hospital for care of the city's indigent population.

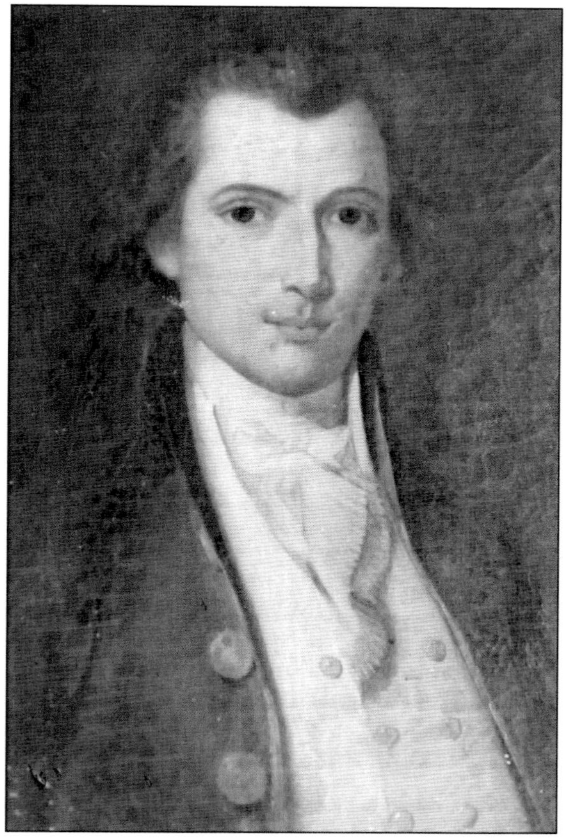

During the late 19th century, the city leased the property and operated City Hospital in the Roper facility. The 1886 earthquake damaged the building, effectively condemned until repairs could be made. By 1891, it was repaired and leased by the Charleston Medical School (different from the Medical College) and later by The Citadel. The building was never used as a hospital again and was converted to apartments. After Hurricane Hugo struck, the remnants of the structure on Queen Street were demolished in 1989.

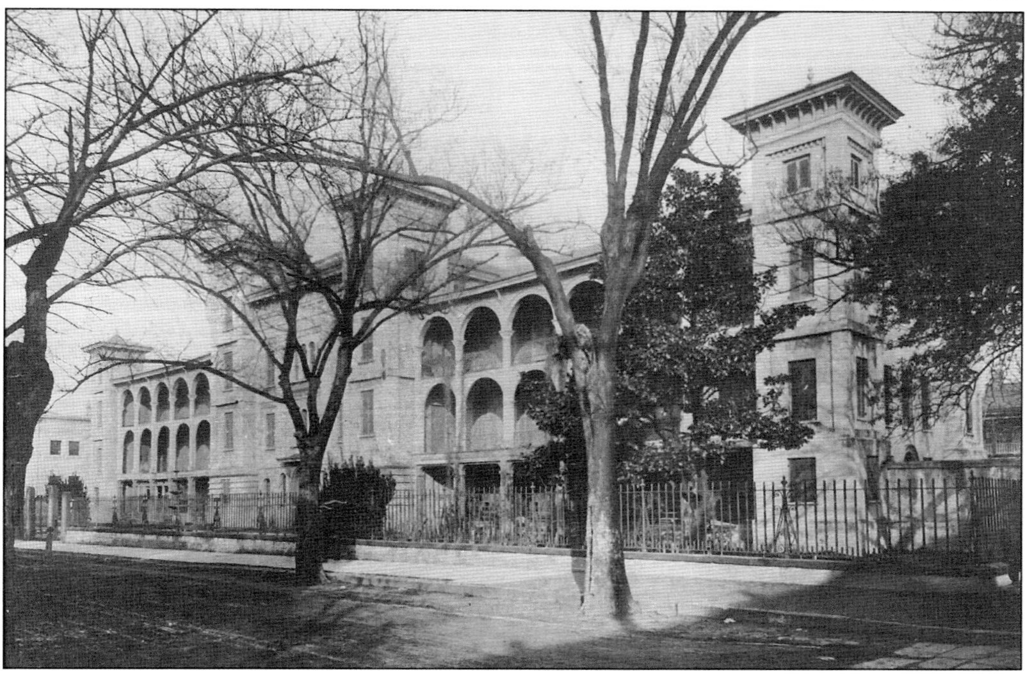

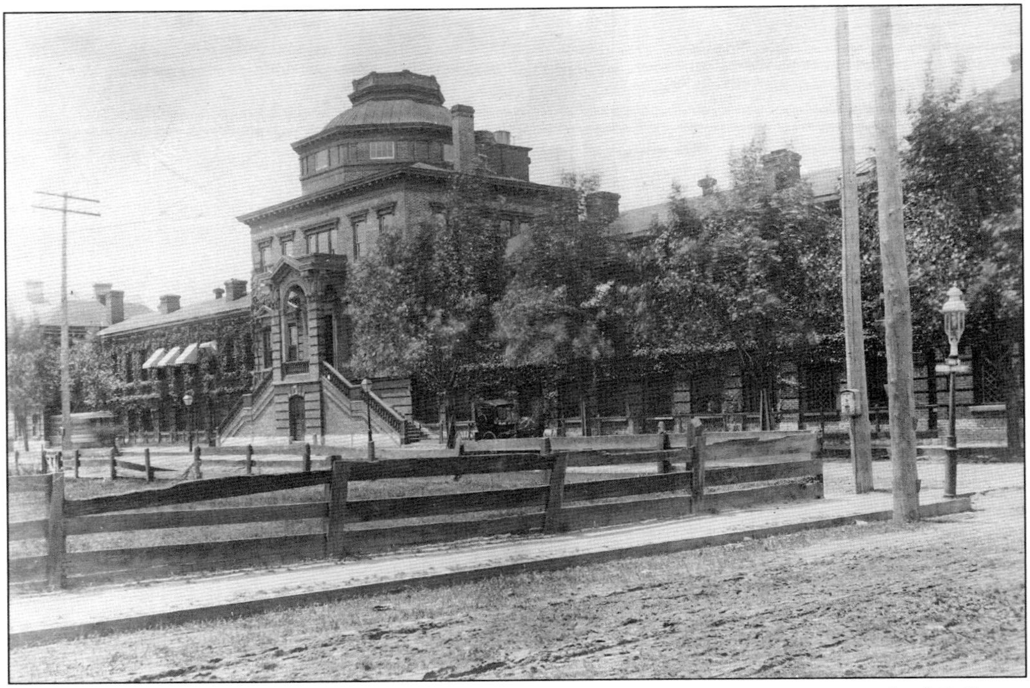

The Memorial (City) Hospital was built on the former Jonathan Lucas property north of Calhoun Street in 1887 to 1888 to replace the earthquake-damaged Roper Hospital. After several years of squabbling between the Roper Trustees and the City of Charleston council, this building was acquired by the trustees, partially demolished in 1904, and rebuilt as a new Roper Hospital.

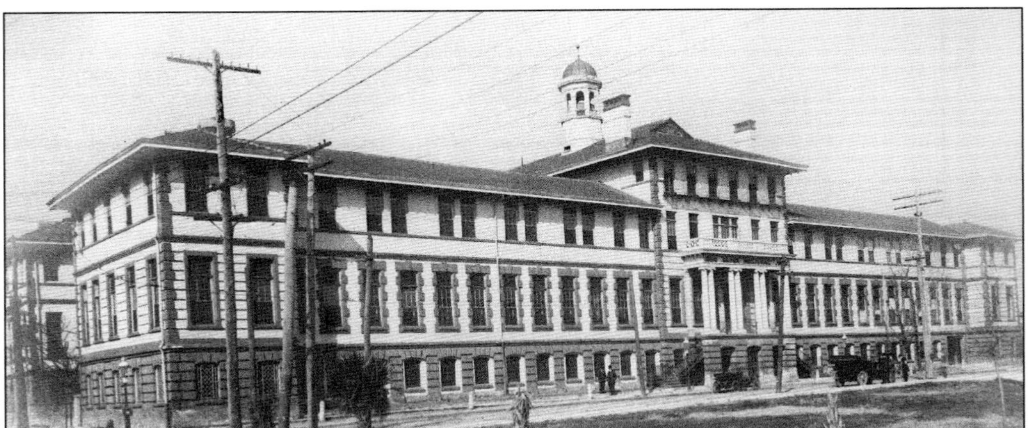

In 1906, the second Roper Hospital was built on the corner of Calhoun and Lucas Streets on the location of the Memorial (City) Hospital, which was directly across the street from the site of the 1914 Medical College Building. This "new Roper" became "old Roper" when the Medical Society built and opened the Roper Hospital Palmetto Pavilion in 1946. "Old Roper" was closed to incoming patients in 1959, demolished in 1967, and replaced by a parking lot.

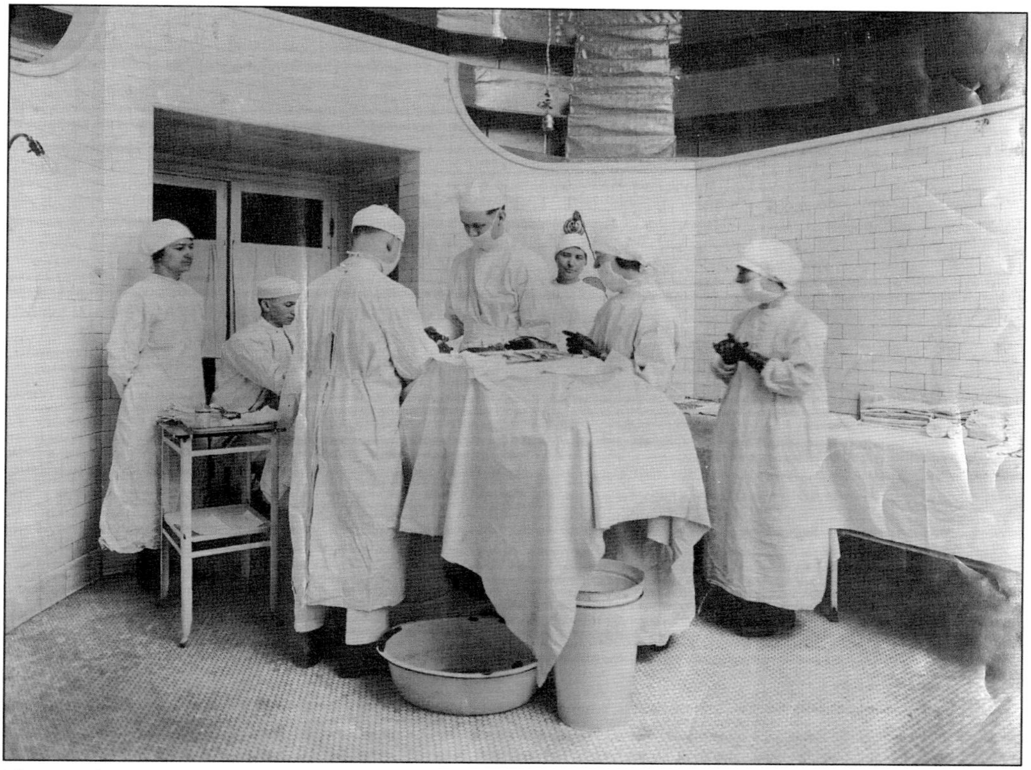

This is the operating room at "Old Roper" Hospital, dating from approximately 1924. In the photograph are, from left to right, Reba Carter, Dr. Dennis Hill (anesthesia), Dr. Murray, unidentified, Marguerite Andell, unidentified, and Lucille Bryan.

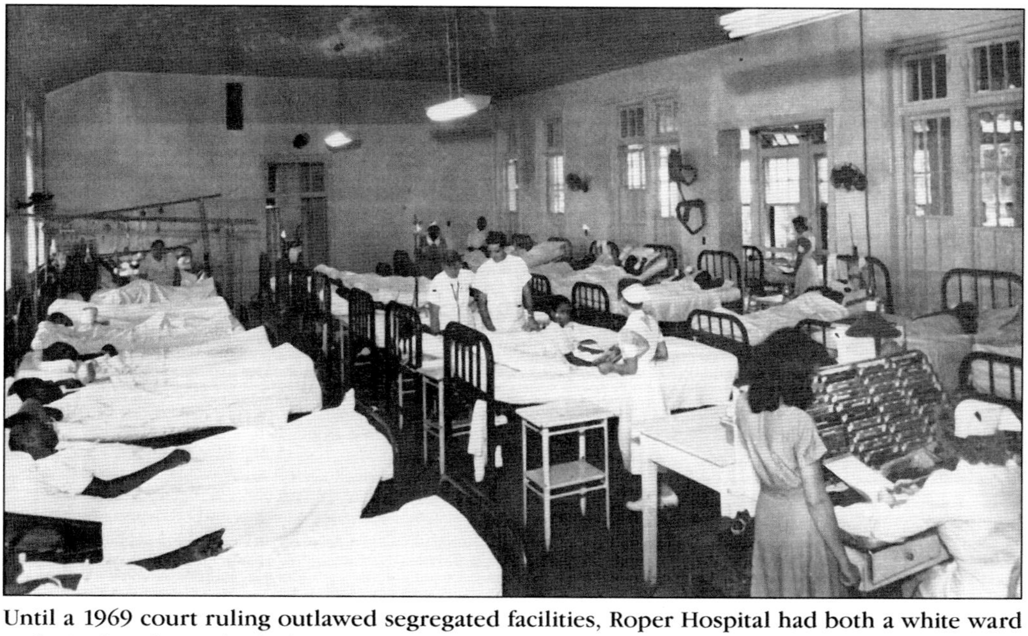

Until a 1969 court ruling outlawed segregated facilities, Roper Hospital had both a white ward and a "colored" ward. The latter is seen here on visitor's day in 1947.

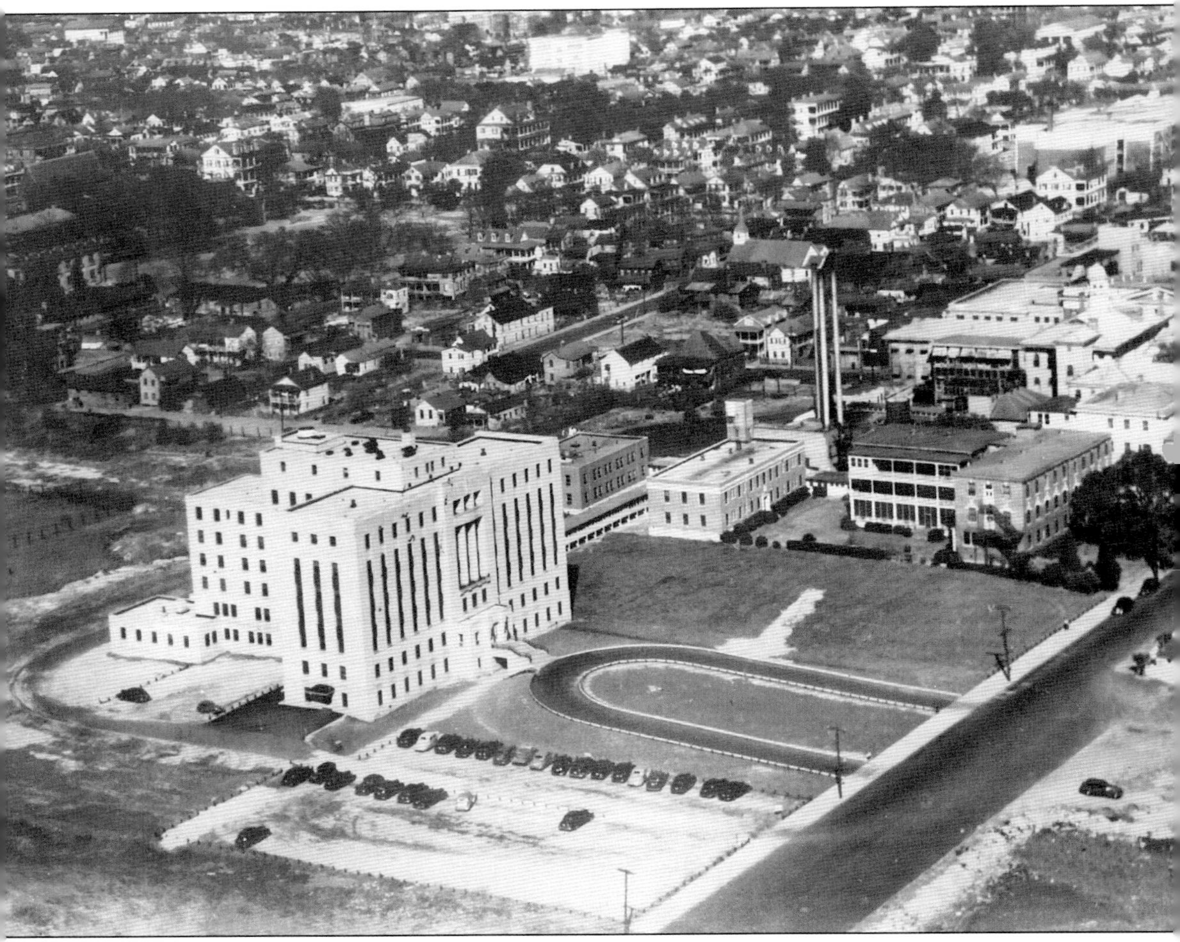

The third Roper Hospital to be built was this one, seen above shortly after construction concluded in 1946. Known originally as Palmetto Pavilion, this facility served the private patients of Roper, while the "Old Roper" on Lucas Street continued to serve the indigent population of Charleston until 1959, when that responsibility fell to the Medical College Hospital.

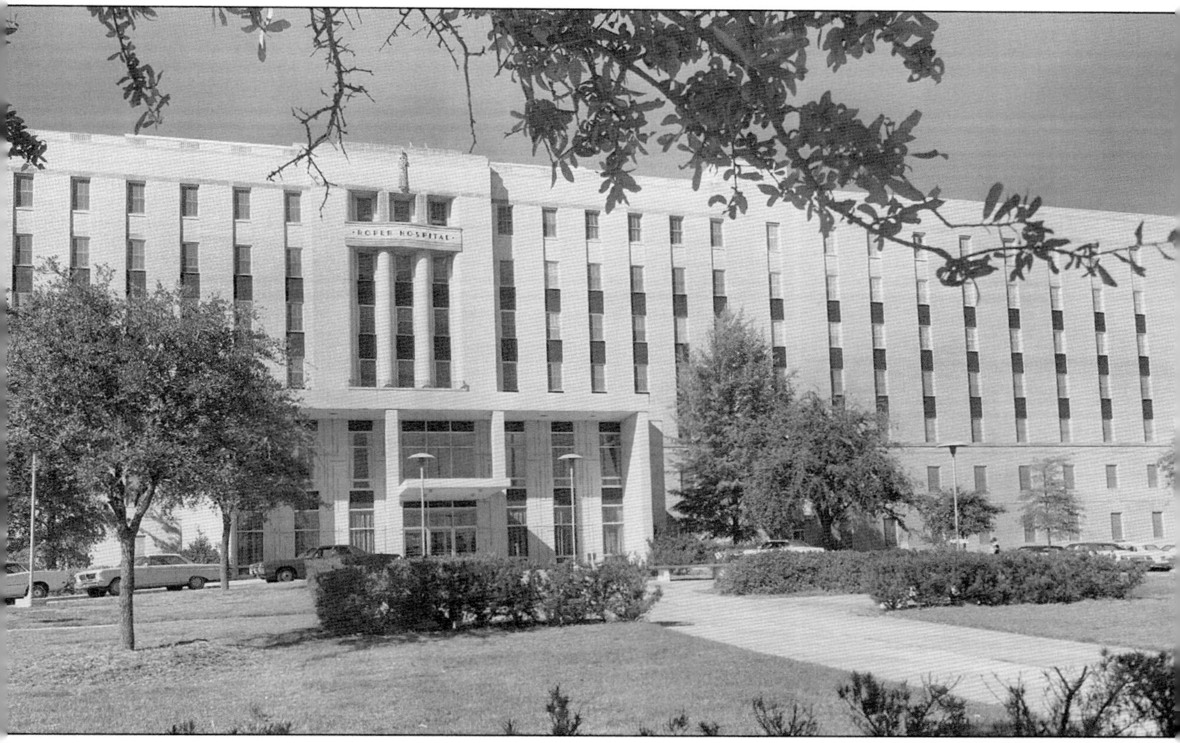

Located at the western end of Calhoun Street, Roper Hospital's Palmetto Pavilion has been renovated and expanded numerous times since its construction. The view above shows the first major round of renovations, which occurred between 1965 and 1975.

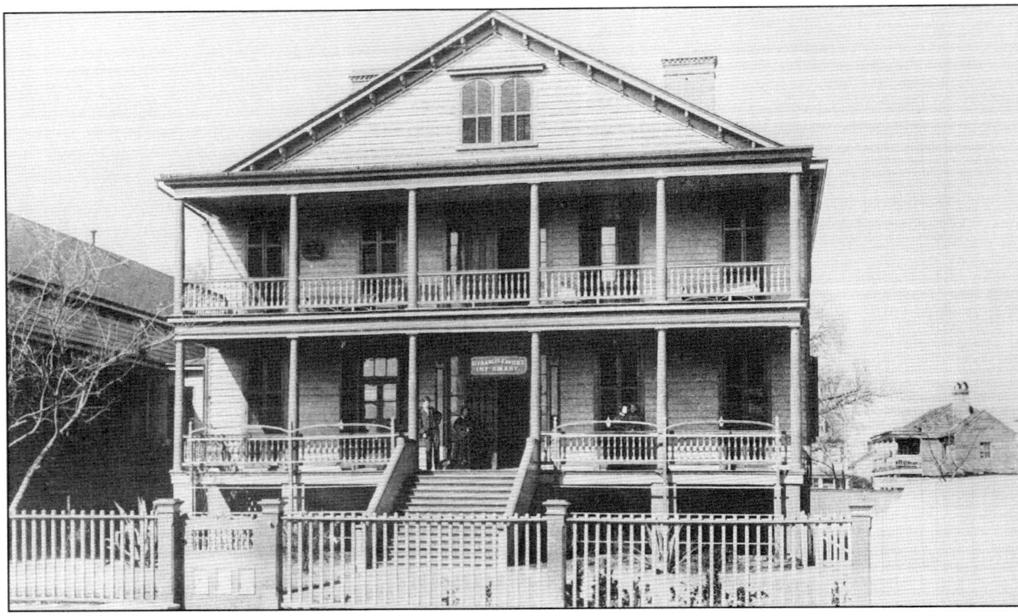

The origins of what became St. Francis Xavier Infirmary began with an outbreak of yellow fever in Charleston in 1838. In response, Catholic bishop John England rented a house on Queen Street and staffed it with five nuns who cared for their predominantly Irish-immigrant congregation. After a break of several years, the Sisters of Charity of Our Lady of Mercy tended to the wounded Confederate and Union soldiers during the Civil War. Officially opened in 1882, the infirmary had 15 beds, five staff nurses, and two surgeons. Soon, it would average 200 patients a year, necessitating the addition in 1896 of a two-story wooden building (below) containing two wards, 20 private rooms with baths, and an operating room.

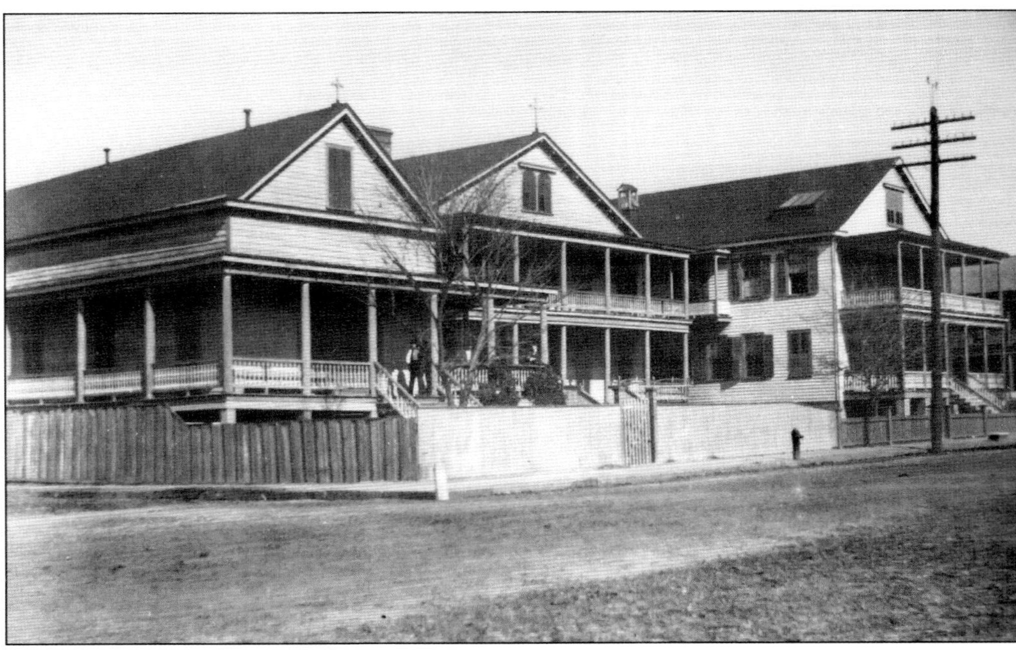

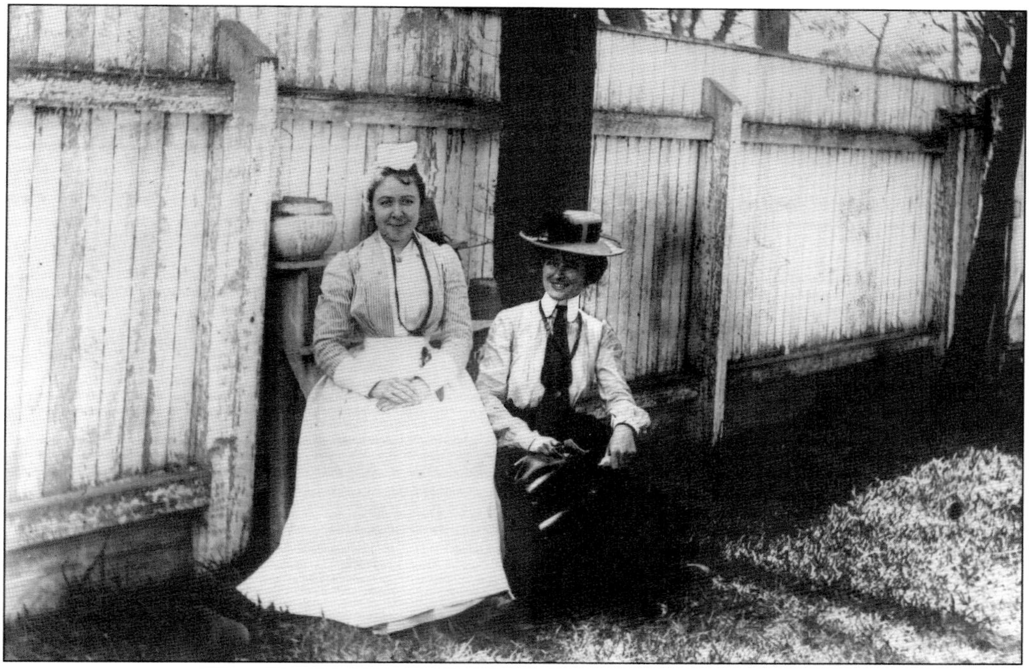

On October 22, 1900, the infirmary opened a nurses' training school. Above are Eva Walpole, class of 1903, and Katherine McGrath, class of 1902. On July 5, 1925, the sisters broke ground on a new three-and-a-half-story Spanish-style hospital (below) facing Calhoun Street. In 1951, the name was changed to St. Francis Xavier Hospital, which was added to throughout the 1970s and 1980s. In July 1989, the Sisters of Charity of Our Lady of Mercy transferred sponsorship of St. Francis Xavier Hospital to the Sisters of Bon Secours, and the hospital became part of the Bon Secours Health System.

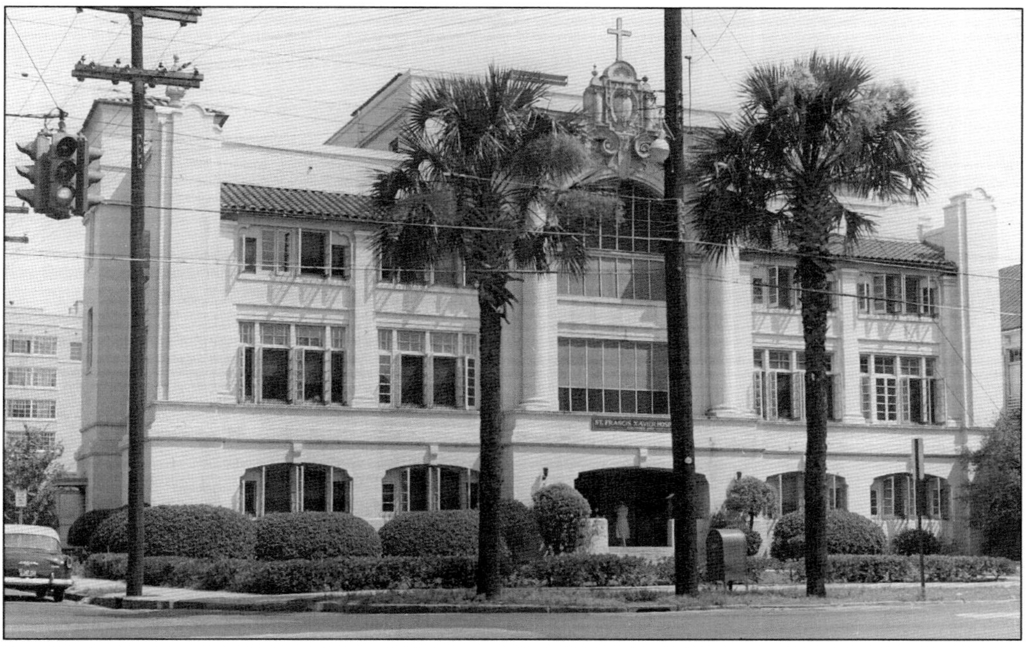

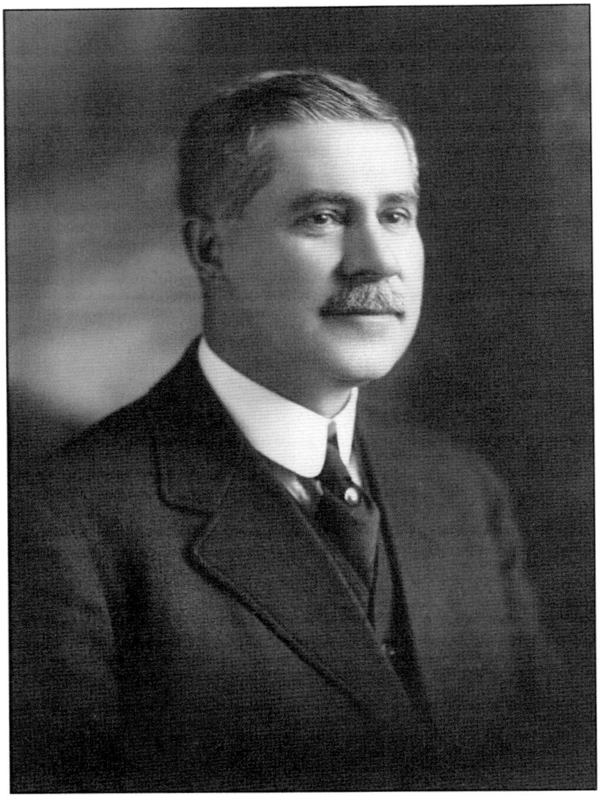

Founded in 1912 by Dr. Archibald E. Baker Sr. (left) of Charleston and Dr. Lawrence Craig of Dillon, South Carolina, Baker-Craig Sanatorium opened on Thanksgiving Day 1912. In 1917, Dr. Baker assumed full control of the hospital and amended the charter so the hospital could operate as a charitable institution. In 1963, the trustees purchased the hospital from the Baker family and renamed it Baker Memorial Hospital. Below is an interior shot of the ward; Dr. Baker is bending over the patient in the bed on the right.

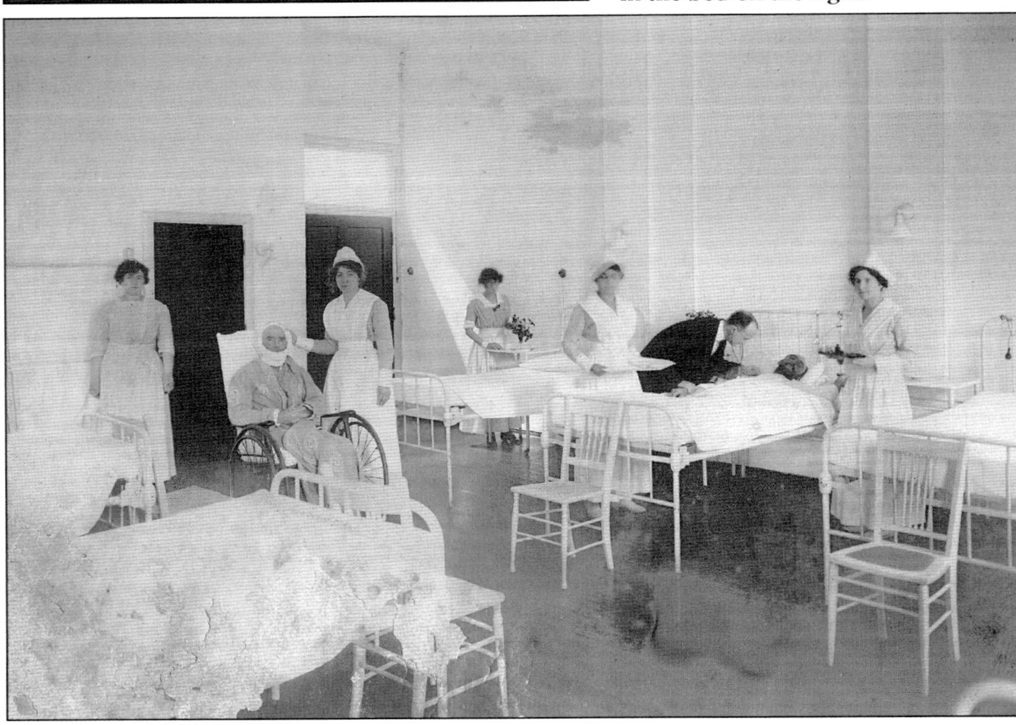

Designed by Charleston architect J.D. Newcomer, Baker-Craig Sanatorium (right) was built at a cost of between $100,000 and $150,000. In 1981, when the hospital moved to a new building in North Charleston, the old hospital was converted to a condo complex called Baker House. It is located at the corner of Beaufain Street and Ashley Avenue on Colonial Lake.

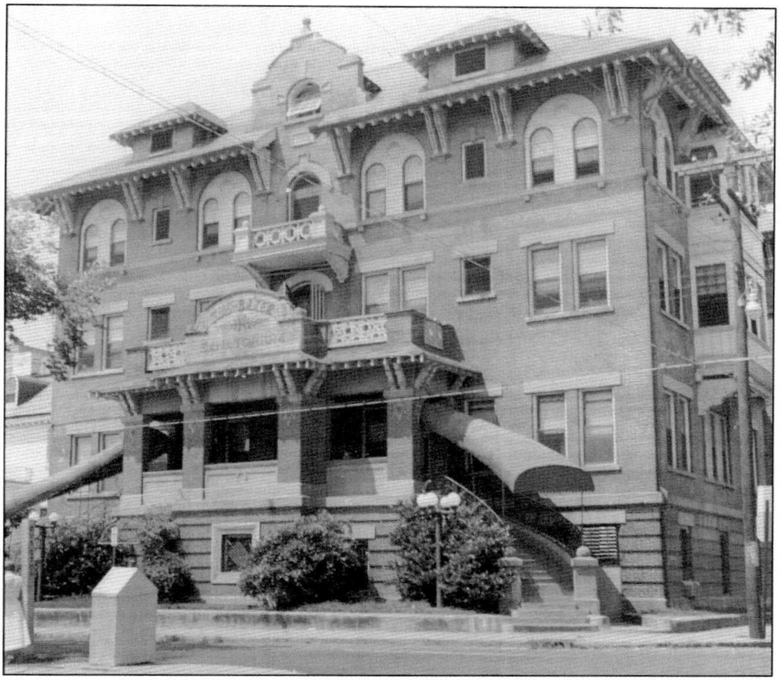

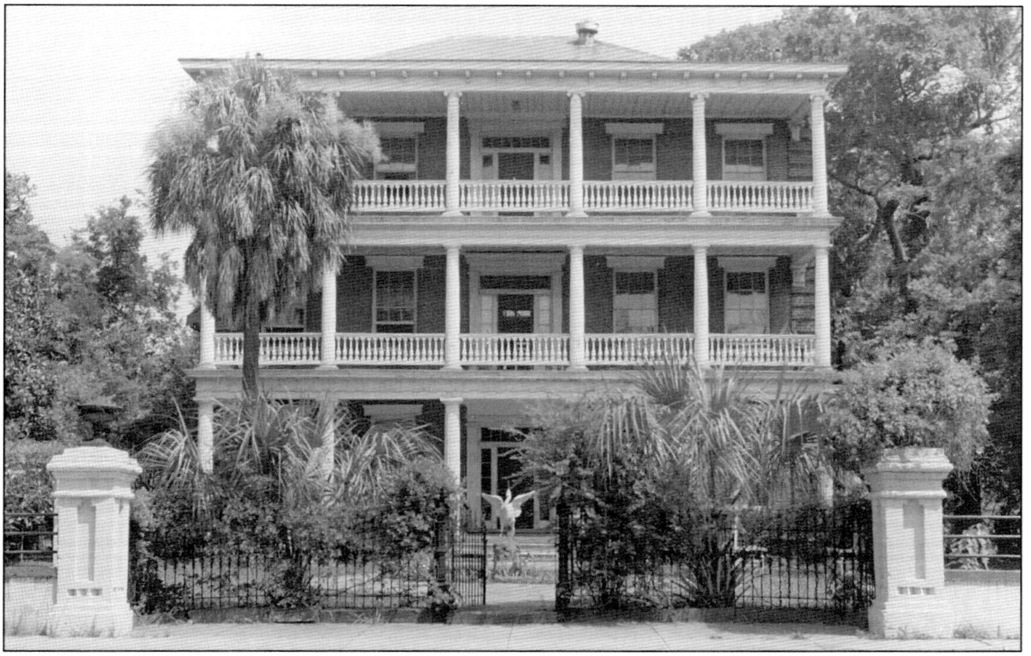

Mercy Maternity Hospital (above) was an obstetrical (or laying in) hospital located at the corner of Ashley Avenue and Bee Street. Originally the home of William Robb, the house, built in 1858, was sold to Mercy Maternity Hospital on April 30, 1920. It operated until 1926 when it was sold to the president of the hospital board, William King McDowell, who renovated the house and transferred it to the Episcopal Church Home and Orphanage in 1927. In 1929, the Episcopal Church Women's Home opened; it closed in 1982 when the property was sold to a developer for apartments.

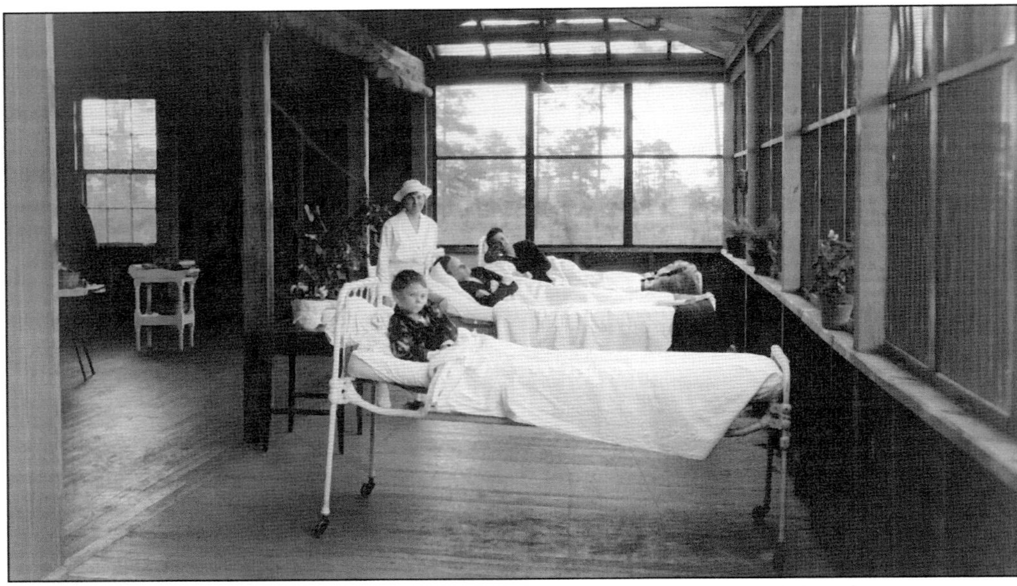

Although tuberculosis was a serious health issue for the city, Charleston did not have a treatment facility until Dr. Leon Banov (below), the City of Charleston's health officer, secured funding from Charleston County for the construction of a TB hospital. The Pinehaven Sanatorium (interior seen above) opened in 1924 just north of the city, adjacent to the US Naval Yard and under the governance of the Charleston County Tuberculosis Association. Regardless of their ability to pay for treatment, patients in all stages of the disease were treated at Pinehaven. The facility treated both African American and white patients, although it was segregated. The Medical College had a cooperative relationship with Pinehaven: faculty of the school offered their services as consultants, while students served as interns at the hospital.

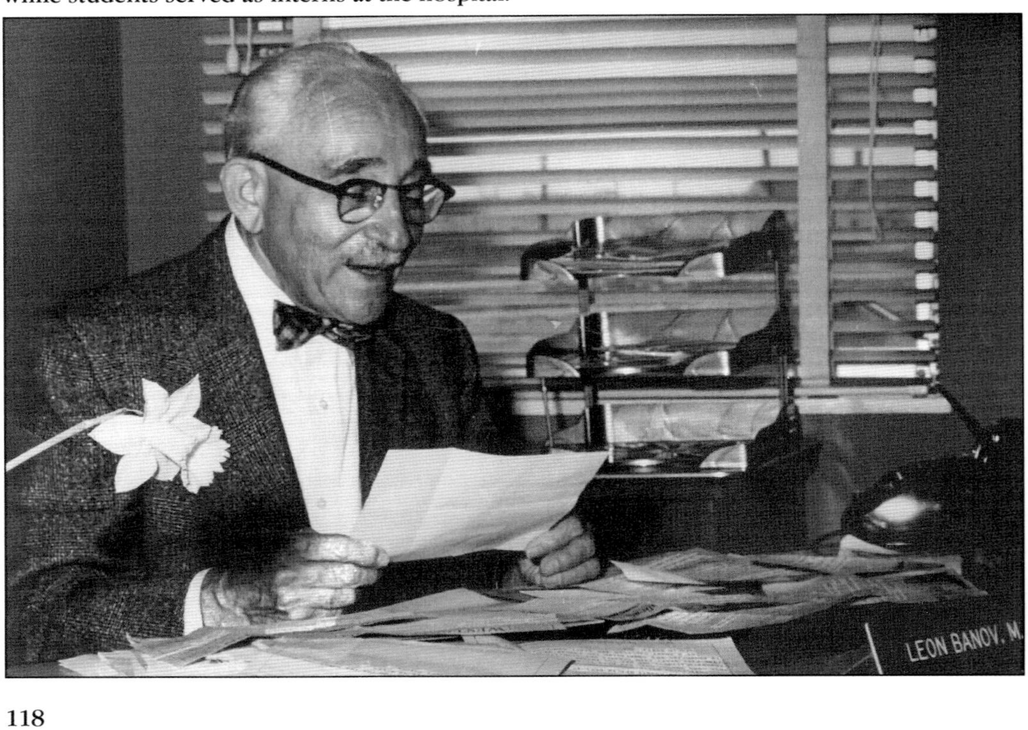

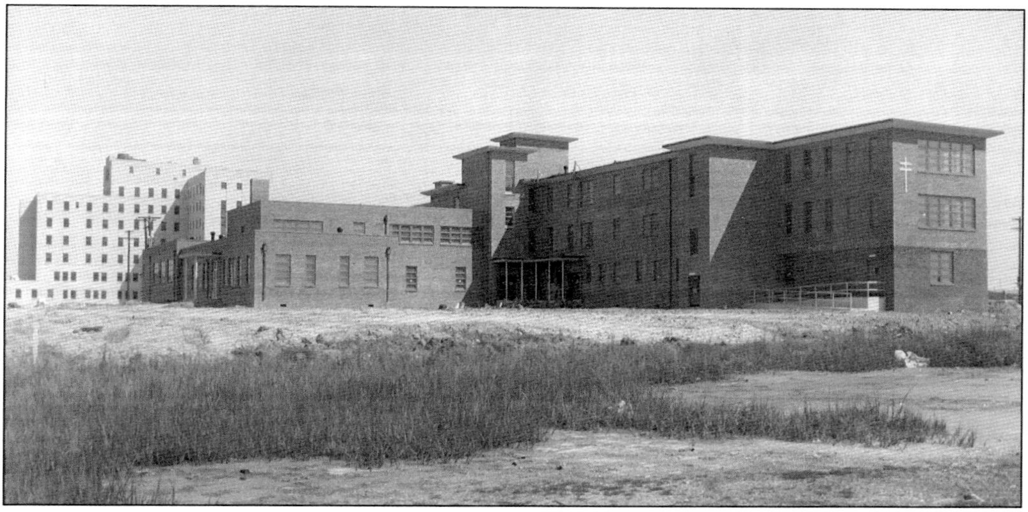

By the late 1940s, many in Charleston felt that the Pinehaven facility was deficient, and plans for a replacement facility were made. In 1953, the Charleston County Tuberculosis Hospital, referred to as "New Pinehaven," opened at 326 Calhoun Street (above), offering more beds and services for patients. In 1965, New Pinehaven became Charleston County Hospital with a wing dedicated to TB patients. The hospital's name was changed again in 1981 to Charleston Memorial Hospital, and it was managed for Charleston County by MUSC starting in 1985 and later purchased by the university.

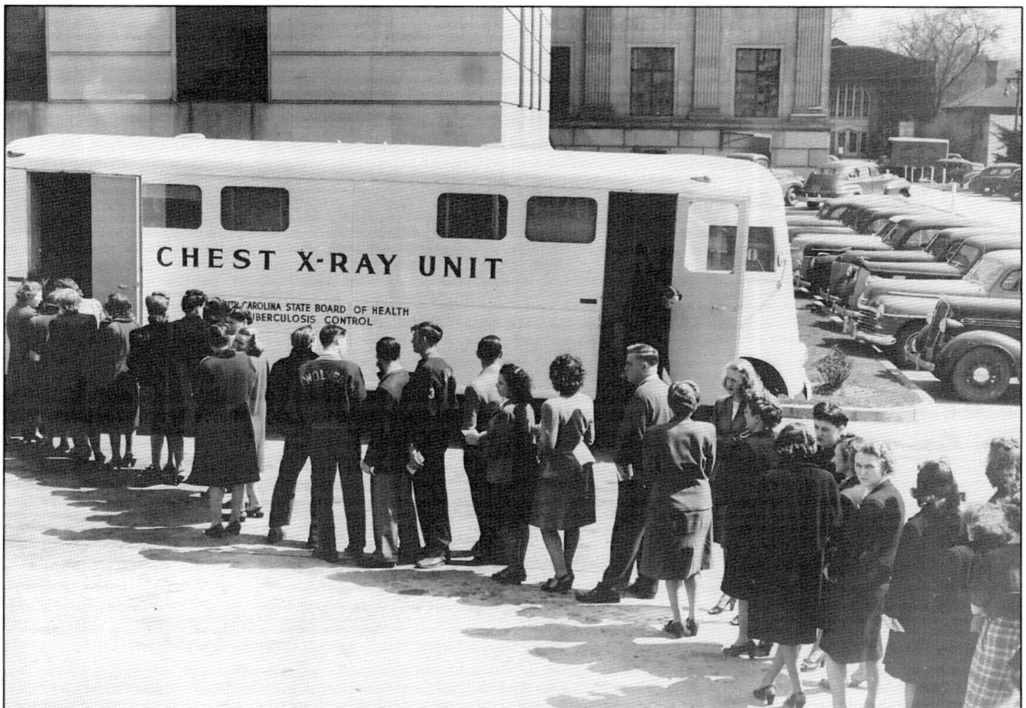

Among its other efforts to fight tuberculosis, the Charleston County Health Department organized a mobile chest X-ray unit (above) to screen as many residents as possible for the "white plague."

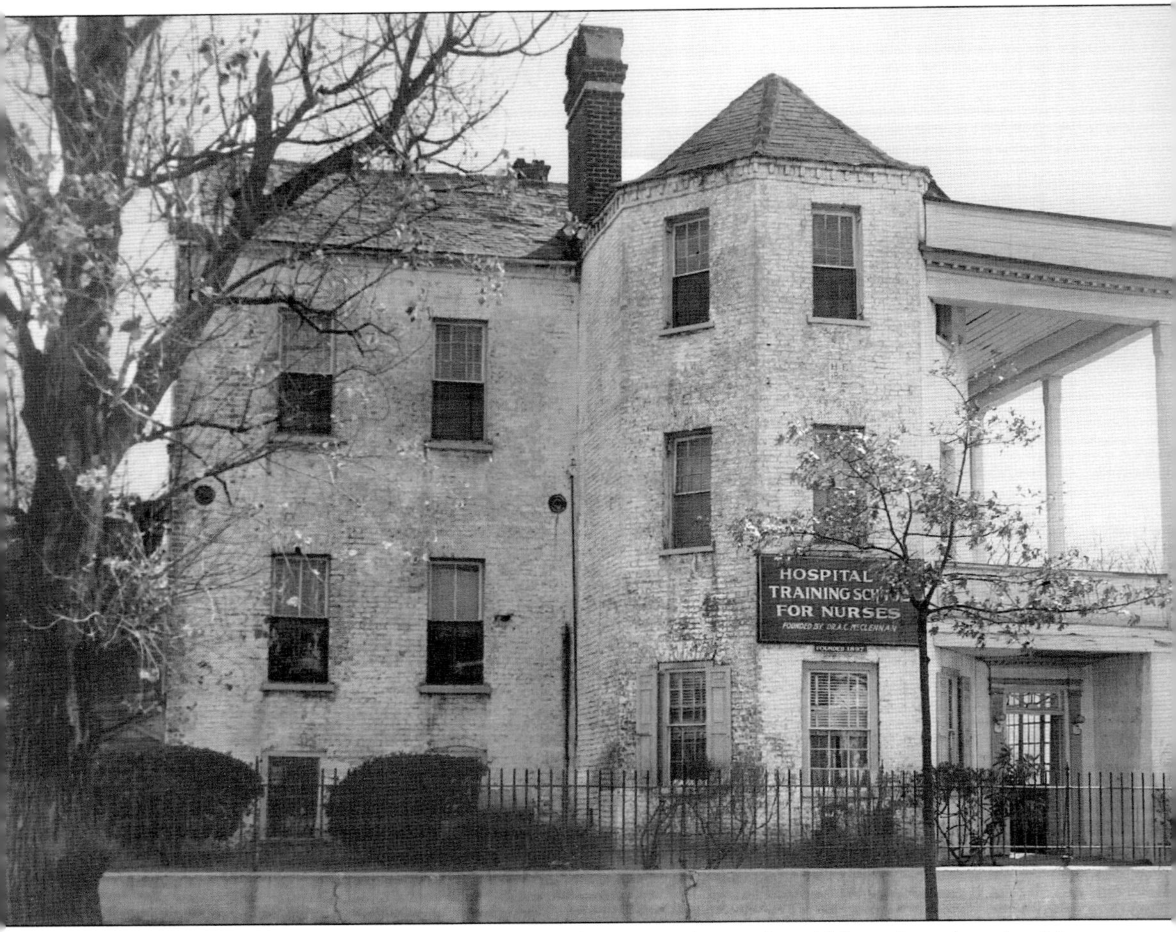

In November 1896, Dr. Alonzo Clifton McClennan and six other African American health-care professionals met to discuss the need for a hospital and nurses' training school for African Americans in the city of Charleston. In July 1897, the State of South Carolina approved the charter for the Hospital and Training School for Nurses. Later that year, it opened its doors at 135 Cannon Street in a three-story brick building, which had been bought for $4,500. The Cannon Street Hospital, as it was also known, provided desperately needed health care for Charleston's African American citizens with 24 beds, nurses' dormitories, an operating room, dining hall, reception room, and office. No patient or physician was denied admission because of race; some white doctors sent white patients to Cannon Street and treated them there.

Alonzo Clifton McClennan was born in Columbia, South Carolina, in 1855. After graduating from Howard University's Schools of Medicine and Pharmacy, McClennan moved to Charleston in 1884 and established the first black drugstore, called the People's Pharmacy, on King Street. He helped found the Hospital and Training School for Nurses and served as its medical director, surgeon-in-charge, and instructor in surgical nursing until his death in 1912.

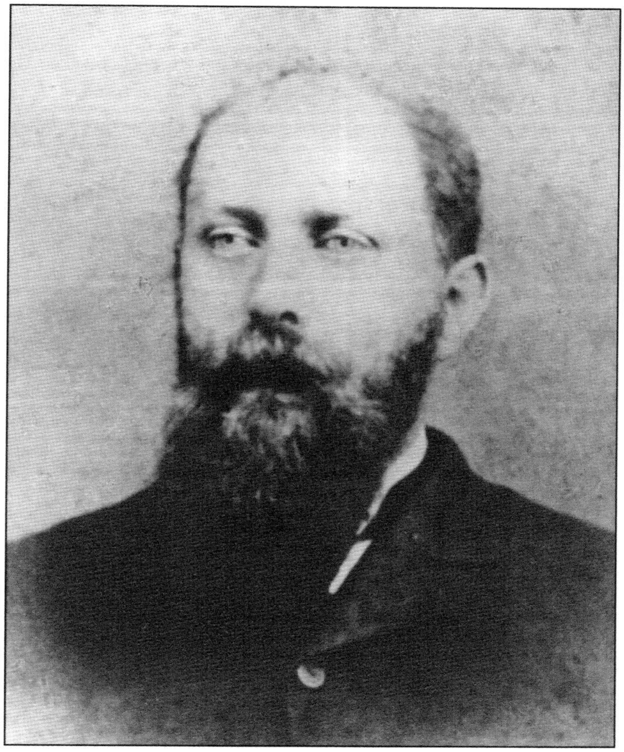

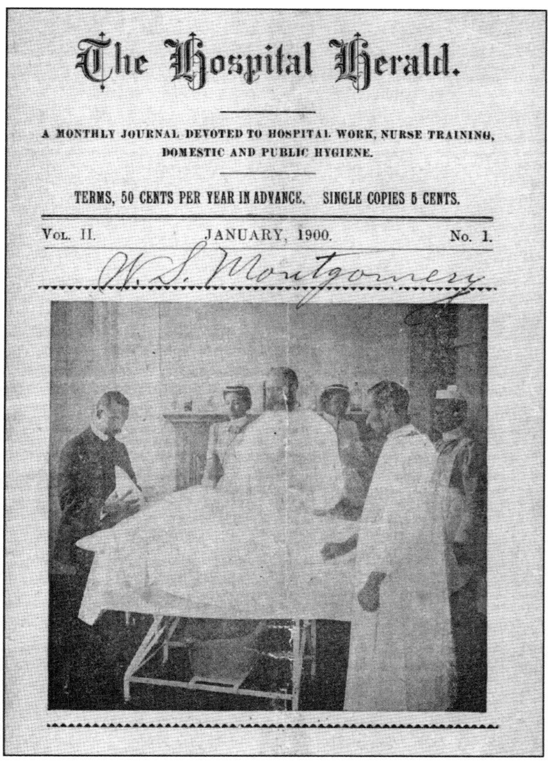

The Hospital Herald.

A MONTHLY JOURNAL DEVOTED TO HOSPITAL WORK, NURSE TRAINING, DOMESTIC AND PUBLIC HYGIENE.

TERMS, 50 CENTS PER YEAR IN ADVANCE. SINGLE COPIES 5 CENTS.

VOL. II. JANUARY, 1900. No. 1.

W. S. Montgomery

Dr. McClennan edited the *Hospital Herald—A Monthly Journal devoted to Hospital Work, Nurse Training and Domestic and Public Hygiene*. In addition to writing about health-related matters, Dr. McClennan used the *Hospital Herald* to promote fundraising events such as community fairs, teas, and, in later years, radio-thons, a telethon, and a "womanless" wedding featuring physicians. In one issue he wrote, "Every penny you give will do something toward the relief of suffering and toward training some deserving colored woman in an honorable and useful profession." Dr. McClennan is seen in the center on the cover image, standing over the patient.

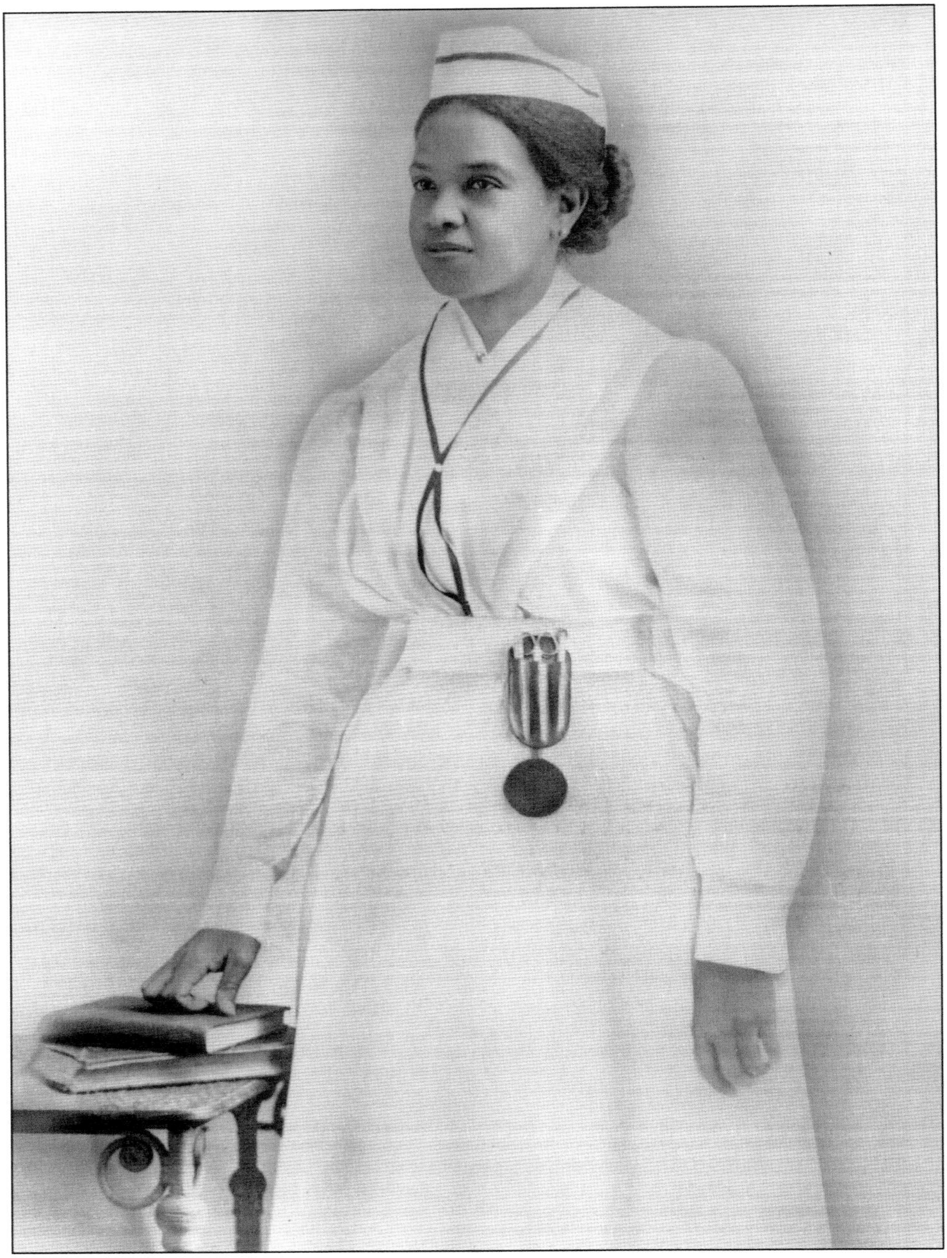

Anna DeCosta Banks was born on September 2, 1869, in Charleston. She was educated in the Charleston Public Schools and graduated from Virginia's Hampton Institute Dixie Hospital of Nursing. Banks was among its first graduates and, in 1895, served as head nurse at the Dixie Hospital. Returning to Charleston, she went to work at the Hospital and Training School for Nurses. After her tenure as head nurse, she subsequently rose to become superintendent of nurses, serving in that capacity for 32 years. Banks once said, "I have found that when a person is sick or in need, it does not make any difference to them who you are or what. If you have come to help them, all are gladly received." When she died in 1930, the Ladies Benevolent Society paid her this tribute: "All ages, classes, races, called her blessed."

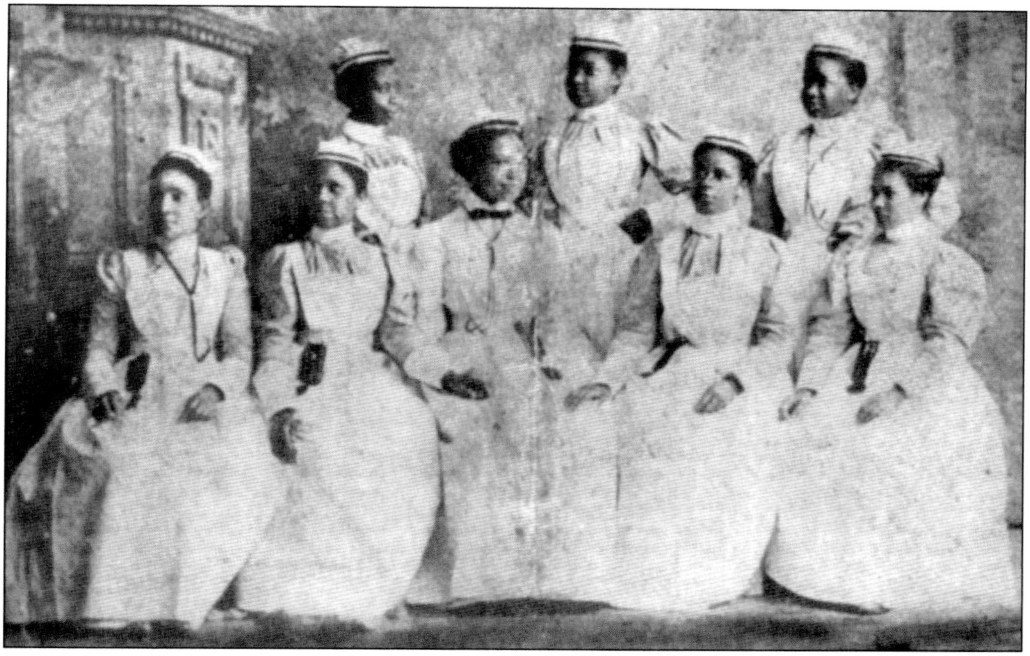

"The colored people have long felt the need of a hospital where their sick can be properly cared for. Many of them have simply died for want of attention. The work has only been going on for one year and within that time we have paid $1,000 on the building, the whole cost being $4,000. The building has two wards, two private rooms, dormitory for the nurses, dining room and kitchen and reading room. We can accommodate fifteen patients at a time," wrote Anna DeCosta Banks in *Southern Workman*, published by the Hampton Normal and Agricultural Institute, where Banks received her nursing education. The image above is of the first graduating class of the Hospital and Training School for Nurses. Below, Drs. Alonzo McClennan (seated left) and Lucy Hughes Brown (seated right) pose with another graduating class of nurses.

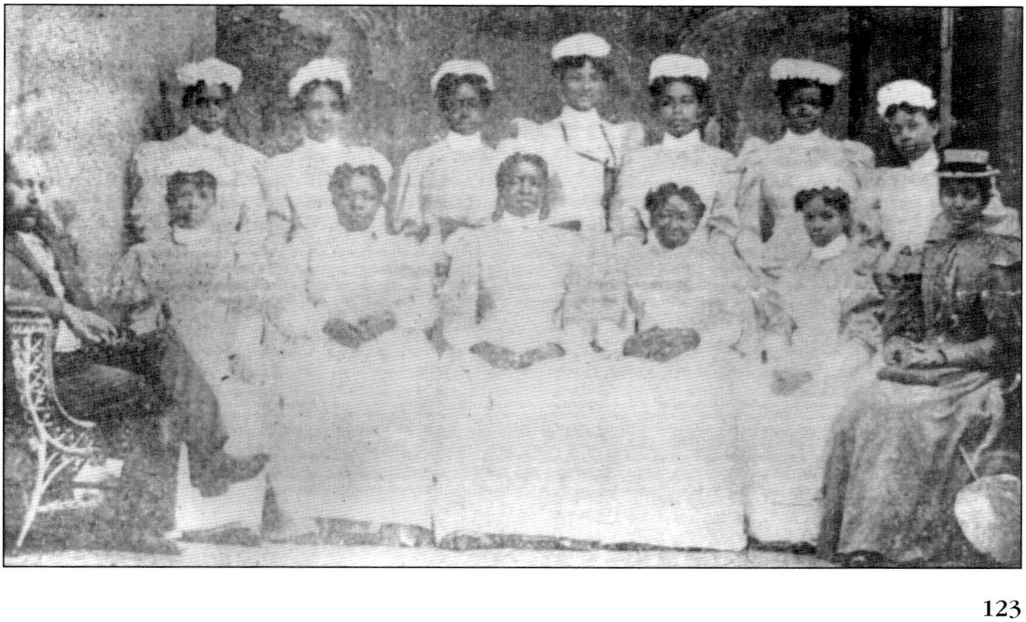

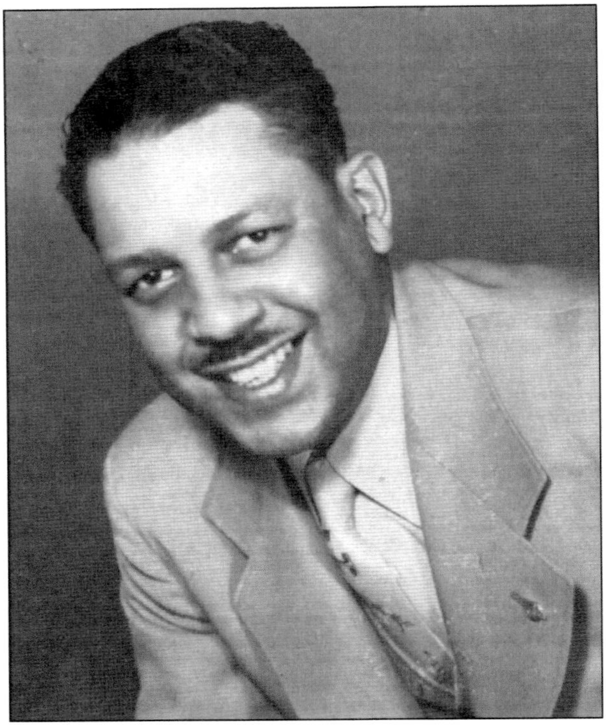

Dr. Thomas Carr McFall was born in Charleston in 1908 and attended the Avery Normal Institute. After receiving his doctor of medicine degree from the University of Michigan School of Medicine, McFall returned to Charleston in 1938 and established a private practice in obstetrics and gynecology. After serving in the US Medical Corps in World War II, McFall returned to his Charleston practice. In 1949, he was appointed to the South Carolina State Hospital Advisory Council to the State Board of Health, the first African American to serve in that capacity. McFall served as the last medical director of the McClennan-Banks Memorial Hospital.

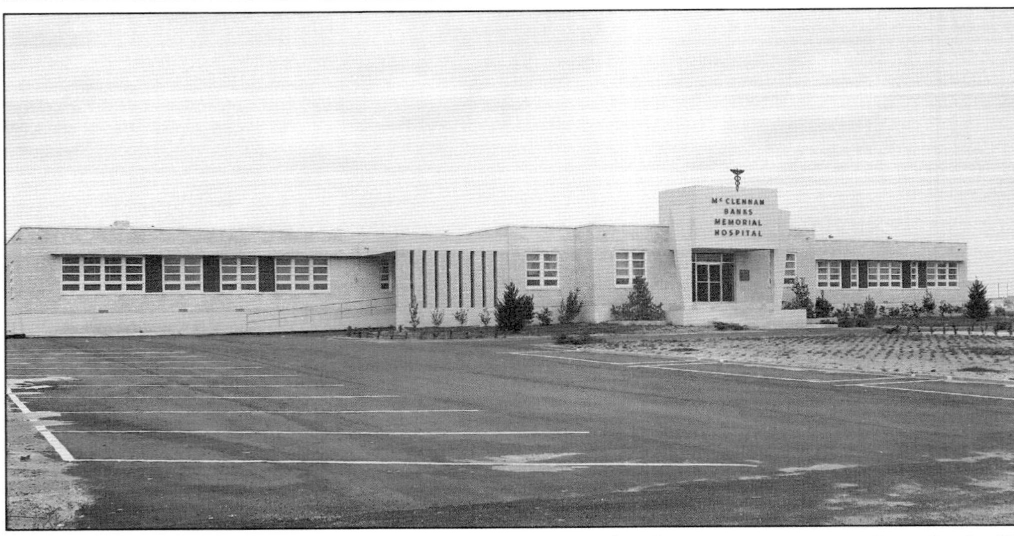

Under the leadership of Dr. McFall, the hospital sought funds to renovate or replace the badly deteriorated building on Cannon Street. In addition to soliciting the city's black community for financial support, McFall appealed to the Charleston County Council for $88,000 for the construction of a new hospital. In 1956, the money was approved and construction began on the newly renamed McClennan-Banks Memorial Hospital at 25 Courtney Drive on the west side of Charleston. The 31-bed facility served as a full-service hospital, continuing the mission and policies of the Cannon Street Hospital until December 31, 1976, when integrated hospital facilities rendered it unnecessary. In 2004, the building on Courtenay Drive was demolished. On its site today stands the Ashley River Tower.

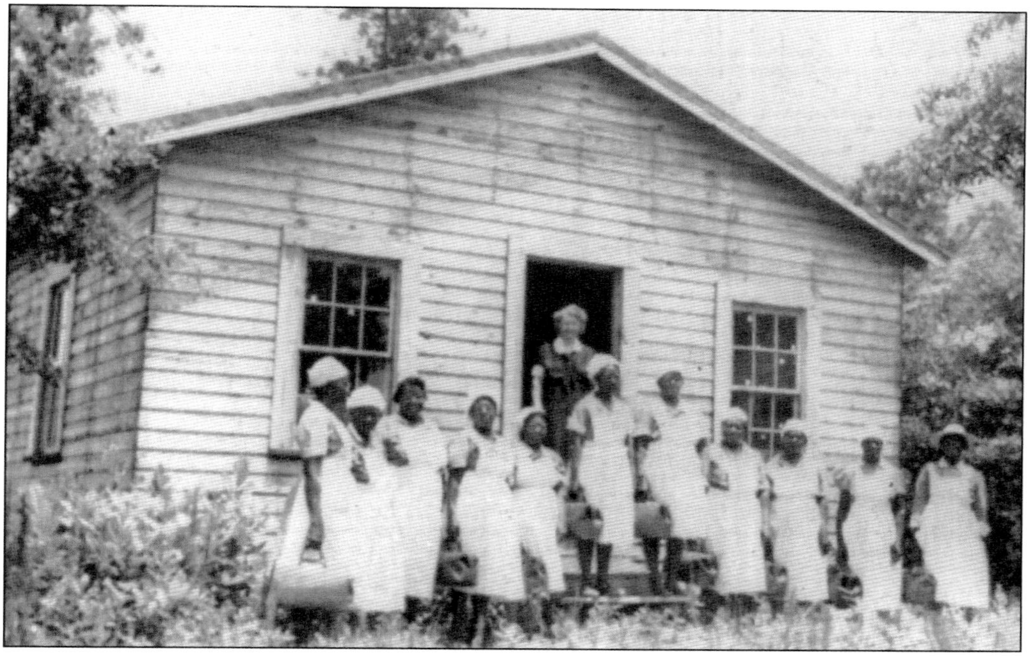

While the Hospital and Nurses Training School provided formal training for African American professional nurses, there remained a need for training and education for midwives, who traditionally played a frontline role in the delivery of health care to rural and underserved communities. To encourage a standard of hygiene and practice, the Charleston County Department of Health (CCDH) sponsored a program to train midwives as early as 1920. Classes were taught and supervised by Roper Hospital nurses and obstetricians and covered sanitation and the simplest procedure of the safe delivery of patients. In addition to training midwives, the CCDH employed a wide range of programs designed to improve the health of Charleston's citizenry. Established in May 1920 under the direction of Dr. Leon Banov, a 1917 graduate of the Medical College (pictured standing, center below), the CCHD worked with the South Carolina Board of Health and the US Public Health Service to implement medical and sanitary programs.

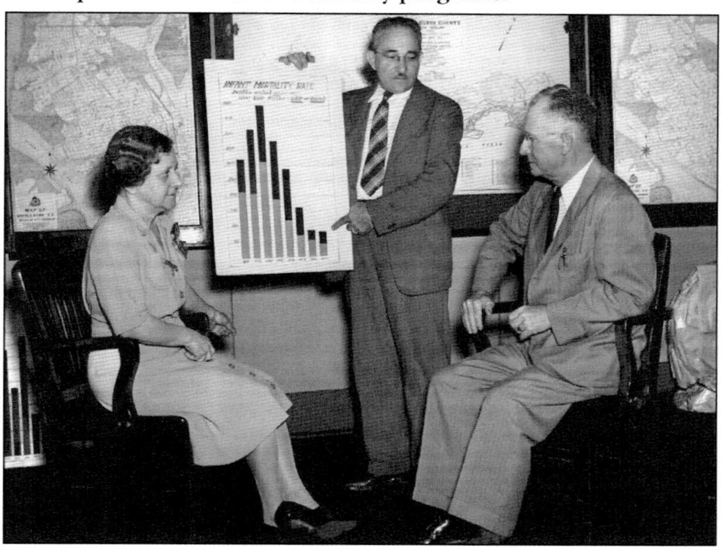

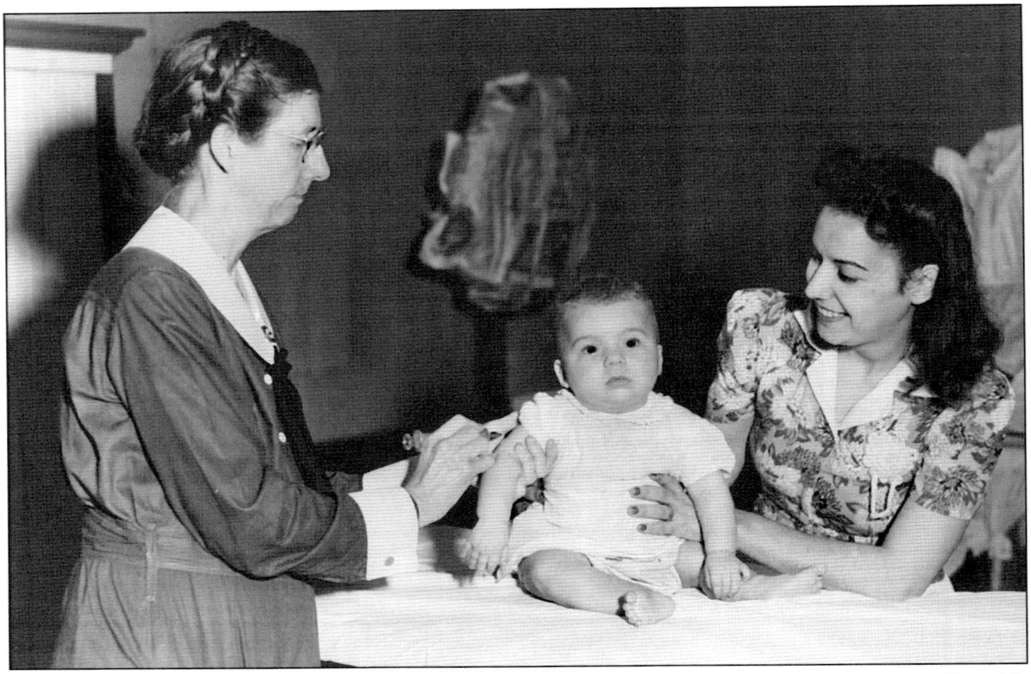

In its effort to improve the health of its constituents, the Charleston County Department of Health sponsored numerous programs to address diverse health issues such as maternal and child welfare, communicable and venereal disease control, environmental sanitation, health education, and biostatistics. In praise of the efforts of the CCDH, Dr. Leon Banov wrote in *A Quarter Century of Public Health* (1946), "Even a casual glance at our past accomplishments and our present program will convince the most skeptical that in the city and the county of Charleston, South Carolina, public health is definitely on the march." Above is a well-baby clinic, and below is a vaccination clinic; both images date from around 1945.

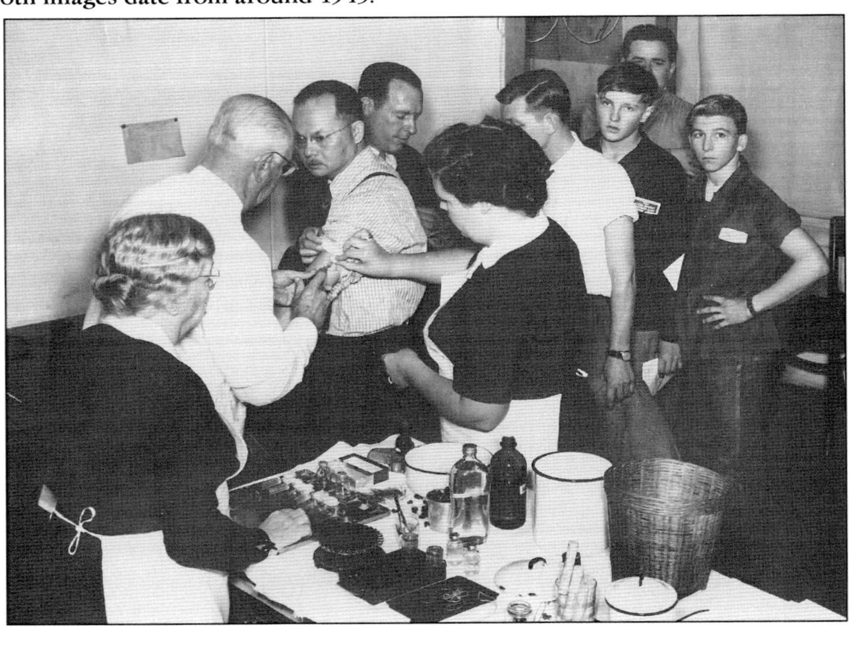

INDEX

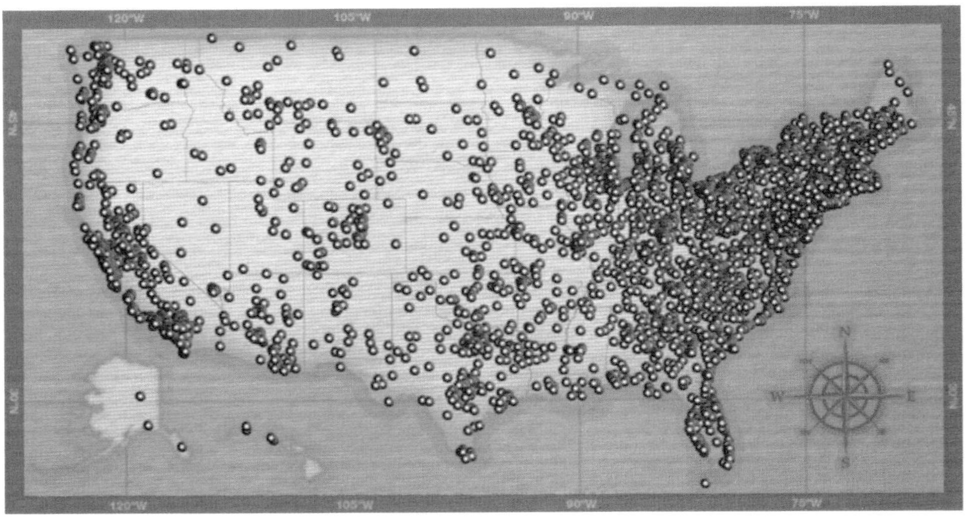